# After Hong Kong

## Some Key Trade Issues for Developing Countries

Edited by
Ivan Mbirimi

COMMONWEALTH SECRETARIAT

ACADEMIC FOUNDATION

Published by the Commonwealth Secretariat
Commonwealth Secretariat, Marlborough House, Pall Mall
London SW1Y 5HX, United Kingdom

and

Academic Foundation
(co-publication partner for South Asia)
Academic Foundation, 4772-73 / 23 Bharat Ram Road,
(23 Ansari Road), Darya Ganj,
New Delhi-110 002, India



Designed by Wayzgoose
Printed by Academic Foundation, New Delhi, India

Wherever possible, the Commonwealth Secretariat uses paper sourced from sustainable forests or from sources that minimise a destructive impact on the environment.

Copies of this publication may be obtained from

(except for South Asia)

The Publications Section,
Commonwealth Secretariat,
Marlborough House,
Pall Mall,
London SW1Y 5HX,
United Kingdom
Tel: +44 (0)20 7747 6342
Fax: +44 (0)20 7839 9081
E-mail: publications@commonwealth.int
Web: www.thecommonwealth.org/publications

ISBN-13: 978-0-85092-838-9
ISBN-10: 0-85092-838-9

(for South Asia only)

Academic Foundation,
4772-73 / 23 Bharat Ram Road,
(23 Ansari Road),
Darya Ganj,
New Delhi - 110 002,
India
Tel: +91 (0)11 2324 5001 - 04
Fax: +91 (0)11 2324 5005
E-mail: academic@vsnl.com
Web: www.academicfoundation.com

ISBN-13: 978-81-7188-641-8
ISBN-10: 81-7188-641-8

## The Authors

**Andrew Charlton** is a Research Officer at the Centre for Economic Performance at the London School of Economics.

**Jane Kennan** is a data policy analyst at the Institute of Development Studies at the University of Sussex

**Ivan Mbirimi** is an economic advisor in the Economic Affairs Division of the Commonwealth Secretariat.

**David Primack** works in the Economic Affairs Division of the Commonwealth Secretariat.

**Christopher Stevens** is coordinator of the International Economic Development Group at the Overseas Development Institute, UK.

**Joseph E. Stiglitz** was awarded the Nobel Prize in economics in 2001 and is a Professor at Columbia University. He was Chief Economist and Senior Vice-President of the World Bank from 1997–2000 and Chair of President Clinton's Council of Economic Advisors from 1995–97.

# Contents

# 1

# Will the Doha Round Deliver for Development?

Ivan Mbirimi

## Introduction

The Doha Round was launched in 2001 without a great deal of enthusiasm among developing countries. From their perspective, the Uruguay Round outcome was unbalanced in two ways: the anticipated benefits fell far short of expectations and developed countries were the main beneficiaries. Developing countries also found it too costly to implement some of the agreements reached. Not surprisingly, they saw the new Doha Round in terms of removing asymmetries in Uruguay Round Agreements as well as ensuring that development became central to the negotiations.

The major developed countries clearly saw things differently, as their negotiating tactics subsequently demonstrated. To them, a development round was mainly a political response to the discontent expressed by developing countries – a discontent that had been exacerbated by the events of 11 September 2001. Thus, over the course of the negotiations, there was a progressive narrowing of the development agenda, so that when the sixth World Trade Organization (WTO) Ministerial Meeting took place in Hong Kong in December 2005, what was being considered as a 'development package' comprised essentially of four issues: a package which would give least developing countries (LDCs) duty-free and quota-free (DFQF) access to developed country markets, erosion of preferences and attention to the needs of small, weak and vulnerable countries, cotton and the new issue of aid for trade.

This book focuses on three of these issues, on which some modest progress was made at the sixth WTO Ministerial Meeting. The needs of the so-called small and vulnerable economies and preference erosion will continue to be addressed. Our main purpose in putting together these papers is to highlight how much remains to be done in order to deliver a development package on these issues. If there is one thread that runs through them, it is that failure to achieve meaningful outcomes is likely to mean that the Doha Round fails to deliver even a minimal development package for around 100 WTO members (the countries which belong to the G90 group). There is, therefore, an urgent need to ensure that further progress is made.

## The Story So Far

At one level, development issues have become hostage to disagreements among the major players. The European Union (EU), in particular, has approached the negotiations in terms of a grand bargain involving an offer to open its agricultural market to imports in return for an agreement by developing countries to open their manufacturing and service sectors.[1] One consequence of this is that the specific concerns of least developed countries, small and vulnerable economies and the 'cotton four' have been used by the major players as bargaining chips in this grand bargain between agriculture, and manufacturing and services. The EU's position on development issues at the sixth WTO Ministerial Meeting in Hong Kong was viewed in this light.[2]

### Aid for Trade

The first issue discussed here is aid for trade (AFT), in a paper by Nobel Prize winner, Joseph Stiglitz, and Andrew Charlton. They set out their ideas about what might constitute an effective aid for trade package. The AFT initiative emerged from the sixth WTO Ministerial Meeting in Hong Kong. The Ministerial Declaration makes it clear that the initiative aims to help developing countries, particularly LDCs, build their supply-side capacity and trade-related infrastructure so as to be able to implement and benefit from WTO agreements.

Stiglitz and Charlton provide a powerful narrative on the need for aid for trade, which in part is about making good the Doha Round's development promise, but is also about building the capacity of developing countries to trade. They see AFT as a necessary complement to the core market access issues in the Round.[3] They also view it in the broader context of increasing the volume and value-added component of exports, and diversifying export products and markets, as well as attracting foreign investment to create jobs and exports. However, approaching the issue in this broad context raises a number of questions, of which the most critical is: where do we draw the line between aid for trade and aid for development? It may be that there are no ready answers to this question.[4] But it is clear that where trade is important for development, this distinction may not be relevant. This also suggests that a 'one size fits all' approach is unlikely to work because developing countries face different economic circumstances.

Issues of definition and scope are not the only contentious area. Others include the volume and type of resources, country eligibility and future predictability of resources. The authors try to deal with these issues by suggesting a number of principles that could guide the establishment of an AFT package. These principles include *additionality of resources*, so that aid for trade does not come at the expense of aid for development budgets; *predictability*, so that there is a degree of certainty about funding; *country ownership*, as the only way to respond to the needs and priorities of a country; and *coherence* – essential in making trade part of the broader development agenda.

Turning to mechanisms for implementing aid for trade, Stiglitz and Charlton consider three options: continuation of existing mechanisms; creation of a new trade specific fund; and reform of existing mechanisms. Having analysed the merits and demerits of each option, they set out their proposal for a special Global Trade Facility (GTF), to be administered by the World Bank, similar to the Global Environment Facility (GEF), which is also administered by the Bank. The concept of an integrated facility would be retained, but the governance structure and location would be different. Where will the

WTO be in all this? The suggestion is that financial resources to be made available to the GTF would be treated as part of binding commitments written into the final Doha Round agreement.

The debate on aid for trade has only just begun and developing countries have only just joined it. Two considerations are paramount in developing countries' thinking: that the debate should not detract from a balanced outcome of the Doha Round that reflects their development concerns; and that an effective aid for trade package should help reduce the adverse effects of the Round, as well as enable them to take advantage of the opportunities it creates.

## Duty-free and Quota-free Market Access for Least Developed Countries

Kennan and Stevens undertook an assessment of the implications of the Hong Kong Declaration on duty-free and quota-free access for least developed countries. The package that emerged from the Hong Kong Ministerial Meeting – offering DFQF for up to 97 per cent of tariff lines – fell short of what the LDCs wanted. The USA and Japan could not countenance 100 per cent product coverage for fear that countries such as Bangladesh and Cambodia, which are competitive in textile products, would create problems for their textile producers. It also argued that 100 per cent product coverage would undermine African preferential market access under the African Growth and Opportunity Act (AGOA).

The central question posed by Kennan and Stevens is whether duty-free and quota-free market access is likely to result in the removal of significant barriers to LDCs' trade. Their starting point is to note the two situations in which the initiative on DFQF might not have a significant impact. One is when few barriers to trade exist and the other is when, although barriers to trade exist, there is scope to restrict trade for sensitive products. Their focus was on the Quad markets (Canada, the EU, Japan and the USA). They conclude that in the case of the EU and Canada, the LDC package will not have a significant impact because there are very few existing barriers. Its principal effect would be to increase certainty and reduce the scope for regime dilution. Based on their analysis, the authors conclude that to make a difference, any new package would have to tackle specifically other barriers to imports from LDCs, such as unduly onerous rules of origin, health standards or other non-tariff barriers (NTBs).

In regard to the USA and Japan, Kennan and Stevens conclude that full implementation of the DFQF package would result in a significant removal of barriers to imports from LDCs. They therefore suggest that the main issue is whether the 3 per cent rule in the 'small print' could allow this effect to be diluted. They argue that if the USA concentrated its exclusions on the highest value items facing tariff peaks, the effect would be to exclude a substantial proportion of imports from Bangladesh, Cambodia, Nepal and Haiti. Otherwise, for the majority of LDCs, the scope for dilution is likely to be limited. In the case of Japan, Kennan and Stevens argue that the 3 per cent exclusion is unlikely to affect substantially the effect of the LDC package on current imports. This is because the country imports a narrow range of goods from LDCs.

Kennan and Stevens conclude by making several recommendations on issues to be followed up. One is that implementation of the LDC package should not be linked to the start of the Doha Round implementation period; another concerns the need for action to clarify and extend the Hong Kong Declaration, in particular in regard to how it might be enforced. Finally, the authors believe that action outside the scope of the Declaration (i.e. on measures other than border measures) may be required.

### Addressing Global Cotton Subsidies

The last paper, by David Primack, deals with cotton. Primack discusses the problem of global cotton subsidies and their impact on poor developing country cotton producers. The issue came to prominence in the WTO in 2003, in the period leading up to the Cancun Ministerial Meeting, when four West African cotton producers argued for a speedy and expedited treatment of the problems faced by cotton exporters. They called for a mechanism to phase out cotton subsidies, with a view to eliminating all support to cotton production, as well as transitional financial compensation to offset injury during the period of elimination. They made a powerful case, which many observers saw as a test of the developed countries' preparedness to observe the rules, and of their seriousness in regard to levelling the playing field and allowing developing countries to reap the benefits of multilateral trade liberalisation.

Primack traces the development of the 'Cotton Initiative' from Cancun to Geneva, where in the July Framework package of 2004, agreement was reached to address the issue of cotton 'ambitiously, expeditiously and specifically', and finally to Hong Kong in December 2005, where only modest advances were made. The Hong Kong Declaration provides for the elimination of export subsidies in 2006 and DFQF for LDC cotton exports at the start of the implementation period. Any benefits flowing from these concessions are likely to be very modest. This is mainly because export subsidies constitute only a small proportion of the subsidies that the USA gives to its cotton producers every year. In the case of the EU, domestic subsidies make up almost all the subsidies provided to cotton producers.

Primack also analyses the impact of the Brazilian challenge to elements of the US cotton support programme, and although he sees some positive effects, he concludes that political economy considerations are likely to interfere with the pressure that Brazil and others are likely to exert on the USA through this avenue.

## Conclusion

Taken together, these analyses show that the prospect of a balanced outcome to the Doha Round – one that responds to the development concerns of poor countries – is remote. In all three cases, there are serious issues and problems to be addressed. Already, there are some who are asking whether any deal is better than no deal at all.[5] It is not difficult to see why this view is taking hold in some quarters.

*First*, the pursuit of an agriculture for manufacturing and services deal, at the expense of other issues, is likely to produce an outcome that would be of little benefit to around 100 developing countries (essentially those belonging to the G90). Yet the costs of such a deal in terms of tariff losses (from opening their markets to industrial goods), adjustment costs and the loss of policy space are likely to be considerable.

*Second*, there remain several ambiguities in the agreements reached on the LDC package and the Cotton Initiative that may be carried forward into the final agreements, should an overall Doha Agreement be reached within the time-frame envisaged at Hong Kong. In other words, the risks of ending with very poor agreements on development issues are considerable, particularly if things are rushed in order to meet the Hong Kong timelines.

*Third*, political will, an essential ingredient for striking trade deals, is clearly in short supply. The change in personnel at the top of the US negotiating team is seen by many as an indication of the downgrading of the Doha Round by the USA.

What then is to be done? The authors of these papers make suggestions as to what needs to be done to achieve development objectives in the areas they have looked at, but the time and space to follow up these suggestions may be inadequate, particularly if a compromise is reached soon on an agriculture for manufacturing and services deal. That may then put pressure on developing countries to accept what is on offer. This is a major risk facing developing countries at this stage of the negotiations. It means that they must remain focused on their objectives and refuse to adopt agreements that do not serve their interests. They must also look at the detail of proposed agreements – the 'small print' – and seek clarity on ambiguous provisions in agreements reached at Hong Kong.

## Notes

1 Andrew Charlton and Joseph Stiglitz, 'The Doha Round is Missing the Point on Helping Poor Countries', *Financial Times*, 13 December 2005.
2 Faizel Ismail, 'An Assessment of the Sixth WTO Ministerial Conference', December 2005
3 Although the authors are sympathetic to the concerns of preference-dependent economies, they do not think compensation is a good rationale for aid for trade.
4 Elizabeth Parsan, 'Reflections on the Aid for Trade Debate', April 2006 (unpublished paper for Commonwealth Secretariat).
5 'A Recipe for Disaster: Will the Doha Round Fail to Deliver for Development?', Oxfam Briefing Paper 87, April 2006.

# 2

# Aid for Trade

Joseph E. Stiglitz and Andrew Charlton

## Introduction

Fifteen years after the Washington Consensus, the world has come to acknowledge that free trade is not a magic wand.[1] Trade may be necessary for sustained industrial development, but it is not sufficient. In the right circumstances, trade liberalisation creates opportunities for development, but other factors determine the extent to which those opportunities are realised. In addition, any 'gross' welfare gains from trade liberalisation must be balanced against its associated costs. Liberalisation incurs adjustment costs as resources are moved from one sector to another in the process of reform, and whereas it may take decades for multilateral trade reform to deliver gains to developing countries, the adjustment costs are automatic and usually upfront.

Furthermore, developing countries will need to incur additional costs if they are to realise the full benefits of new market opportunities. In many cases they lack the necessary exporting infrastructure (for example, efficient ports, adequate roads, reliable electricity and communications) or lack the necessary technology and knowledge to meet product standards prevailing in high value markets (sanitary measures, technical barriers, certification, etc.). To benefit from liberalisation, developing countries will need to make public investments in infrastructure and institutions, as well as private investment in productive capacity.

The aid for trade agenda reflects the realisation that, for developing countries, the necessary investments are particularly large, and the capacity to meet them is particularly small. There is an emerging consensus that the current WTO Doha Round will require adequate trade-related assistance to mitigate the detrimental effects of trade reforms, and to enhance the trading capacity of developing countries.

The next two years represent a critical opportunity for progress on trade-related development assistance. Following the G8 and EU summits in 2005 and various other recent commitments by developed countries, annual development aid is expected to increase by US$50 billion between now and 2010. This will make more resources available for all kinds of support. However, aid for trade will be given a special focus. This is partly because donors are aware that increased aid flows may have unintended negative

The authors would like to acknowledge the comments of participants at the conference 'An Assessment of the Doha Round after Hong Kong', held on 2–3 February, 2006, organised by the Initiative for Policy Dialogue at Columbia University and hosted by the Brooks World Poverty Institute at Manchester University. They have benefited from comments by Ricardo Melendez-Ortiz, Julia Nielson, Dan Curiak, Sheila Page, Susan Prowse, Hilde Johnson, Dirk Willem te Velde, Simon Evenett, and Roman Grynberg, without implicating them in the opinions expressed.

consequences for developing countries[2] if more aid leads to real exchange rate appreciations (Dutch disease) which reduce their international competitiveness. The threat of such an outcome will focus donors' attention on counterbalancing programmes, including trade development, trade facilitation and other programmes to boost competitiveness.[3] The next two years are also a critical period for the WTO, during which it hopes to reach a conclusion to the Doha Round.[4] The imperative to make good on the development promise of the round provides a political focus for aid for trade. For a broader discussion of the development potential of the Doha Round, see Stiglitz and Charlton (2005).

Aid for trade involves the flow of development finance from rich to poor countries for the purpose of enhancing the world trading system. The design of an aid for trade framework involves three key questions. There is a 'needs' question: 'What should be funded?'; there is an instrument question: 'In what form should the money be given?'; and there is an institutional question: 'Who should manage the transfer?'.

In the context of trade, the answers to these questions depend critically on the purpose of the fund and its relationship to the trading system – fundamental issues which remain unresolved. Several (non-exclusive) purposes for trade-related development assistance have been floated and these have very different implications for the design of an aid for trade mechanism.

First and most straightforward is the political motivation often ascribed to the rich countries, namely that aid for trade is an instrument to 'buy' progress in the Doha Round. Put bluntly, this view conceives of aid for trade as 'your normal negotiating side payment'[5] necessary to ensure that the Doha Round package results in Pareto improvements for all developing countries – arguably a necessary condition for progress in the WTO's bargaining process, which is characterised by both a single undertaking and consensus agreement (Evenett, 2005b). This view leads to the conclusion that aid should be directed to those countries that would be net losers from the Doha Round and therefore have an incentive to block its progress.[6]

A second argument for aid for trade is discernible in the demands for compensation levelled by preference-dependent countries, net food importers and those facing costs associated with industrial restructuring following the end of the textiles agreement. This compensation motivation appears to be based on the view that developing countries should be compensated for losses arising from specific elements of the agreement, independent of their gains in other areas and in the deal as a whole. This rationale leads some proponents of aid for trade to envisage compensatory schemes to address specific categories of adjustment costs arising from changes to the world trading system following implementation of the agreement.

A third (related but more general) rationale for aid for trade is fairness. There is no doubt that an ambitious Doha Round will deliver significant gains to the rich countries, and that these gains will far outweigh the gains to poor countries. For some, aid for trade is a mechanism of redistribution through which the reality of the unbalanced outcome can be squared with the rhetoric of the 'Development Round'.

All of these three rationales see aid for trade as an exchange: either a payment, compensation or gift in return for complicity in the multilateral trade liberalisation agenda. While we believe that each of these rationales has some merit, we have several concerns with their application.

The basic problem is that all three rationales place several undue and unhelpful constraints on aid for trade. First, limiting aid for trade to a 'compensation' concept limits the pool of donors. For example, the problem of preference losses is arguably an issue between the recipients and the granters of preferences (the EU and to a smaller extent the USA), and other rich countries may be reluctant to commit resources to resolve a problem they did little to create. A more important concern is that a compensation approach limits the beneficiaries of aid, and may prevent aid for trade reaching the most needy countries. Losses from preference erosion, for example, are heavily concentrated in the handful of countries that have managed to benefit from preferential access, and these are not, for the most part, the least developed countries. Moreover some have expressed concerns about whether the erosion of rents arising from historical preferential schemes gives rise, as an ethical matter, to a right to compensation.[7] Another question is how losses in some areas of the agreement should be treated relative to losses in other areas (i.e. should losses arising from terms of trade effects related to the elimination of export subsidies be compensated in the same way as losses arising from preference erosion; and should losses from preferential access in free trade agreements be treated in the same way as preferential schemes; and should losses from previous rounds, for example the costs of the TRIPS agreement, be included as well?). In our view the most serious reservation about the compensation approach is that it does not necessarily imply that funds would be directed to the poorest countries, or even to those countries facing the largest net losses from the round as a whole.

With these concerns in mind, we use a fourth rationale to motivate aid for trade in this report. Rather than seeing aid as an exchange for progress in the Round, we see it as a necessary complement to the core market access issues at the centre of the Round. Lack of supply capacity is a barrier to trade which limits market access for poor countries. Aid for trade should be seen as an essential component of market access offers to the poor countries. The message from least developed countries in the Doha negotiations should be: 'aid for trade must be part of the market access agenda. It is meaningless to give us tariff-free entry if we are unable to use it. In the context of supply constraints, giving access to your markets must mean giving us both free entry and aid to ensure we can use it.' Of course, in the past the hope was that new market access by itself would spur investment in new supply capacity in the LDCs. However the lessons from the Everything but Arms (EBA) and AGOA experiments indicate that this has not happened to any meaningful degree.

In our view, aid for trade should be motivated by the imperative of creating 'effective market access' by removing internal barriers to trade. We acknowledge that countries facing adjustment shocks (preference-dependent countries, LDCs facing adverse terms of trade shocks and tariff losses) should all receive funding. However, while adjustment costs should motivate donors and identify recipients, aid disbursements should have the purpose of promoting future exports, not compensating for the loss of past exports.

The objective should be to put resources into increasing the volume and value-added component of exports, diversifying export products and export markets, and attracting foreign investment to generate jobs and exports.

The primary instruments to achieve this should focus on private sector development by facilitating the improvement of the business environment for exporters. This involves helping developing countries to design and implement a trade development strategy as part of a broader national development strategy. It also means helping developing countries to improve credit markets both through the creation of new multilateral instruments to mitigate risk and through assistance in improving local financial markets. It also involves development aid to finance investments in trade-related infrastructure, especially customs, ports and roads, as well as investments in institutions.

This expansive definition of aid for trade raises the question of how it differs from development aid in general. When a road is built, how close does it have to be to the port to become an aid for trade project? If there is no clear dividing line between aid for trade expenditure and general development expenditure, is there merit in complicating the aid system by creating separate frameworks and structures for trade-related assistance? We recognise, on the one hand, that there is value in a separate approach to aid for trade to the extent that it is useful to recognise that the world trading system is imposing costs on developing countries, and that the beneficiaries of the system should meet those costs. The WTO is a useful forum in which to recognise these costs and commit funds to redress them, to ensure that the aid itself is not just a political instrument, to be withdrawn if the country does something that the donor country does not like (such as voting the wrong way at the UN). The Doha Round agreement provides a contract in which these commitments could be made binding, and the dispute settlement system could then be utilised to enforce them. We recognise, on the other hand, that the WTO has no capacity to manage or disburse aid funds, and that there is little value in reinventing the wheel to create a new channel through which to deliver aid for trade.

Multiple channels already exist to deliver trade adjustment assistance, including the IMF's Trade Integration Mechanism (TIM), bilateral aid for trade programmes, several World Bank programmes and the Integrated Framework for Technical Assistance to Least Developed Countries (IF) coordinating mechanism. In this chapter it is proposed that the scale and scope of aid for trade should be broadened and it is stressed that this will require significant reform to the existing aid for trade system. New options for aid for trade need to be developed within the context of the 'new aid framework' (see Hoekman and Prowse, 2005), which emphasises coordination between donors and coherence with national policies and priorities. Although new structures will be required to deliver increased trade assistance, these should build upon the progress of existing programmes and leverage the capacity of existing institutions, rather than stand apart from them.

To summarise our recommendations, we propose significant reform to the existing channels of delivery. A new mechanism would have the following components:

- Existing multilateral aid for trade structures, particularly the Integrated Framework, should be consolidated under the management of the World Bank where a new Global Trade Facility should be housed in much the same way as the Global Environment Facility is already housed within the World Bank.
- The six agencies currently participating in the Integrated Framework would continue to operate in an advisory capacity. They would continue to promote harmonisation and to ensure that trade development is not considered in isolation, but as part of an overall package of domestic policy reforms and economic planning.
- The facility would receive a stream of funding (additional to existing aid commitments) agreed to as part of binding Doha Round agreements.
- These commitments would be subsequently enforceable within the WTO. The GTF could directly bring a charge of non-compliance against any country not meetings its aid commitments, and would have the right to auction off any enforcement action. All countries agreeing to contribute to the GTF would subscribe to a Maintenance of Effort Commitment that current aid levels would not be reduced; such Maintenance of Effort Commitments would also be binding.
- The facility would have a broad mandate to finance technical assistance, trade-related capacity building, enterprise development and infrastructure projects through a combination of grants and concessional loans.

## Principles

The goal of expanded trade-related development assistance should be to enhance the export capacity of developing countries. Programmes must be linked to overarching development strategies and complement, rather than replace, other development priorities. Until recently the existing aid for trade approach was to provide modest amounts of aid on an *ad hoc* basis – primarily to cope with specific bottlenecks, or to support participation in WTO negotiations. In this section we identify some of the principles that should guide the expansion of the aid for trade system.

**Additionality:** *'Developing countries need aid for trade and such aid must not come at the expense of aid for development.'*[8]

Aid for trade has entered the WTO agenda partly because of the widespread view that the trading system is unfair and that previous agreements have been unbalanced and have had the effect of marginalising the developing countries in the world trading system. In recognition of this, aid for trade should supplement, not replace, existing aid commitments.

But assessing the additionality of aid commitments is a difficult task. As Prowse (2005) points out, care needs to be taken in interpreting aid figures. A large proportion of the increase in the dollar denominated value of aid in the last five years is accounted for by exchange rate changes. In 2002, over half the increase in official aid was due to debt relief to just two countries (Afghanistan and Pakistan) and in 2003/4 87 per cent of the increase was accounted for by reconstruction aid to Iraq. Since the UN Conference on Financing for Development, held in Monterrey, Mexico in 2002, the increment flowing to low-income countries has in fact been very small. Aid for trade commitments must provide funds that complement those provided as aid for development. It should not merely rename or divert resources from existing programmes.

**Predictability:** *'It is easy to be taken in with promises of bilateral aid, and make seemingly innocuous commitments in bilateral agreements.'*[9]

Experience in the Uruguay Round demonstrated the need for a mechanism that provides a level of commitment to promises of assistance from rich countries and gives poor countries a degree of certainty about their funding. In the past, 'best endeavour' promises to provide assistance have often not materialised, leaving poor countries sceptical about the merits of agreeing to binding trade disciplines in return for unbound promises of help with implementation and adjustment.

Part of the problem is that while the WTO has enforcement mechanisms that apply to the liberalisation elements of agreements, it has not yet attempted to specify and enforce promises of assistance embedded in the agreement. Moreover, the WTO has no capacity to manage aid flows, requiring instead that they be channelled through other international organisations. These facts significantly reduce the negotiating leverage of developing countries, whose liberalisation commitments are made and enforced within the WTO, but whose receipts of aid are handled and distributed outside it. To be credible, the aid for trade mechanism must include monitoring capacity to ensure that the funds are being provided.

**Country ownership:** *'Development cannot be imposed, it can only be facilitated.'*[10]

Best practices in aid delivery indicate that donors must be responsive to partner countries' priorities for aid financed projects.[11] This is particularly true for aid for trade, where export promotion projects will be ineffective unless they are tailored to the needs of the private sector; and technical assistance and government support must form part of a local administration's broader development plan. Donors must ensure that aid complements and strengthens a country's own plans, budgets and structures, rather than undermining them by setting up a parallel donor-run administration.[12]

Trade-related assistance has a mixed record on country ownership. In some cases, technical assistance has seemed to focus on assisting local bureaucracies to participate in negotiations with the donor countries with a view to ensuring progress in trade agreements, instead of focusing on the practical difficulties faced by local agricultural producers, industry cooperatives or individual enterprises. Particularly during the Cancun WTO meeting, many developing countries felt that offers of technical assistance reflected 'less a burning desire to accelerate development' than to provide 'the bare minimum to keep them afloat so they don't break the system by walking away'.[13]

**Coherence:** *'Trade liberalisation must be carefully managed as part of comprehensive development strategies.'*[14]

Related to the principle of country ownership is the need for coherence. Not only must aid for trade must be linked with broader development programmes, but its effectiveness also depends on the ability of donors to coordinate their efforts with a broad national development strategy. These two requirements create a trade-off for the design of mechanisms for aid for trade. On one hand, the establishment of a stand-alone aid for trade fund would centralise trade facilitation financing and potentially enhance the coherence of different programmes. But on the other hand, a stand-alone fund would be less likely to successfully integrate trade projects into broader national poverty reduction and development strategies.

Currently, coherence in trade-related aid projects is managed by the Integrated Framework, which is intended to ensure that aid for trade corresponds to country priorities and focuses on poverty reduction. Six multilateral agencies, led by the World Bank, use the IF to coordinate aid for trade programmes. The IF proposes to assess each LDC's needs, report these to donors and eventually integrate trade promotion programmes into the country's Poverty Reduction Strategy Paper (PRSP). While the IF's diagnostic studies are valuable tools for promoting coherence, it is not clear that the IF structure will be able to manage the imminent changes in the volume and nature of aid for trade financing. High-level coordination mechanisms might be too slow and unwieldy to offer useful guidance to aid for trade strategies, particularly programmes involving private sector development. In addition, an institution that is, in principle, jointly managed by six agencies, is probably too cumbersome to administer aid delivery.

**Private sector:** A drawback of many aid programmes is that they often tend to focus too much on the role of the public sector and of government planning. The Monterrey Conference stressed the need to foster private sector actors to promote development. This is particularly important in aid for trade, where capacity building and export promotion rely on the ability of donors to identify and remove roadblocks to private sector development.

For the poorest and least creditworthy countries, direct grants to governments will continue to be the primary means of addressing development needs, but for countries with existing industrial capacity, donors should devote greater attention to the private sector and attempt to implement programmes which act as catalysts and facilitators for enterprises to establish themselves, grow, adopt technology, acquire finance and reach international markets.

**Instruments: loans v. grants:** *'Many have rallied to the idea of dropping the debt. I say let's rally to the idea of stopping the debt.'*[15]

Since the Meltzer Report (2000),[16] multilateral development banks have shifted their support towards performance-based grants and away from loan instruments. This has been a welcome move since they prevent the accrual of unpayable debt, which has proved so problematic in the past.

But donors should not turn their back entirely on soft loans in favour of grants. The type of trade expansion projects being financed by aid will vary widely from long-term public institutional development to short-term finance for individual industries or enterprises. One form of assistance may, for instance, be to create lending institutions to finance export-oriented investments. Funds provided to the private sector should be largely on a commercial basis, with the expectation that they generate returns large enough to make them self-liquidating.[17] In this context there are merits to embracing a multiplicity of instruments. The level of the concessional element should vary depending on the type of project, the level of development of the recipient country and the type of recipient (government, NGO or enterprise).[18]

## Adjustment Needs

*'Not only are there gains from trade, there are also "pains from trade".'*[19]

Trade liberalisation creates adjustment costs as resources are moved from one sector to another in the process of reform. When tariffs are reduced, import-competing firms may reduce their production in the face of new competition, causing some of their workers and capital to lie idle for a period. The firm's laid-off workers will incur costs while searching for new jobs and may need to invest in retraining. Governments will be called upon to provide assistance to the unemployed, while also incurring costs associated with implementing the new systems to manage reform.

Significant trade liberalisation will also affect the distribution of income among factors of production: the relative price of the factor which is in relative scarcity will decline, while that of the abundant factor will increase.[20]

Even the elimination of distortionary policies has costs. Agricultural subsidies are capitalised in the price of land, and landowners will lose substantial amounts when such subsidies are eliminated.[21] Because there are large distortionary costs associated with taxation, there are large societal costs associated with the compensation designed to mitigate these effects.[22]

Trade liberalisation may impose further costs: the movement from quotas to tariffs, whatever its merits, may expose countries to additional risks.[23] Developing countries with weak social safety nets will have to devote more resources to strengthening these safety nets and to mitigate the cost of risks. This too should be viewed as part of the cost of trade liberalisation.

Given the severe constraints on developing countries in raising taxes, the opportunity cost of funds diverted for even partial compensation and to strengthen safety nets may be very high.

In one sense, these adjustment costs can be thought of as the 'price' to be paid for the benefits of multilateral tariff reduction. Together, these adjustment costs and trade benefits determine the net effect of trade reform for each country. The Doha Round has placed renewed emphasis on the importance of sharing the benefits of trade reform fairly among developed and developing countries. However, less attention has been paid to the distribution of adjustment costs among countries.

A theme that runs through the empirical evidence is that the adjustment process resulting from the proposals emerging from the Doha Round will impact particularly harshly on the people and governments of developing countries – especially small developing countries. There are several reasons for this asymmetry. First, developing countries are particularly vulnerable to policy shocks because their export industries are the least diversified – many are dependent on the export and hence on the world price of just one or two commodities. Second, developing countries are likely to need to make the largest changes to comply with international regulations. Third, the structure of world trade is most distorted in the industries of importance to developing countries. World markets for agriculture, processed foods, textiles and other critical goods are the most distorted by developed countries' tariff policies. Consequently, these industries will be highly impacted on by liberalisation – even where reform has long-run net positive effects for developing countries, they will have to cope with adjustment costs, investment costs, and redistributive effects. Fourth, and most importantly, developing countries are home to the world's poorest people and the weakest credit markets. Poor people are particularly vulnerable to adjustment costs. Fifth, almost by definition, markets are less well developed in developing countries; their economies are marked by much larger market imperfections. Well functioning markets enable resources to be redeployed easily. In poorly functioning markets, such redeployments are more likely to be slow, with longer periods during which resources are not fully utilised.[24] For all these reasons, adjustment to new trading rules is a radically different experience for developed and developing countries.

## Fiscal losses

Trade liberalisation reduces tariff revenue. In some countries tariff revenues make up a substantial part of total government revenue. Many of these countries are concerned that trade liberalisation will have a significant adverse effect on public revenue and the ability to fund public expenditure.

Taxes on international trade account for around 1 per cent of government revenues in developed countries and around 30 per cent in the least developed countries. Small countries are the most reliant on tariffs. For example, tariffs make up 62 per cent of tax revenue in the Bahamas, 54 per cent in the Solomon Islands, and 75 per cent in Guinea (Ebrill *et al.*, 1999). Changes in tariff revenue resulting from trade reform will have disproportionate effects on developing countries: African governments are most reliant on revenue from tariffs, followed by Middle Eastern and Asian/Pacific countries.

Governments can, of course, attempt to replace lost tariff revenue with other sources of income, but these may be limited and have high associated costs. Thus, either public expenditure is reduced or other taxes are increased: either may have significant adverse effects on growth.[25] The desirability of replacing revenue from trade taxes with domestic revenue sources raises the issue of the relative efficiency of alternative forms of taxation. There is some theoretical evidence suggesting that reducing trade taxes and replacing them with a consumption tax is welfare enhancing (Keen and Lightart, 1999) on the basis that they are broader and less distortionary. More recently, however, Emran and Stiglitz (2004) have shown that in developing countries with an informal sector in which, say, a value added tax (VAT) cannot be imposed, it is desirable to retain some trade taxes, for example to tax imports at a higher rate than domestic production.

The effect of trade liberalisation on government revenues is difficult to predict. Senegal pursued trade liberalisation in the mid-1980s, following which there were large revenue shortfalls. Lost tariff revenue combined with slow growth in trade volumes, and weaknesses in economic management led to dire fiscal consequences. To raise more revenue, the tariff reductions were quickly abandoned and the liberalisation process delayed. In contrast, trade liberalisation in Morocco was accompanied by programmes to broaden the domestic tax base, including the introduction of a VAT in 1986. As a consequence, Morocco was able to reduce its reliance on trade taxes while maintaining a stable ratio of public revenue to GDP.

The main point is that global trade reform has significant consequences for the fiscal structures of developing countries, whereas developed countries are by and large immune. Developing countries rely on tariffs as a source of revenue far more than do developed countries, largely because tariffs are an administratively efficient way of raising revenues; switching to other sources of revenue not only entails switching costs, but there may be permanently higher administrative burdens.

As a result, developing countries are likely to suffer either a loss of total tax revenue, or at best a large administrative cost – and even more economic distortions – associated with the implementation of a new taxation system.

## Net food-importing countries

Agricultural liberalisation presents developing countries with the benefits of increased market access, but also the (potential) costs of higher prices for domestic consumers. The reduction in tariffs, domestic support and export subsides for agricultural products that has been agreed to will impact on developing countries largely through higher international prices of previously protected and supported products. The World Bank has estimated that total losses for net food importers would be between $300 million and $1.2 billion per year (Mitchell and Hoppe, 2006). Depending on assumptions, between 7 and 16 countries risk having food import bills increase by 5 per cent or more.[26]

The existence of net losses for developing countries in some areas of reform should not imply that no reform is required – rather it suggests that a selective and gradual approach to agricultural liberalisation is needed and that considerable adjustment assistance may be required for the negatively affected countries. Even countries who receive net gains from agricultural reform will incur costs associated with managing the internal distributional consequences of higher food prices. The fundamental point is that consumers benefit from lower prices that result from large agricultural subsidies, and producers lose.[27] The producers are typically poor farmers, who are often far worse off than the urban net consumers. Given the limited capacity of developing countries to effect redistribution, there can be a significant welfare loss from such adverse distributional impacts.

## Preference erosion

Several developed countries offer non-reciprocal preferential market access which reduces the tariff rates on the goods of least developing countries below most favoured nation (MFN) rates. Many LDCs fear that reductions in MFN tariff rates through multilateral trade liberalisation would harm their exports by eroding their preferential margins.

Preferential tariffs for LDCs have formed an important part of the global trade architecture since the inception of the Generalised System of Preferences (GSP) in 1968. Recently there have been a number of initiatives in OECD countries to further discriminate in favour of LDCs. Most notable among these are the EU's Everything but Arms initiative and the USA's African Growth and Opportunity Act.

Estimates of the benefits of preferences for LDCs (often calculated as the costs LDCs would experience if they were eliminated) are different from estimates of the costs of preference erosion through reduced MFN tariff rates. The chief difference is that in the case of preference erosion, LDCs are compensated for the loss of competitive advantage in donor countries by increased market access in all other countries. As a result, the costs to LDCs of preference erosion through MFN tariff reductions are likely to be smaller than the costs of preference elimination. The net effect on LDCs of preference erosion through reduction in MFN tariffs depends on whether the loss of 'trade diversion' (the negative switching or substitution that occurs as the margin of their preferences declines) exceeds the gains from 'trade creation' (the increase in global trade resulting from improved market access).

Most research, for example Waino and Gibson (2003) and Low *et al.* (2005) indicates that the average effect of preference erosion on LDCs is unlikely to be large. However, this is not true for all industries in all countries. Industries that are particularly reliant on preferences could be seriously damaged by preference erosion. Large effects on a small group of countries and a small group of sectors cannot be ignored. While preference erosion is not a consideration that should impede multilateral liberalisation, it does suggest that the small group of net losers will need assistance to manage adjustment.

In general, the higher the dependency of countries on preferences, the larger the potential loss from MFN tariff cuts. Addressing the problems of adjustment in critical industries in vulnerable countries should be a key component of any multilateral reform proposal. There are many examples of critical industries – particularly in small countries – which face large negative consequences from preference erosion.

Assistance for critical industries and their workers is a preferred solution to the maintenance of preference margins. There are two reasons to prefer assistance to delayed MFN liberalisation. First, delayed liberalisation discriminates against developing countries which do not benefit from preferences. The second reason for preferring assistance is that the maintenance of long term preferences induces beneficiaries to specialise in activities in which they may not be competitive once preferences are removed. This discourages industrial diversification and increases adjustment costs when the preferences are eventually removed.

At the same time, it should be recognised that providing even temporary preferential access can sometimes provide long-term gains. By excluding some critical products (particularly bananas, rice and sugar) from immediate zero tariff under the EBA in 2001, the EU may be missing the opportunity to provide these industries with a foothold in their markets in advance of MFN liberalisation.[28]

## Implementation costs

Implementation costs are another example of how WTO agreements may impact differentially on poor and rich countries.

There are few reliable estimates of the implementation costs associated with multilateral trade reform. Finger and Schuler (2000) produced extrapolations based on case studies from the Uruguay Round. Their research concluded that while tariff reductions are relatively easy to implement, regulatory changes impose a burden on developing countries which may in some cases be large compared to the benefits they receive from new market access opportunities.[29]

Compliance with WTO agreements is harder for developing countries, whose administrative systems usually require larger reform to meet agreed standards. In addition, developing countries have the weakest government institutions and most constrained public resources. Implementation of an agreement incorporating regulatory changes requires expenditure on system design and drafting of legislation, capital expenditure on buildings and equipment, and personnel training, as well as the ongoing costs of administration and enforcement.

Finger (2000) points out that the implementation of regulatory agreements will often draw money from the development budgets of poor countries. For this reason such agreements should be analysed in terms of their rate of return and compared to the alternative development priorities on which the same money could be spent. Finger estimated the implementation of three of the Uruguay Round's six agreements that required regulatory change (customs reform, intellectual property rights, and sanitary and phytosanitary (SPS) measures). His analysis suggests that the average cost of restructuring domestic regulations in the 12 developing countries considered could be as much as $150 million. In eight of these countries this figure is larger than the entire annual development budget.

Many developing countries have been unable to meet their Uruguay Round obligations because of these high costs. By January 2000, up to 90 of the WTO's 109 developing country members were in violation of the SPS, customs valuation and Trade-Related Intellectual Property Rights (TRIPs) agreements. Estimates of the cost of compliance with the Uruguay agreements vary widely depending on the quality of existing systems and the strength of institutions in each country. Hungary spent more than $40 million to upgrade the level of sanitation of its slaughterhouses alone. Mexico spent more than $30 million to upgrade intellectual property laws. Finger (2000) suggests that for many of the least developed countries in the WTO, compliance with these agreements is a less attractive investment than expenditure on basic development goals such as education.

The costs of implementing the regulatory agreements that could potentially emerge from the Doha Round will vary widely across countries. However, these costs are likely to be smaller than for the Uruguay Round because the agenda is smaller, the developing countries are being asked to do less and there are fewer regulatory issues on the table (particularly since three of the Singapore issues have been dropped).

However, the costs of the remaining Singapore issue, trade facilitation, could be large for some countries. For example, the World Bank assisted Tunisia in its programme of streamlining and modernising its customs procedures. The total value of World Bank loans to Tunisia for this purpose was $35 million in 1999. Similarly, the World Bank lent $38m to Poland for upgrading the physical and managerial infrastructure of its port facilities.[30] Projects to implement the WTO Agreement on Customs Valuation, which also includes broader customs reform, have been estimated to cost between US$1.6 million and US$16.2 million. For example, a six-year programme in Tunisia to computerise and simplify procedures cost an estimated US$16.2 million (Finger and Schuler, 2000). Bolivia implemented a broad customs reform programme that cost US$38.5 million.

The important lesson from the Uruguay Round is that regulatory changes impose a large and (in the case of the many non-compliant countries) unacceptable burden on developing countries. The rules seemed to be developed with little awareness of development problems and little appreciation of the institutional capacities of least developed countries.

## Building Capacity Needs

*'The LDCs have neither the surplus of exportable products nor the production capacity to take immediate advantage of new trade opportunities. They will need substantial investment and technical assistance in order to expand their production.'* Kofi Annan[31]

Market access on its own is not sufficient to bring the benefits of trade to developing countries. LDCs are in many cases unable to take significant advantage of new trading opportunities because their supply capacity and competitiveness are extremely limited. LDCs have been granted new market access opportunities in successive rounds of trade negotiations, as well as in a range of preferential market access schemes. In each case, studies are produced to assess the potential benefits of these opportunities and invariably make large claims about the anticipated effect on LDCs' exports and welfare. These studies make a number of optimistic assumptions about supply elasticity in LDCs and in most cases, *ex post* analysis has found that new market opportunities have led to little increase in LDC exports. Time and time again, we learn that without decent roads, efficient ports, and the technical capability to produce and distribute goods of sufficient quality, new trading opportunities are meaningless for the poorest countries.[32]

Despite decades of multilateral liberalisation and increasingly 'generous' preferential schemes, LDCs' share of world trade has fallen over the past 20 years. There can be no doubt among WTO members that tariff reductions must be accompanied by concerted efforts to ensure that poor producers are able to capitalise on new trading opportunities. In the context of low productive capacity, a deficient policy environment, poor infrastructure, poor access to technology and non-existent or imperfect markets (especially financial markets), liberalised markets will not stimulate the development required to enable LDCs to take advantage of new trading opportunities.[33]

Some attention has been given to this issue within the WTO since the commencement of the Doha Round. Paragraph 41 of the final Declaration of the WTO Doha Ministerial Meeting – which was warned by the G77 countries about the lack of technical assistance in recent years – reiterates the importance of technical assistance and 'reaffirms ... the important role of sustainably financed technical assistance and capacity-building programmes'. Easing supply constraints requires a broader interpretation of the responsibilities covered by technical assistance – i.e. going beyond bolstering public institutions to promoting private enterprise and financing infrastructure.

Assistance to build supply capacity is of three type, each of which should be the focus of an expanded aid for trade agenda:

- **Trade policy and regulations** – to help countries participate in the multilateral trading system and reform their own trade policies;
- **Enterprise development** – to help private sector enterprises to trade and create a favourable business climate;
- **Infrastructure** – to assist in the identification of infrastructure bottlenecks and finance infrastructure projects.

## Trade policy and regulations

A core need which should be addressed by aid for trade is the lack of trade policy capacity in many developing countries, which simply do not have the staff, finance or depth of skills to adequately represent their interests in trade negotiations and integrate their own trade policies into changing environments. This is particularly true as demands on trade policy officials increase because of the proliferation of bilateral trade agreements.

Trade policy capacity building is too often narrowly focused on encouraging developing countries to participate in negotiations that are of interest to rich countries. Too often it is focused on one-off issues, rather than contributing to building national capacity to understand, negotiate and implement trade agreements in a way that maximises development. Perhaps the rich donor countries do not necessarily want to increase the knowledge and negotiating skills of the developing country officials with whom they are bargaining?

Ideally, trade policy capacity building would involve research, training and institutional funding with the aim of creating trade-related knowledge networks. Much of this is already occurring through bilateral donors and the World Bank – the challenge is to continue the development of national and regional institutions, for example the Caribbean Regional Negotiating Machinery (CRNM), and to ensure that funding leads to long-term results – whether in terms of trade policies, negotiations, implementation, or the resolution of supply-side constraints and the realisation of expanded market opportunities.

The WTO regulations designed to create a level playing field may, however, circumscribe traditional, as well as innovative, approaches to development. For instance, some are concerned that the kinds of strong industrial policies which played such an important role in the success of the East Asian countries might be circumscribed by current WTO rules.[34] As with any new and untested body of law, there is uncertainty about interpretation, and developing countries are subject to pressure (especially when they are the recipients of preferences that can be taken away at will) to accept the interpretations demanded by the advanced industrial countries. There has been concern, for instance, about pressure brought to bear when some countries attempted to use the flexibilities built into TRIPs to issue compulsory licenses for life-saving medicines. An important form of assistance is to help developing countries redesign their development policies in ways that are consistent with their broad development and social agendas.

Aid and trade policy advice should also encompass training government officials on how to implement new trade agreements and on building the capacity within institutions that is necessary to carry out the terms of the agreements.

## Enterprise development

While public sector capacity building is an important precondition, the ultimate objective of aid for trade programmes is to enhance the capacity of the private sector to develop into new markets. Aid for trade schemes need to constructively promote the development of new productive capacity without crowding out private investment, promoting inefficient industries or stifling entrepreneurial activity.

For many exporters in developing countries the costs imposed on them by tariffs, quotas or rules of origin are small relative to the costs imposed on them by an unfavourable business environment and inadequate local financial development. The costs associated with setting up a business, acquiring credit, getting reliable access to utilities and transporting goods from plants to ports all impose a burden on the productive sector of most developing countries.

The aim of aid for trade should be to expand exports and enable companies to do a better job of responding to export opportunities. A key component of private sector development is improved access to finance: to take advantage of new opportunities for exports, there must be export finance. In countries with underdeveloped financial sectors, inadequate finance is a major constraint inhibiting exports. To the extent that the poor are involved in trading activities, they may struggle to obtain access to the trade credit they need because of particular difficulties in assessing the creditworthiness of exporting firms and because the firms do not have sufficient collateral.[35]

In addition to improving access to knowledge and credit, more attention needs to be given to helping the development of competent institutions in developing countries and removing the obstacles ineffective institutions place in the way of exporting firms. These include effective customs authorities, more accountable policing and more efficient port authorities.

## Infrastructure

Inadequate infrastructure is also an important source of supply constraints. Poor transport infrastructure can prevent local farmers from accessing large domestic markets and international ports; poor storage facilities can increase inventory costs; and bad energy and water supplies can disrupt production or increase costs. In addition, institutional capacity can affect trade costs if customs procedures, inspections or certifying bodies are run inefficiently.

For example, in Uganda poor infrastructure cripples local exporters. More than 50 per cent of Ugandan roads are in poor condition,[36] placing a large burden on farmers. Increased transport costs associated with poor roads add the equivalent of an 80 per cent tax on exported clothing. Most companies rely on generators to bridge periods of blackout and to avoid damage to equipment from power fluctuations. This is far less efficient than grid power. For example, the average generator installed by small and medium-sized enterprises (SMEs) in Uganda costs about $25,000 to purchase and imposes considerable ongoing maintenance and fuel costs.[37] Power generation can increase business start-up costs by more than 30 per cent. For businesses in countries without decent infrastructure, tariff barriers are inconsequential when compared to the costs imposed by domestic obstacles. EU Commissioner Pascal Lamy acknowledged that 'duty-free access alone is not enough to enable the poorest countries to benefit from liberalised trade. We need to help them build their capacity to supply goods of export quality and we reaffirm the Commission's commitment to continued technical and financial assistance to this end' (European Commission, 2005).

Despite the importance of these 'behind the border' costs, aid for infrastructure has been falling for a decade. There is now recognition in development quarters that donor-supported public funding is an essential prerequisite for boosting or upgrading supply capacity and infrastructure building in LDCs. Improved infrastructure, combined with strong macroeconomic conditions, complements investment in supply capacity building and increases export competitiveness. The increased focus on infrastructure needs is reflected in the World Bank's plans to increase infrastructure lending by $1 billion per year to around $10 billion by 2008 and in the G8's Gleneagles Agreement to '*boost growth, attract new investment and contribute to Africa's capacity to trade'* through the establishment of the Infrastructure Consortium for Africa, jointly supported by African countries and by the European Commission, G8 and key multilaterals.[38]

However, in order to achieve trade-related policy objectives, infrastructure improvements must be coupled with good policies. Research indicates that returns to infrastructure projects can vary widely and are affected by the quality of the business environment. For example, good roads and port facilities alone do not guarantee an expansion of trade. The value of infrastructure projects is easily eroded by poor economic policies or inefficient and corrupt customs services.[39]

## New Mechanisms for Aid for Trade

In recent years a number of institutions have made concerted efforts to deal with trade adjustment and capacity building. These include the Integrated Framework for Trade-Related Assistance and the IMF's Trade Integration Mechanism. At the same time, bilateral aid for trade has been increasing and multilateral development banks have stepped up their technical assistance programmes and increased support for trade-related investments.

As aid flows begin to significantly increase and the scope of trade development projects widens, it is appropriate to consider alternative mechanisms to deliver aid for trade more effectively – in particular to ensure predictability, coherence, country ownership and additionality. There are three options:

- Continue with existing mechanisms
- Create a new trade specific fund
- Reform existing mechanisms

Existing mechanisms have been relatively successful in managing the policy dimension of aid for trade – they have made some progress in integrating aid for trade into national poverty reduction strategies and they have increased the coherence of programmes run by multilateral institutions. The Integrated Framework emerged from the 1996 WTO Singapore Ministerial Conference, as part of the WTO Action Plan for LDCs, to boost their participation in the world trading system. The IF is made up of six multilateral institutions: the World Bank, WTO, IMF, ITC, UNCTAD and UNDP. Its objectives are to embed a trade agenda into national poverty reduction strategies (country ownership); and to assist in the coordinated delivery of trade-related technical assistance from multiple donors (coherence).[40] However, the IF has extremely limited resources – its mandate to date has been essentially one of policy advice. But without funds to back up its recommendations, the IF will find it difficult to convince developing countries that they should include large unfunded trade development projects in their poverty reduction strategies. Moreover, even if the IF was equipped with funds, its institutional structure is ill-equipped to translate policy into delivery and implementation of aid for trade.

Its management is too diffuse and it has insufficient in-country presence to manage projects. Existing structures would not be effective in managing the delivery of large volumes of funds earmarked for trade development, and they are unlikely to be the best mechanisms through which to deal with the specific concerns of developing countries arising from the prospective Doha Round agreement.

By the same token we are sceptical about the merits of a new stand-alone fund dedicated to aid for trade. Page and Kleen (2004) propose that a new fund be established within the WTO to deal with preference dependent economies. Its funding would come from contributions from developed countries which would be determined by various criteria, and commitments would be 'legally irrevocable'. Funding would be allocated to recipient countries according to the estimation of their loss of preferences. Similarly, Grynberg and Silva (2004) suggest the creation of a Special Fund for Diversification to benefit preference dependent countries. An attractive feature of this scheme is that a share of funds would be allocated for a private sector development including start-up financing for SMEs. However, a dedicated fund would be costly to set up. It would lack coherence with existing efforts, and would be less likely to consider adjustment needs in the context of broader development efforts and policy reforms which constitute a holistic approach to development assistance.

A second attractive feature of dedicated funds is that by identifying specific costs to developing countries arising from the trade round (i.e. preference losses), they create well-defined obligations on the rich countries. However, these obligations are ultimately forms of compensation. This means that there is no reason in principle that the aid must be related to trade development rather than channelled as direct transfers.[41] Indeed, the proposed funds would be slow to develop the institutional experience and in-country presence necessary to manage and implement complex trade development programmes effectively. There is also a concern that if aid for trade is conceived of as compensation for one specific set of losses (preferences), assistance will be focused on those countries that are most disadvantaged by preference loss, rather than those countries who are most in need overall. Those who have the most to lose from preference erosion are not necessarily the poorest or most vulnerable – and it is unclear why countries which have benefited from a historical preference should be compensated above those whose needs are greater now. While the problem of preference erosion is important and will require funds to overcome, a new aid for trade facility should encompass broader objectives.

For this reason, we propose significant reform to existing mechanisms, rather than the establishment of a new fund. The IF concept should be retained, but rather than being controlled by a cumbersome alliance of six institutions, its management should be more firmly concentrated within the World Bank. In particular, dedicated funds for aid for trade – donated through specific binding commitments in the final Doha agreements and subsequently enforceable within the WTO – should be allocated to a special facility to be administered by the World Bank, in much the same way as the Bank administers the GEF. Location within the bank would allow the new facility to take advantage of the administrative capacities of the Bank and the possibly strong synergies between the GTF and the Bank's other lending activities. Of particular relevance is the Bank's private sector arm, the International Finance Corporation (IFC), which should work closely with the GTF in enterprise development. (Clearly other international organisations would be involved in the identification of trade development needs, and a wide variety of organisations would be delegated to execute projects.) It will be important, however, for the governance of the GTF to remain separate from that of the World Bank, to ensure that the funds are used in the way intended.

Because the GTF is the result of a negotiated global trade agreement, the governance structure should be different from that of the World Bank, where voting is dominated by the donor countries. Indeed, one of the principle responsibilities of the GTF is to enforce the obligations and commitments of the advanced industrial countries. The following structure is proposed: a board of 24, with eight seats reserved for low-income countries, eight for middle-income countries and eight for advanced industrial countries. A 60 per cent supermajority would be required for major decisions. The seats would be held by WTO members on a rotating basis, chosen to ensure a diversity of geography and economic interests: for example no more than three seats (within any of the groupings) would be held by countries in any one region, with at least one seat reserved for an agricultural exporter.

Any aid for trade initiative, including the proposal for a GTF enforceable within the WTO framework, would require developed countries to make commitments. While the size and distribution of those commitments will inevitably be a matter of intense negotiation among WTO members, the following proposal suggests a set of principles which might guide the discussions.

Any meaningful aid for trade facility must be large enough to actually make a difference, yet not so large that it would overwhelm other aid initiatives, including those for social purposes or for protecting the environment (the GEF). The international community has made a commitment to provide 0.7 per cent of advanced industrialised countries' GDP for assistance.[42]

It also makes sense to relate the aid for trade commitments to the size of the benefits from global trade, and particularly trade with developing countries. Finally, those countries that impose large costs on developing countries through their failure to liberalise (eliminate agriculture subsidies) should make additional commitments. Overall, the failure to achieve fair liberalisation (eliminating agricultural subsidies, higher tariffs on the products of developing than developed countries) accounts for much of the disappointment with liberalisation in many developing countries. Such a levy would have the further advantage of providing an incentive to eliminate distortionary and inequitable policies.

Hence we propose a three-part commitment:

(a) The advanced industrial countries would contribute 0.05 per cent of their GDP to the GTF. This means that the aid to trade facility would comprise approximately 7 per cent of the total commitment (of 0.7 per cent of GDP) to developing countries, an amount that seems balanced within the framework of overall development needs;

(b) There would be an *additional* commitment of a small percentage of the value of their exports to LDCs. This would be a partial substitution of the revenues that would have been received as tariffs; but it would take advantage of the greater administrative capacity of the developed countries, and avoid all the distortionary and political economy 'costs' associated with tariffs. The advanced industrial countries need not actually levy the amount as a tax on exports, but could simply pay the amount (small relative to the GDP of the advanced industrial countries) out of general revenues;

(c) There would be an *additional* commitment of 5 per cent of all agricultural subsidies and 15 per cent of all arms sales to developing countries, partially reflecting the costs that these impose on developing countries.

We believe that the middle-income countries should also make a contribution directed towards those with lower incomes. It might be appropriate for the contribution to be at a significantly lower rate (say a half or a quarter of the rate of that for the advanced industrial countries); some of their contribution might be *in kind*, rather than in dollars: for instance, designing training programmes for the less developed countries to explain what they have done to expand and facilitate trade.

These contributions to an aid for trade facility must not be made at the expense of other forms of assistance. There has to be some Maintenance of Effort Commitment. There are several problems in defining an appropriate commitment: debt write-offs, for example, should not be included, especially in the case of debts that would not in any case have been repaid. They should, perhaps, be defined in terms of net flows of funds to developing countries for assistance purposes (as a percentage of GDP) over the last five years. We are concerned with development assistance, not military assistance. We suggest that the Maintenance of Effort Commitment should be defined, accordingly, as assistance *exclusive of reconstruction activities in war zones* and *exclusive of all military assistance*.

## Instruments

There are many factors that constrain export growth in developing economies. A broad aid for trade effort should focus on removing these and creating a favourable environment for private sector development. Of course, ongoing support for institutional capacity building is an essential complement to enterprise development. Support should be extended to programmes to enhance in-country expertise and policy formulation, as well as research and trade development diagnostic studies. In the long run, regulatory and legal frameworks are essential to successful business environments.

But in the short run, a key feature of an expanded aid for trade agenda should be to promote investments in new productive capacity. If new aid is to catalyse, rather than stifle, private sector resources it must take a bottom-up approach beginning with action to create the a favourable business environment and an effective credit market.

An aid for trade fund should prioritise programmes to mitigate risk for enterprises in developing countries, and to promote the development of local financial markets. High levels of risk in developing countries are a major barrier to investment. In particular, political risk and exchange rate risk cause foreign investors to shy away from developing countries. There are several ways that multilateral finance could be mobilised to reduce risk and enhance credit. For example, a multilateral credit insurance facility could subsidise financial guarantee insurers – providing projects in developing countries with access to monolines[43] which would facilitate access to large volumes of credit. Similarly, a multilateral securitisation facility could help national and subnational developing countries to bundle different cash flow streams into a single asset against which they could borrow at a lower rate. Currency risk is perhaps the greatest threat to developing countries' ability to trade and attract investment. The development of multilateral assistance programmes to pool currency risk and subsidise hedging costs should be the subject of research. The GTF could work with existing initiatives, for example the Asian Bond Fund, as well as expanding such initiatives to other regions. At the same time, the GTF could work with the World Bank and other multilateral banks to encourage bond markets in local currencies and/or baskets of local currencies.

Infrastructure projects to address specific bottlenecks need to be financed, but they also should be driven by local users. There is a critical need to ensure that good projects are identified and matched quickly to finance and implementation. This will require increased financial support for project development capacities: feasibility studies, demand assessments and project proposal documents. A wide range of different levels of government, civil society groups and private interests should be eligible to apply for finance. And public private partnerships should be harnessed to expand finance for infrastructure. However, in most cases projects will require significant subsidies – in many developing countries, basic infrastructure projects are either not commercially viable at all, or not profitable unless they charge fees which inhibit universal access.

One of the major changes in thinking about development during the past decade is the realisation that what separates developed and less developed countries is not just a gap in resources, but a gap in knowledge. There is widespread concern that TRIPs, the intellectual property provisions of the Uruguay Round, may have impaired access to knowledge for development. This is reflected, for instance, in the initiatives taken within the World Intellectual Property Organization (WIPO) by the Friends of Development to create a more development-oriented intellectual property regime.[44] The GTF could support the development of institutions capable of facilitating the transfer of technology (for example science and technology-oriented universities, research centres and standards centres). It could help organise global internship programmes, in which students from developing countries learn from the practices of the advanced industrial countries.

We referred earlier to the fact that one of the important adjustments facing developing countries arises from a reduction in one of their major sources of revenues, tariffs.

Alternatives often have higher administrative costs and are often less progressive. This is particularly true of VAT, which is widely employed in advanced industrial countries (outside the USA); but the regressive nature of VAT in these countries is mitigated by the existence of highly progressive income taxes. Most developing countries, however, do not have the capacity to administer such a tax effectively. The GTF should also engage in helping developing countries develop effective and efficient progressive tax structures, that can make up for the loss of revenues from tariffs. These (perhaps second best measures – appropriate for a second best world) may include the design of progressive excise taxes, progressive housing taxes (based on the square footage of a house), financial transactions taxes, severance taxes, excess or windfall profits taxes on natural resources (when prices suddenly shoot up) or taxes on monopoly/oligopoly profits.

It is important that the aid for trade programme (for example the GTF) should not be subject to the usual conditionalities, and in particular that there should be no macroeconomic or political conditionality.[45] The only exception to this principle should be in enforcing matters vital to the well-being of the entire world, for example nuclear proliferation and global environmental agreements (in particular, those affecting global warming). Countries do not have to be signatories to such global agreements for these matters of global concern to be used as conditionality.

In the first instance, funds should be directed to countries facing large adjustment costs, and to projects which will be of benefit to those most adversely affected by trade liberalisation and any new trade agreement. Even though the aid is not intended as compensation, appropriately designed aid programmes can ensure that there are as few losers from trade liberalisation as possible. The aid should be designed to facilitate job creation in areas most adversely affected, and to help those who have lost their jobs obtain alternative employment.

In the longer run, projects and proposals should be evaluated in terms of: (i) their economic and social rates of return; (ii) the income of those who benefit from the programme; and (iii) the magnitude of the adverse trade shocks (liberalisation) to which those who benefit (or their country) have been subjected. This takes into account the fact that countries which have been more adversely affected are in a poorer position to provide adjustment help for individuals and firms which have been adversely affected.

Administratively, it may turn out best to allocate money using three baskets: one devoted to countries and areas which are most adversely affected; another based on broader metrics of income and trade; and a third, where countries would be encouraged to submit innovative projects which would be judged competitively. The relative allocation of funds to these three baskets could change over time, with more money being allocated initially to the first basket.

## Conclusion

For several years, the governments of many developed countries have argued that 'trade not aid' is the answer to the problems of the developing countries. The insincerity of their approach has been revealed in successive rounds of trade negotiations in which they have been reluctant to open their markets to poor countries. And more recently their claims have also been exposed as fundamentally inaccurate, as liberalisation has failed to result in either export growth or development for the poorest countries.

Increased aid is vital for the poor countries if they are to grasp the opportunities provided through trade and meet transition costs. Adjustment to a post-Doha trading regime will be disproportionately costly and difficult for developing countries because of the loss of preference margins, the loss of revenue from trade taxes, institutional weaknesses including the absence of adequate safety nets, implementation costs, lack of finance required to restructure the economy and the limited ability of poor populations to manage short-term unemployment.

However, our proposal to provide new resources to meet adjustment needs does not suggest that trade, when combined with aid, will be a panacea for developing countries. Interactions between trade, aid, and broader development policies and reforms are important. Trade reform is just one of many potential shocks and opportunities faced by developing countries, and internal as well as external reforms will be essential in ensuring that these countries realise their development potential.

## Notes

1 Pascal Lamy made this point by bringing a wand to the opening session of the Hong Kong Ministerial, 13 December 2005.

2 This goes beyond the traditional concerns of aid dependency.

3 For a discussion of aid for trade, see Page (2006).

4 Although there are concerns that the Round may not be finished within two years, see Evenett (2006).

5 Gary Hufbauer of the Institute for International Economics. Comments at a meeting of trade experts hosted by International Trade Canada, Ottawa, 3 March 2006.

6 The relevance of this concern is highlighted by the fact that so many developing countries were actually worse off after the last round of trade negotiations. UNDP (1997).

7 Page (2005): 'One argument could be that there is no case for adjustment assistance: the countries knew that their income depended on preferences, and knew that trade policies could change, so their losses could have been anticipated. There are two reasons for rejecting this, one practical, one developmental: the first is that if they are not offered some compensation, they will have an incentive to delay or frustrate a settlement, which will damage other countries' welfare. The second is that they are developing countries and should have some advantage in WTO agreements, particularly in a Development Round.'

8 UN Secretary General Kofi Annan's statement at the WTO's Fifth Ministerial Meeting in Cancun, Mexico, 2003.

9 *Pop of the World*, Equity Watch, Center for Science and Environment, 25 October 2002.

10 President Benjamin Mkapa of Tanzania, November 2004.

11 Country ownership has become a basic principle of initiatives like the Millennium Challenge Account or the Millennium Development Goals. Various new donor organisations, including the Global Fund to Fight AIDS, Tuberculosis and Malaria, have implemented financing instruments to fund projects which are both proposed and implemented by local organisations. Implementation is carried out by a wide variety of stakeholders, including the academic sector, government, non-governmental and community-based organisations, the private sector, religious organisations and multi- and bilateral development partners.

12 The Heavily Indebted Poor Countries (HIPC) debt relief initiative was one of the first aid schemes to successfully implement the country-led approach to development assistance. Eligible countries were asked to incorporate debt relief into national poverty reduction strategies which demonstrated how the extra money would be used to further the country's own development goals.

13 Henri-Bernard Solignac Lecomte, quoted in *Interaction* (2005), 'Strengthening the Connection Between Trade and Development by Reorienting Trade Capacity Building Assistance', Interaction Working Paper, March 2005.

14 UN Secretary General Kofi Annan's statement at the WTO's Fifth Ministerial Meeting in Cancun, Mexico, 2003.

15 George W. Bush (2000). Remarks by the President on Global Development, Inter-American Development Bank, 14 March 2002.

16 Metzler (2000), 'Report of the International Financial Institution Advisory Commission', US Congressional Report, March 2000.

17 It has also been argued that because lending requires repayment, it generates more ownership and commitment from the recipient country than a grant does. To the extent that that is true, it is an argument for blending grants and loans.

18 A main concern with the shift from loans to grants is that the reflows will not be be available for helping developing countries, and that the net flows to developing countries may actually be reduced, as governments classify debt forgiveness – even when the moneys would never in any case have been repaid – as 'aid', subtracting that amount from what otherwise would have been given.

9 Term originally coined by Sapir (2000). Sapir, A. 2000. 'Who Is Afraid of Globalization? The Challenge of Domestic Adjustment in Europe and America', CEPR Discussion Paper 2595, Centre for Economic Policy Research, London.

20 This is the implication of the renowned Stolper and Samuelson (1941) theorem; but even if the restrictive conditions under which it holds are not satisfied, there is a presumption that relative rewards to different factors will change in the way indicated.

21 The numbers can be large. A $4 billion annual cotton subsidy translates, if fully capitalised in land values at a 5 per cent interest rate, into $80 billion.

22 Thus, even if the dollar value of the gains to the winners from liberalisation are greater than the dollar value of

the losses to the losers, when the costs of compensation are taken into account, trade liberalisation may not be welfare enhancing.

23 That is, countries are now more subject to the vagaries of international prices. See P. Dasgupta and J. E. Stiglitz, 'Tariffs Versus Quotas as Revenue Raising Devices Under Uncertainty', *American Economic Review*, 67(5), December 1977, pp. 975–81. More generally, trade liberalisation may make countries more vulnerable to external shocks, and for countries in which trade looms large in GDP, the result may be greater macroeconomic volatility.

24 Even in developed countries, there is evidence that less well educated workers who are displaced experience greater adjustment costs.

25 Many countries have shifted to greater reliance on VAT, but as Stiglitz has argued, this switch may have adverse effects on development. See J. E. Stiglitz, 'Development Oriented Tax Policy', paper presented to 59th Congress of the IIPF, Prague, 24–25 August 2003.

26 See Eiteljorge and Shiells (1995), Tokarick (2005) and Phillips, Page and te Velde (2005).

27 There is another reason to be wary of an excessive focus on agriculture. Development requires less developing countries to move into sectors with higher rates of potential productivity improvements, to develop their dynamic comparative advantage, not just their static comparative advantage.

28 Although for some of these products, it is unlikely that there will be MFN liberalisation in the near future. Moreover, market 'loyalty' is likely to be less important in 'commodity' trade than in trade in manufacturers.

29 Many developing countries have been unable to meet their Uruguay Round obligations because of these high costs. By January 2000, up to 90 of the WTO's 109 developing country members were in violation of the SPS, customs valuation and TRIPs agreements. Estimates of the cost of compliance to the Uruguay agreements vary widely depending on the quality of the existing systems and the strength of institutions in each country. Hungary spent more than $40 million on upgrading the level of sanitation of its slaughterhouses alone. Mexico spent more than $30 million on upgrading its intellectual property laws. Finger (2000) suggests that for many of the least developed countries in the WTO compliance with these agreements is a less attractive investment than expenditure on basic development goals such as education.

30 Wilson (2001).

31 Quoted in *Financial Times*, 5 March 2001, in the context of Annan's response to the EU's 'Everything but Arms' initiative.

32 Fugazza (2004) shows, for example, that Africa's ability to reap benefits from improved market access has been constrained by the poor development of supply capacity factors.

33 One way of understanding the problem is the following: there are both natural (economic) barriers to trade and man-made barriers to trade (tariffs). Trade liberalisation reduces the man-made barriers. For developed countries, with good roads and ports, these are the *major* barriers, while for developing countries the natural barriers are the major barriers. In effect, trade liberalisation reduces the barriers to trade by a much larger percentage for developed than for developing countries.

34 Others ask whether it is possible for them to adopt versions of America's Community Reinvestment Act, requiring banks (whether domestically or foreign owned) to invest in underserved communities (or, in a slight extension, in SMEs). Still others ask if the kinds of affirmative action requirements that Malaysia used so effectively in addressing its problems are proscribed by the WTO.

35 Where there is an absence of private credit, there may be a role for publicly funded institutions to increase access to finance for low-income producers. For example, the Development Bank of Mauritius (DBM) played a key role in providing finance for the expansion of existing business and the establishment of new firms in Mauritius. Among several other activities, the DBM was involved in building industrial estates to encourage development in export processing zones, setting up foreign exchange schemes for SMEs, providing working capital through micro-credit and extending preferential credit schemes.

36 IMF (2004). *Uganda Poverty Reduction Strategy Paper: Progress Report*, IMF.

37 D.J. Donaldson, F. Sader and D.M. Wagle (1997). 'Foreign Direct Investment in Infrastructure – The Challenge of Southern and Eastern Africa', Foreign Investment Advisory Service Occasional Paper 9. Washington, DC: World Bank.

38 EC (2005). 'Conclusions of the Council and of the Representatives of the Governments of the Member States Meeting within the Council on Aid for Trade', Brussels, 14 December 2005.

39 Anke Hoeffler, 1999. 'Challenges of Infrastructure Rehabilitation and Reconstruction in War-affected Economies', background paper for the African Development Bank Report 1999.

40 In this way the IF mechanism embodies many features of the 'new aid framework' which aims to improve harmonisation between the providers of trade assistance and place trade within the context of a country's broader development strategy.

41 There are other problems with adopting compensation as the basis underlying the aid for trade programme. Compensation should really be directed at the individuals who are hurt. Aid for trade may in fact fail to reach those individuals. If compensation were directed at the country, one could argue for an offset for the gains, resulting in a contentious analysis of the magnitude of the *net* losses. There are further problems: many of the preferences have always been temporary, though they were continually renewed. Does the country (individual) need compensation *as if* they were permanent (which could be large), or only for the period of the explicit programme (in which case they might be very small.)

42 Reconstruction activities are important, but they should not be at the expense of the broader commitment to development.

43 Financial guarantee insurance (monolines) is widely used in the developed world – particularly by municipal governments – to facilitate long-term, low-cost access to large amounts of credit.

44 In particular, the endorsement of that initiative by the General Assembly of WIPO in October 2004. Developing countries believe that while their access to knowledge may have been impaired, TRIPs provided insufficient protections for Traditional Knowledge.

45 Concerns about macroeconomic conditions in the country may, of course, shape the nature of the lending programme. But it is important that the new facility be viewed as another instrument for leveraging into particular policy stances.

## References

Anke Hoeffler (1999). 'Challenges of Infrastructure Rehabilitation and Reconstruction in War-affected Economies', background paper for the African Development Bank Report 1999.

Commission for Africa (2005). *Our Common Interest: Report for the Commission for Africa*. London: Penguin Books.

Dasgupta, P. and Stiglitz, J.E. (1977). 'Tariffs Versus Quotas as Revenue Raising Devices Under Uncertainty', *American Economic Review* 67(5), pp. 975–81.

Donaldson, D.J., Sader, F. and Wagle, D.M. (1997). 'Foreign Direct Investment in Infrastructure – The Challenge of Southern and Eastern Africa', Foreign Investment Advisory Service Occasional Paper 9, Washington, DC: World Bank.

Ebrill, L., Stotsky, J. and Gropp, R. (1999). 'Revenue Implications of Trade Liberalization', IMF Occasional Paper, No. 180.

European Commission (2005). 'Conclusions of the Council and of the Representatives of the Governments of the Member States Meeting within the Council on Aid for Trade', Brussels, 14 December 2005.

Eiteljörge, Uwe, and Shiells, C. (1995). 'The Uruguay Round and Net Food Importers', IMF Working Paper 95/143.

Emran, M.S. and Stiglitz, J.E. (2004). 'On Selective Indirect Tax Reform in Developing Countries', *Journal of Public Economics* 89(4).

Evenett, S. (2005a). 'Some Tough Love On 'Aid For Trade', November 2005. Forthcoming in *Intereconomics*.

Evenett, S. (2005b). 'Can the WTO Rise to the Challenge of Economic Development?', Forthcoming in *Aussenwirthschaft*.

Evenett, S. (2006). 'The WTO Ministerial Conference in Hong Kong: What's Next?', mimeo, University of St Gallen.

Finger, J.M. (2000). 'The WTO's Special Burden on Less Developed Countries', *Cato Journal* 19(3): 425.

Finger, J.M., and Schuler, P. (2000). 'Implementation of Uruguay Round Commitments: The Development Challenge', *The World Economy* 23(4): 511–25.

Grynberg, R. and Silva, S. (2004). 'Analysis of a Special Fund for Diversification', mimeo, Commonwealth Secretariat.

Hoekman, B. and Prowse, S. (2005). 'Economic policy responses to preference erosion: from trade as aid to aid for trade', World Bank Policy Research Working Paper 3721.

IMF (2004). *Uganda Poverty Reduction Strategy Paper*, Progress Report, IMF.

Interaction (2005). 'Strengthening the Connection Between Trade and Development by Reorienting Trade Capacity Building Assistance', Interaction Working Paper, March 2005.

Keen, M. and Lightart, J.E. (1999). 'Coordinating tariff reduction and domestic tax reform', IMF Working Paper WP/99/93, Washington, DC.

Low, P., Piermartini, R. and Richtering, J. (2005). 'Multilateral Solutions to the Erosion of Non-Reciprocal Preferences in NAMA', World Trade Organization Economic Research and Statistics Division Working Paper, ERSD-2005-05, October.

Metzler (2000). 'Report of the International Financial Institution Advisory Commission', US Congressional Report, March 2000.

Mitchell, D and Hoppe, M. (2006). 'From Marrakesh to Doha: Effects of Removing Food Subsidies on the Poor,' in Newfarmer, R. (ed.), *Trade, Doha and Development: A Window into the Issues*, Washington, DC: World Bank.

Page, S. (2005). 'A Preference Erosion Compensation Fund: A New Proposal to Protect Countries from the Negative Effects of Trade Liberalisation', *Overseas Development Institute Opinion* 35, January.

Page, Sheila (2006). *Trade and Aid: Partners or Rivals in Development Policy?*, London: Cameron May Ltd.

Page, S. and Kleen, P. (2004). 'Special and Differential Treatment of Developing Countries in the WTO', for the Ministry of Foreign Affairs, Sweden. Overseas Development Institute.

Page, S. (2004). 'Preference Erosion: Helping Countries to Adjust,' ODI Briefing Paper, available at *www.odi.org.uk*

Phillips, L., Page, S. and te Velde. D.W. (2005). 'Aid for Trade: What does it mean? Why should aid be part of WTO negotiations? And how much might it cost?', *ODI Opinions*, December 2005.

Sapir, A. (2000). 'Who Is Afraid of Globalization? The Challenge of Domestic Adjustment in Europe and America', CEPR Discussion Paper 2595, Centre for Economic Policy Research, London.

Stiglitz, J.E. (2003). 'Development Oriented Tax Policy', paper presented to 59th Congress of the IIPF, Prague, August 24–25, 2003.

Stiglitz, J.E. and Charlton, A. (2005). *Fair Trade for All: How Trade Can Promote Development*, Oxford: OUP.

Tokarick, S. (2005). 'Aligning Aid with Adjustment, Finance and Development', March.

UNDP (1997). *Human Development Report 1997*, New York/London: Oxford University Press.

Waino, J. and Gibson, P. (2003). 'The Significance of Nonreciprocal Trade Preferences for Developing Countries', Contributed paper presented at the International Conference on Agricultural Policy Reform and the WTO: Where are we Heading?, Capri, Italy, 23–26 June 2003.

# 3

# Implications of the Hong Kong Ministerial Declaration on Duty-free and Quota-free Access for Least Developed Countries

Jane Kennan and Christopher Stevens

## Introduction

This chapter provides an analysis of the potential implications of the statement included in the Ministerial Declaration issued at the end of the WTO Hong Kong conference, held in December 2005, to offer duty-free and quota-free market access to least developed countries. It presents the results of a desk-based study which has analysed the current market access regime applied by Canada, the EU, Japan and the USA to imports from LDCs.

This analysis has been used to determine whether or not the DFQF initiative is likely to result in the removal of significant barriers to LDC trade. There are two completely different reasons why the initiative might not remove significant barriers in a specific market. One is that there are few barriers to be removed. The other is that barriers exist, but there is scope in the small print to continue restricting some significant sensitive items. The chapter examines both issues.

Given that the scope of the chapter is tightly specified, it may be helpful to list some of the important issues and questions that fall *outside* its remit. One obvious limitation is that the DFQF initiative applies only to LDCs. Although there are some exceptions, it is reasonable to expect these countries to have a relatively low potential to expand exports – that is why they are LDCs. This does not remove the value of a trade initiative limited to LDCs: the proportionate effects on the countries concerned could be significant. But it must be borne in mind that the Hong Kong initiative excludes most of the countries which have the greatest capacity to expand their exports rapidly.

Another area which is not covered by the report is rules of origin. To the extent that the rules of origin applied by Quad countries (Canada, the EU, Japan and the USA) require an unrealistically high level or type of processing for a good to acquire originating status, the effects of DFQF will be restricted. There is sufficient evidence that the rules applied by some Quad members are beyond the capacity of LDCs and other poor countries to fulfil to lead one to expect that this will dampen the supply response to DFQF.

Finally, the Hong Kong initiative applies specifically only to two types of border measure. There are wide variations between Quad members as to the range and value of imports from LDCs, even on goods for which tariffs or quotas are non-existent or non-constraining. Clearly, many other factors affect the level of imports, some of them directly or indirectly affected by governments, while others are market determined.

The Hong Kong Declaration refers to measures that may be required on rules of origin and on the removal of other barriers to imports from LDCs, but they are not specified in detail. These are not dealt with in this chapter, which is limited to the most specific of the commitments made.

### The DFQF Commitment

The Hong Kong statement is brief (para. 47 and Annex F) and possibly open to interpretation. We have had to make assumptions about the precise meaning of the commitment in order to assess its potential effects. These assumptions are set out below and their implications for the analysis is dealt with in more detail in the next section. An important conclusion of the chapter is that, because there exists scope for different legitimate interpretations of the DFQF commitment which could alter radically its impact on specific countries, it is important that LDCs and their supporters take action during the remainder of the Doha Round to clarify how it will be implemented.

Para. 47 of the Hong Kong Ministerial Declaration commits 'developed-country Members' as well as 'developing-country Members declaring themselves in a position to do so' to 'implement duty-free and quota-free market access for products originating from LDCs' in accordance with the details set out in Annex F (reproduced as Annex 1 to this chapter). Annex F introduces two caveats to the bold statement in the main text. One concerns the date for implementation, which is set at '2008 or no later than the start of the implementation period …'. The implication is that the DFQF proposal may not be implemented unless and until the Doha Round comes to a successful conclusion.

The other caveat is the subject of this chapter. Clause 36(a)(ii) allows 'Members facing difficulties' to provide DFQF 'for at least 97 per cent of products originating from LDCs, defined at the tariff line level …' and to take progressive steps to achieve full access. How large is this loophole? To answer this question assumptions need to be made about the following issues:

- How many goods will be liberalised;
- How many goods can be exempted initially from liberalisation;
- Which goods will be excluded from liberalisation;
- Countries to which DFQF will apply.

#### What liberalisation?

Annex F (36(a)(i)) states that developed country members will 'Provide duty-free and quota-free market access on a lasting basis, for all products originating from all LDCs …'. This is taken to mean that, when fully implemented, DFQF will apply to any import from any LDC on any product in the entire Harmonised System (HS) nomenclature.

There is no mention in this clause of any limitation related to the current pattern of imports from LDCs. In other words, the commitment is not merely to offer DFQF for all the products imported at present by a developed country member from an LDC.

## What exemptions?

Annex F (36(a)(ii)) allows 'Members facing difficulties at this time' to restrict the full application of DFQF. But nonetheless they must provide access conforming to the provisions of 36(a)(i) 'for at least 97 per cent of products originating from LDCs, defined at the tariff line level ...'. Four elements of this seem to be clear. They may appear to be mere semantic distinctions but, as will be seen below, they are directly relevant to the task of assessing the potential impact of clause 36(a)(ii). They are that:

- The commitment is expressed in terms of what must be liberalised (i.e. 97 per cent) and not what may be excluded;
- Any temporary exemptions from DFQF (during the period this chapter refers to as 'the transition phase') can be inferred to be restricted to a group of items that do not exceed 3 per cent of products originating from LDCs (i.e. actual imports) 'defined at the tariff line level ...'; and that therefore
- They relate to actual imports (and not to all of a country's tariff lines);
- At any given time (since no 'base year' is indicated) the number of items that must be liberalised and the number that may be excluded will change as the range of goods imported from LDCs changes.

### Tariff-line level

What is the tariff-line level? It would appear to mean the level of product disaggregation used by a Quad member when setting its tariffs. The UNCTAD/WTO International Trade Centre defines it as 'the classification codes ... applied to merchandise goods by individual countries that are longer than the HS-6 digit level'.[1] This is the sense in which the term appears habitually to be used in the WTO to distinguish it, for example, from the HS6 level of disaggregation. For example, clause 2(b)(ii) of the Annex on Modalities and Product Coverage of the Singapore 'Ministerial Declaration on trade in information technology products' specifies that modifications to a country's tariff schedule be made 'in the case of the products specified in Attachment B, by attaching an annex to its Schedule including all products in Attachment B, which is to specify the detailed HS headings for those products at *either* the national tariff line level *or* the HS 6-digit level' (italics added).[2]

### The permitted number of exclusions

It seems clear that the number of exclusions is linked to the number of items imported. Suppose a developed country Member's tariff schedule runs to 10,000 lines and there are imports from LDCs in 500 tariff lines. We take Annex F as requiring DFQF to be applied to 485 lines and allowing it to be withheld temporarily from 3 per cent of 500 tariff lines (i.e. 15 lines) and not from 3 per cent of 10,000 lines (i.e. 300 lines). If the number of imports increased to 600 items, the importing state would be required to offer DFQF to an additional 97 items and be permitted to withhold it from an additional 3 items. In other words it can exclude from DFQF any number of items that are not imported at all – but once such imports commence, even at the tiniest values, it must remove tariffs on 97 per cent of the new total.

## Which imports?

There is ambiguity over which 'imports' the 3 per cent refers to, and this has major implications for the methodology used. The assumptions made on this point will have a significant effect on the assessed impact of the Hong Kong Declaration.

There are four possible interpretations of the population to which the 97 per cent and the 3 per cent refer.

- *Interpretation 1:* of the developed country Member's imports from the LDC in question;
- *Interpretation 2:* of the developed country Member's imports from all LDCs;
- *Interpretation 3:* of all developed country Members' imports from the LDC in question;
- *Interpretation 4:* of all developed country Members' imports from all LDCs.

Interpretations 3 and 4 seem to be ruled out on grounds of practicality in the implementation and enforcement of Annex F. The HS trade classification is common only to 6 digits and most countries sub-divide some HS6 codes to 8 or 10 digits and set their tariffs at this level. Since these 8- and 10-digit codes are unique to each state, it is difficult to see how Interpretations (3) and (4) could be implemented. Suppose Quad state A sub-divides 10 of the HS 6 sub-heads into 100 8-digit items (for which it sets different tariffs) and Quad B splits them into 20 8-digit items, 15 of which are the same as A's and 5 of which are different. A and B together will be importing under 105 separate tariff lines and will each be required to remove all barriers on 97 per cent of these – or 102. Since each has fewer than 102 lines, it would have to liberalise on everything and exclude nothing.

Moreover, it is hard to see how any particular Quad state could be held to account since its compliance (or lack of it) would depend partly on what all other Quad states were doing. A decision by one Quad state to increase or reduce the number of exclusions would affect the target for all the others. For these reasons, Interpretations 3 and 4 have been discounted in this chapter.

No such *a priori* exclusion applies to Interpretations 1 and 2. The choice between them has major implications for the analysis. Under both interpretations a country which currently imports many items from one LDC may withhold DFQF treatment from a larger number of tariff lines than can a country which imports only a few items.

Interpretation 1 would allow a Member to exclude more items from an LDC that exported to it a wide range of products than from one that did not. Quad state A, which imports 1000 items from LDC 1, would be able to exclude 30 of them, but if it imports only 660 items from LDC 2, it could exclude just 20 of these. Under Interpretation 2, on the other hand, the number of possible exclusions from any one LDC would be related to the range of goods imported from all LDCs. Quad state A could exclude the same number of items from both LDC 1 and LDC 2. If 460 of its imports from LDC 2 were also being imported from LDC 1, it could exclude 36 items from each (3 per cent of the 1200 separate items it imports). This would be equivalent to 3.6 per cent of its imports from LDC 1 and 5.5 per cent of its imports from LDC 2. But Quad B (which imports just 900 separate items) could exclude only 27.

For reasons related to the practical implementation of DFQF, it is assumed that Interpretation 2 is the most likely. But analysis of the impact of Interpretation 1 is a necessary precursor to that of Interpretation 2. For this reason, we provide an analysis using both interpretations, starting with Interpretation 1 and then explaining how the situation would be different under Interpretation 2.

In summary, we assume that the Hong Kong Declaration commits developed country members to:

- Remove all tariff and quantitative barriers to imports from LDCs on any item in any sub-head of the HS system;
- *Save that*, this can be deferred for a basket of goods that:
  - on Interpretation 1, does not exceed in number 3 per cent of the items currently being imported by the developed country Member from a specific LDC (at the tariff line level); or
  - on Interpretation 2, does not exceed in number 3 per cent of all the items (at the tariff line level) imported by the developed country Member from all LDCs.

## Which countries?

The analysis considers only four developed country Members: the Quad. Not all Quad members offer LDC tariff treatment to all countries on the UN list of LDCs. This may be because the countries concerned have not completed the necessary administrative requirements (such as the establishment of an approved authorising authority). Or it may be because the Quad state concerned does not, as a matter of policy, offer LDC tariff treatment to the country in question.

It is assumed that the Hong Kong Declaration refers to all countries on the UN list of LDCs and that any LDC which is a WTO Member could take a case through the dispute settlement procedures on the grounds of discrimination if it was denied preferences made available to its LDC competitors (other than through the application of the 3 per cent rule).

It is beyond the scope of this chapter to check out in each case the determining factor for the non-provision at present of LDC access by some developed Members to some countries on the UN list. Nonetheless, we have identified separately the implications of offering DFQF to all of the countries currently given LDC treatment by the Quad state, and then to all the other countries on the UN list of LDCs that are not treated in this way at the present time.

The next section describes the methodology applied to derive the results described here and the sources of the data used. The chapter then considers the impact of DFQF on the two Quad members in which it might be expected to have least effect because most tariff and quantitative barriers have already been removed: these are the the EU and Canada. The following sections consider the potential application of DFQF in the USA and Japan. These countries have not yet removed almost all tariffs and quotas on imports from LDCs. The analysis is focused, therefore, on the extent to which the 3 per cent exclusion provision could enable a government wishing to adopt a minimalist approach to avoid substantial market opening during the transition phase. It must be borne in mind that only potential is assessed: the analysis does not suggest that these countries will wish to take a minimalist approach.

## Methodology

The Hong Kong Declaration requires developed country members to offer DFQF treatment to at least 97 per cent of their imports from LDCs with effect from 2008 or the start of the period for implementing decisions agreed in the Doha Round, and to extend this 'progressively' to all imports over an unspecified period of time. To avoid confusion we call the period between the dates on which 97 per cent and 100 per cent DFQF are granted 'the transition phase'.

If developed country members are allowed to exclude from DFQF 3 per cent of their imports from LDCs during the transition phase, would this be sufficient to avoid liberalisation on many sensitive items, or only a few? This is the major question that is addressed in this chapter and, as already indicated, it is far from straightforward. While the basic methodology employed to answer the question is simple, the assessed impact will vary sharply according to what is assumed about the unpredictable decisions that will be required to implement the Declaration.

Uncertainty over the meaning of 'LDC imports' affects the total number of items that can be excluded from DFQF, but even more problematic is the attempt to predict either what form the exclusion will take or which items will be excluded. Yet it will be these implementation decisions that will determine the impact of the Declaration on many LDCs. The methodology must provide some means that at least sets limits to the range of possible outcomes.

This chapter covers only a subset of developed country Members: the Quad. One of these, the EU, will offer full DFQF to all LDCs by 2009 under its Everything but Arms policy (at the expiry of temporary restrictions on three products: bananas, rice and sugar). The first task for the study in relation to the other Quad states has been to derive for each of them their imports from every LDC in order to determine the number of products that fall into the 3 per cent potential exclusion basket. These imports have then been ranked according to their apparent sensitivity and value to identify the items that might be excluded. This has allowed us to determine how substantial DFQF would be if the member in question took full advantage of the 3 per cent potential exclusion and applied it according to several alternative definitions of 'most sensitive products'. As explained above, the exercise has been performed twice, according to different interpretations of the way in which the 3 per cent rule will be applied. Three basic assumptions have been made to deal with the problems inherent in deriving the impact of any exclusions.

## Criteria for assessing potential impact

On one point the Ministerial Declaration is very clear: this is how the 97 per cent is to be derived. It is not 97 per cent by value of imports from an LDC, but of the products defined at the tariff line level. This is the level of product disaggregation at which a country normally sets its tariffs – and is usually 8 or 10 digits. It is referred to here as the national tariff line (NTL). In other words, if a member imports a hundred items it would be able to exclude three of them.

Using this guide, it is possible to identify the maximum number of items a Quad state is allowed to exclude from DFQF, but *which items* will be selected can only be speculated. This gives rise to serious methodological problems when seeking to identify the impact of such exclusions on LDCs, particularly minor exporters.

Until the precise range of exclusions is known, it is unclear whether they account for 75 per cent or more of the value of imports or for only a trivial proportion of import value. Yet without such information, no assessment can be made of the impact of DFQF (or of its limitations during the transition phase).

One assumption used to assess the potential implications of the partial DFQF exemption under Interpretation 1 is that the allowable exclusions are concentrated on the items with high tariffs that are imported to the largest value. This shows the maximum value of trade that could be excluded from full DFQF treatment.

A second assumption, used in both Interpretations (1) and (2), is that it is the highest tariff items that are excluded. This will not necessarily exclude the largest share of trade since very high tariffs are often so restrictive that there are few imports. Other smaller imports may be more sensitive – and are small precisely because the existing tariff is constraining, given the conditions in that particular market. A developed country Member might feel obliged to exclude some of these items even at the 'cost' of liberalising on the large-value items. This is a measure, therefore, less of the potential quantitative than of the qualitative impact of the DFQF limitation: which product groups from which LDCs could be restricted under the 3 per cent rule?

A third assumption takes one step further the point that the items imported to the largest value may not be the most sensitive. It seeks to identify from among a relatively large population of items that face high tariffs the ones that are the most sensitive. While it is not possible here to identify such items precisely, attention is directed to some potential candidates.

This has involved creating for each LDC a 'revealed supply capacity' list made up of its exports of every item to all of the Quad states.[3] Where appropriate the share of the item in the imports of one state can be compared to its share in the imports of all Quad states to identify proportionately low trade. This is not a definitive indication, of course, of whether an import is being artificially suppressed by current import barriers. There could be alternative explanations for exports going disproportionately to some Quad members (as, for example, in the case of sugar-exporting LDCs that have good commercial reasons to concentrate their exports on the EU). But it is a good place to start.

## Dealing with non-trade

This possibility could be taken further: what if a developed country Member chose to exclude products that are *not* imported. There are two possible reasons for the non-existence of the trade. One, which will apply in many cases, is that the LDC concerned does not have the capacity to supply the product either at all, or at the quality levels demanded in the Quad market. It is possible that legitimate questions may be raised in some of these cases about the effect of origin rules or health standards in preventing LDCs from exporting, but such concerns are not the subject of this report.

An alternative explanation, though, is that the LDC does have a supply capacity, but is prevented from exporting anything because of very high protectionist barriers. This possibility is relevant, but appears unlikely to reduce the intended impact of DFQF because of the way the Hong Kong Declaration is set out (according to our interpretation). Temporary exclusions are subject to a positive, not a negative, list: any item that is not positively excluded from DFQF must be included. If a Member chooses to use a part of its basket of allowable exclusions to remove from DFQF treatment an item in which there are no imports at present from an LDC, it will have to forgo the use of this exclusion against an item that is imported. It seems unlikely that such a choice will be made frequently and, if it is, it cannot, by definition, dilute the impact of DFQF on current trade.

## The implementation of DFQF

### Tariff free or quota free?

Consider how states are likely to implement the Hong Kong Declaration. If a Quad state excludes from DFQF a particular item, it will do so by limiting either the 'duty-free' or the 'quota-free' aspects of full implementation – or both. The incidence between LDCs of retaining tariffs may be different from that of keeping quotas: for the former there is no scope for differentiating between LDCs, while there is for the latter.

If a Quad state decides to withhold duty-free treatment for a particular good, it will do so by establishing in its tariff schedules that imports of this item from LDCs are not covered by the Hong Kong commitment.. What tariff (if any) a specific LDC must pay will then be determined by the broader provisions of the Quad's import regime. In some cases the tariff may be at the standard MFN level or there may be a preferential level that is generally applicable to developing countries, such as the GSP. In other cases there may be geographically restricted regimes for which some but not all LDCs are eligible offering still lower or zero tariffs (such as the US African Growth and Opportunity Act). Whatever the regime that applies to a specific LDC, the item will be excluded entirely from the Quad's Hong Kong commitment schedule; there appears to be no provision within the Hong Kong Declaration allowing a Quad state to apply different tariffs to different LDCs during the transition phase.

By contrast, if the Quad state offers duty-free access but limits it through tariff quotas (TQs), differentiation between LDCs will be possible. It can be achieved by setting the TQ at a level that is constraining for major but not for minor suppliers and applying it separately to each supplier. This will require it to apply national rather than global TQs, and its ability to do this may be constrained by other elements of any Doha package. But, as practice stands at present, there would seem to be some scope for any TQs on the 3 per cent excluded items to be set at a national level (and, indeed, for no cap necessarily to be imposed on the smallest suppliers).

The assumption made in the analysis reported below is that when items are excluded from DFQF it is through the retention of a positive tariff (at the current rate applicable to the generality of LDCs) rather than through duty-free access limited by TQs. This is because the primary goal of the study is to assess the maximum possible limitation to DFQF arising from the 3 per cent exclusion possibility. As noted above, the chapter includes no analysis of the *likelihood* of Quad states restricting access in this way, only of their right to do so.

**Which items?**

When considering each LDC in isolation from the rest it is not difficult to make plausible assumptions about where the axe will fall: this is what is done in the sections of this chapter that analyse the effect of DFQF on Interpretation 1. But, having selected which items to exclude from one LDC, the non-DFQF regime will then apply to imports from all LDCs. The blanket application to all LDCs of items selected for exclusion in relation to just one will create problems for both the importing and exporting states.

For the Quad state, Interpretation 2 means that the exclusion list cannot be fine-tuned to the perceived 'threat' from each LDC: trade-offs will be required. If, say, a Quad state can exclude 50 items and it chooses to apply all these exclusions to the most sensitive imports from the most competitive supplier, it will have none left to deal with isolated sensitive items which are exported by other LDCs but not by the dominant one. If it 'saves room' for these isolated cases, it can exclude fewer from the dominant supplier.

The impact of its exclusions on each LDC will depend on:

1. The extent to which the exclusion list has been compiled in relation primarily to that country or to another;

2. If the latter, the extent to which it exports the items so selected;
3. Whether the exclusion is effected through a positive tariff or only a TQ;
4. If the latter, whether the TQ is constraining.

The extent to which less competitive minor LDC states will be affected by the limitations of DFQF during the transition phase will depend, therefore, on how far they export to the Quad state the items that are excluded. In some cases, there may be no overlap. Some LDCs could emerge completely unscathed, even though some of the items they actually export may be considered 'sensitive': this would come about if they do not export any of the items that have been excluded or do so at levels well below the TQ. Others could find that DFQF results in no improvement whatsoever in their situation, if all their exports (though of minor value) are of items that have been excluded because they are exported on a large scale by another LDC. It all depends on *precisely* how the Quad state selects its exclusions, in what way it restricts DFQF and the commodity composition of each LDC's exports.

Making an assumption about how each Quad state makes its exclusion selection is thus of central importance for either Interpretation 1 or Interpretation 2 – but for the latter it both has a greater impact on the assessed effect of DFQF and is more imponderable (because it will involve trade-offs by the Quad state such that no clearly uncontroversial assumption can be made). In the sections of this chapter dealing with Interpretation 2, the assumption made about how exclusions will be selected is related to the characteristics of each Quad country's trade. In the case of the USA, for example, it is assumed that the exclusions will be primarily in relation to perceived threats from the most dominant and competitive LDC sources. This assumption does not work with Japan (for reasons explained below), so a more plausible assumption is used.

The sequence in which the potential impact of exclusions is analysed reflects these difficulties. Using Interpretation 1, the task of identifying the items to be excluded is less problematic. Since this interpretation is that the 3 per cent rule is applied on a country-by-country basis, the analysis can show how many items may be excluded for each LDC on the basis of their current pattern of imports. This analysis, in turn, identifies both the dominant LDC supplier and its most sensitive export items. The analysis is then used to underpin the impact assessment using Interpretation 2: that Quad states may select for exclusion a group of products that does not exceed 3 per cent of items imported from all LDCs.

The effect of this approach is to provide an upper and lower boundary for the potential impact on specific LDCs in relation to each Quad market of the allowable limitations to DFQF during the transition period. It will also establish for each LDC whether they are likely to be 'winners' or 'losers' from a particular interpretation. This information is brought together to identify *inter alia* a set of targets for fine-tuning the Hong Kong Declaration so that any particularly egregious outcomes can be avoided.

## Data use

### Sources

The chapter is based on data for 2004 supplied by three of the four Quad states.

The sources used for imports are: Statistics Canada, the Japanese Ministry of Finance (MoF) and the United States International Trade Commission (USITC).[4] Because of the pre-existence of EBA, no useful purpose would have been served *for this study* (given its sharp focus) in replicating this exercise for the EU. However, the EU's import data for 2003 were used to compile the list of 'revealed LDC supply capacity', and the current EU tariff regime was examined to check on the treatment of imports from all countries on the UN list of LDCs.

The Japanese and US tariff data used were obtained from UNCTAD's *Trade Analysis and Information System* (*TRAINS*) database, and Canada's from the Canadian Border Services Agency.[5]

### Analyses made

For each Quad country (apart from the EU), imports have been analysed in the following sequence. We have listed all imports from every country on the UN list of LDCs, regardless of whether they are currently eligible for the Quad state's 'LDC trade regime'. For each LDC source we have calculated the size of the potential exclusion basket. This has been done by counting the number of tariff lines in which there are imports and establishing the number represented by 3 per cent.

In some cases there are so few imports that even one tariff line represents more than 3 per cent of the total. A literal interpretation of the Hong Kong text implies that in these cases it is not possible for a Quad state to exclude any products from DFQF (unless, of course, it creates additional NTLs). Because of this, cases where one tariff line represents more than 3 per cent of the total imports by a given Quad state from a given LDC have been disregarded from the main analysis, but taken up again in the sensitivity analysis.

For the remainder, a comparison has been made between the size of the potential exclusion basket (in terms of the number of tariff lines) and the number of very high tariffs. For the purposes of this report, very high tariffs have been defined as an *ad valorem* tariff of 15 per cent or more (i.e. a tariff peak in terms of the Doha Round) or any specific duty.[6] It is beyond the scope of this chapter to calculate the *ad valorem* equivalents for specific duties, but typically this form of tariff is applied in the case of sensitive items where there is some protectionist intent.

In many cases this process produces two categories of LDCs.

1. There are those in which the number of high tariffs exceeds the permissible number of exclusions under the 3 per cent rule. In these cases, a Quad country will need to select among sensitive items in order to exclude some and liberalise others.
2. In the other group, the reverse is the case: the number of very high tariffs is lower

than the permissible number of exclusions. In these cases, it is assumed that the Quad country would be able to exclude all the high tariffs and, if it wished, some items facing *ad valorem* tariffs of less than 15 per cent in addition.

Country-by-country treatment is given to the first category of LDCs to give a flavour of the choices available. Clearly, it is beyond the scope of this chapter to consider the political economy of each Quad state in order to identify which of these sensitive items will be excluded and which liberalised. But one illustrative piece of information is provided. We make a comparison of the import share of each sensitive item in the Quad state under review and in all Quad states. Although this is necessarily at the HS6 level, and so lacks detail, the aim is try to identify cases facing high tariffs in which imports into the Quad country in question are disproportionately small. This may provide an indicator of particular sensitivity and therefore give a clue as to which items will be excluded.

## The EU and Canada

These two countries are taken first because they provide a benchmark, given the current extent of DFQF coverage of imports from LDCs under their current autonomous commitments. A principal potential effect of DFQF in these two cases may be to increase certainty and predictability. Because their current regimes are autonomous, they could be withdrawn or amended (although this would presumably have to be done in relation to all LDCs and not just a few to avoid a potential WTO dispute). When the Hong Kong commitment becomes binding (which we assume is only after the successful completion of the Doha Round – see above), this flexibility will no longer exist.

### The EU

Under the EU's EBA initiative, enacted through an amendment to its GSP scheme, access to all imports other than armaments from all LDCs is either currently DFQF, or will be so by 1 September 2009. EBA came into force in March 2001, with the immediate abolition of tariffs and quotas on everything except bananas, rice and sugar. Since then the tariffs on these three items have been progressively reduced: bananas became duty-free on 1 January 2006, sugar will do so on 1 July 2009 and rice on 1 September 2009.

While the EU will, by 2009, be offering DFQF equivalence to LDCs, it is not currently doing so for all the countries on the UN list. Indeed, the number of UN recognised LDCs that apparently are not being granted EBA by the EU is longer than is the case for any of the other Quad states. Although all 50 LDCs on the UN list are listed in the GSP regulation as eligible for EBA (although Myanmar is suspended from the GSP), 18 of these 50 'have not yet nominated a GSP certificate issuing authority' and 'their goods cannot be admitted at GSP rates of duty'.[7] Since all these states are African, Caribbean and Pacific (ACP) countries, for which Cotonou already offers duty-free access for most exports, it may be that the failure results from their perception that EBA currently serves no practical purpose (given their export basket), rather than from any protectionist intent on the part of the EU.

## Canada

Canada is currently in a similar position to that of the EU, but with more gaps in coverage. It already offers LDCs duty-free access for most, though not all, items in the nomenclature. Only poultry, dairy products and eggs are not duty free. Hence the main effect of the Hong Kong commitment would be to provide the additional guarantee that treatment would not be changed, as well as the possibility of closing some of the current gaps. This section examines the scope for Canada to avoid closing the gaps during the transition phase through the use of the 3 per cent dispensation using Interpretations 1 and 2.

### Interpretation 1

Under Interpretation 1, the length of Canada's exclusion list is related to the number of items it imports from any given LDC. In 2004 Canada imported goods from 48 of the 50 countries on the UN's list of least developed countries and accorded LDC tariff treatment to 46 of them (Table 3.1).[8]

**Table 3.1. Canada: The Potential for Exclusions**

| Country[a] | # tariff lines comprising 3% | Country[a] | # tariff lines comprising 3% |
|---|---|---|---|
| Bangladesh | 32.7 | Mozambique | 1.3 |
| Nepal | 20.3 | Yemen | 1.3 |
| Cambodia | 15.0 | Somalia | 1.2 |
| *Myanmar* | 11.8 | Togo | 1.2 |
| Madagascar | 9.5 | Zambia | 1.1 |
| Haiti | 9.0 | Central African Republic | 1.1 |
| Sierra Leone | 8.0 | Congo DR | 1.1 |
| Afghanistan | 6.0 | Benin | 0.7 |
| Niger | 5.3 | Comoros | 0.7 |
| Ethiopia | 3.6 | Vanuatu | 0.7 |
| Senegal | 3.5 | Angola | 0.7 |
| Laos | 3.4 | Burundi | 0.6 |
| Tanzania | 3.4 | Djibouti | 0.6 |
| Mali | 3.2 | Rwanda | 0.5 |
| Lesotho | 2.7 | Eritrea | 0.5 |
| Mauritania | 2.6 | São Tomé and Principe | 0.5 |
| Uganda | 2.3 | Liberia | 0.4 |
| Gambia | 1.8 | Cape Verde | 0.4 |
| Maldives | 1.7 | Solomon Islands | 0.4 |
| Chad | 1.5 | Bhutan | 0.3 |
| Sudan | 1.4 | Kiribati | 0.3 |
| Burkina Faso | 1.4 | *Timor-Leste* | 0.3 |
| Guinea | 1.4 | Samoa | 0.3 |
| Malawi | 1.4 | Equatorial Guinea | 0.2 |

[a]The countries in italics are not eligible for LDC (or GSP) treatment in Canada. No imports were recorded from Guinea Bissau or Tuvalu

*Source:* Derived from data obtained from Statistics Canada.

In 31 of these cases the product breadth of imports is sufficiently wide that a single tariff line represents less than 3 per cent of the total. For the remaining 15 current LDC tariff (LDCT)[9] recipients not a single item could be excluded from full DFQF treatment as to do so would result in Canada failing to liberalise on 97 per cent of its imports. Even for the 31, only two countries should have paid any duty at all in 2004 on any of their exports to Canada given the breadth of its current zero-duty LDC regime (Table 3.2). These are Niger, which exported one dutiable product (butter), and Myanmar which is not covered by the LDCT.

**Table 3.2. Canada: Tariff Peaks**

| Country[a] | # tariff lines comprising 3%[b] | # tariff peaks |
|---|---|---|
| Myanmar | 11 | 225 |
| Niger | 5 | 1 |

[a]Rounded down to the nearest whole item
[b]Over 15% *ad valorem* or AVE
*Source:* Derived from data obtained from Statistics Canada.

Since the 3 per cent rule would allow ample scope for Canada to continue to exempt butter from DFQF (and given that Myanmar is currently excluded from LDC treatment) it seems clear that under Interpretation 1 the Hong Kong Declaration need not require any change in the *status quo*.

### Interpretation 2

The findings under Interpretation 2 are identical. On this interpretation, the number of items that Canada could exclude from DFQF would be set at 3 per cent of the total number of different goods imported from all LDCs.

In 2004 Canada imported a total of 1729 items from all countries on the UN list of LDCs (although it did not accord GSP treatment to two of these, Myanmar and Timor-Leste). This total would allow it to exclude 52 items from DFQF. As only one of the imports (butter from Niger) pays a duty under the current LDCT, this exclusion possibility would allow Canada to avoid including it for DFQF treatment.

### Conclusions

Unless it results in more countries being accorded the LDC trade regime in the EU and Canada, the principal effect of a DFQF commitment under Doha will be to increase certainty and reduce the scope for regime dilution. DFQF offers no apparent improvement over the EU's EBA in terms of the numbers of products exempted from tariff and quota restrictions. Nor does it require any improvement on Canada's current regime under either Interpretation (1) or (2). To make a real difference, a new initiative would need to tackle specifically other barriers to imports from LDCs, such as unduly onerous rules of origin, health standards or other non-tariff barriers.

## The USA

The USA is central to this study. It imports many goods from many LDCs but fails currently to offer DFQF for a large proportion of these. Hence, implementation of the Hong Kong Declaration *could* have a substantial impact. How much impact depends critically on how the 3 per cent tolerance is applied during the transition phase. This chapter identifies a range of possible outcomes under both Interpretations 1 and 2.

### Interpretation 1

In 2004 the USA imported goods from 48 of the 50 countries on the UN's list of least developed countries and accorded LDC tariff treatment to 41 of them. The second column of Table 3.3 shows the number of items that could be excluded from each state on

**Table 3.3. USA: The Potential for Exclusions**

| Country[a] | # tariff lines excluded on | | Country[a] | # tariff lines excluded on | |
|---|---|---|---|---|---|
| | Interpretation 1 | Interpretation 2 | | Interpretation 1 | Interpretation 2 |
| Bangladesh | 17.1 | 48 | *Liberia* | 0.8 | – |
| Nepal | 13.6 | 17 | Cape Verde | 0.8 | 5 |
| Cambodia | 10.1 | 28 | Gambia | 0.8 | – |
| Haiti | 8.1 | 19 | Central African Rep. | 0.8 | 1 |
| Madagascar | 6.9 | 20 | Samoa | 0.8 | – |
| Sierra Leone | 4.9 | 10 | Equatorial Guinea | 0.7 | – |
| Ethiopia | 3.1 | 12 | Mauritania | 0.7 | – |
| Mali | 3.0 | – | Djibouti | 0.6 | – |
| Tanzania | 2.9 | 5 | Togo | 0.6 | – |
| *Senegal* | 2.7 | 3 | *Maldives* | 0.6 | – |
| Niger | 2.6 | – | *Solomon Islands* | 0.6 | – |
| Guinea | 2.2 | – | Benin | 0.5 | – |
| Afghanistan | 2.1 | 1 | *Eritrea* | 0.5 | – |
| Congo DR | 2.1 | – | Chad | 0.5 | – |
| Lesotho | 1.8 | 17 | Vanuatu | 0.5 | – |
| Uganda | 1.7 | 5 | Rwanda | 0.4 | – |
| *Laos* | 1.6 | 9 | São Tomé & Principe | 0.4 | – |
| Malawi | 1.6 | 14 | Bhutan | 0.3 | – |
| Mozambique | 1.3 | 2 | Comoros | 0.2 | – |
| Burkina Faso | 1.2 | – | Kiribati | 0.2 | – |
| Zambia | 1.1 | 1 | Burundi | 0.2 | – |
| Somalia | 1.1 | – | Tuvalu | 0.2 | – |
| Yemen | 1.0 | – | *Sudan* | 0.1 | – |
| Angola | 0.9 | – | Guinea–Bissau | 0.1 | – |

[a]The countries in italics are not eligible for LDC treatment in the USA. Senegal, Solomon Islands and Eritrea are eligible for GSP treatment; Laos, Liberia, Maldives and Sudan are eligible for MFN only. No imports were recorded from Timor-Leste or Myanmar, both of which are also eligible only for MFN treatment

*Source:* Derived from data obtained from USITC.

Interpretation 1, which relates exclusions to the number of items imported from each LDC. It shows that the 3 per cent rule would allow items to be excluded only in the case of the 23 states for which the product breadth of imports is sufficiently wide that a single tariff line represents less than 3 per cent of the total.

Imports from these 23 countries have been analysed further to identify tariff peaks (defined as an ad valorem tariff of 15 per cent or more or any specific duty or any unknown tariffs). In each case a count has been made of the number of items facing a tariff peak and the result compared to the total number of permissible exclusions under the 3 per cent rule (Table 3.4).

**Table 3.4. USA: Tariff Peaks**

| Country | # tariff lines comprising 3%[a] | # tariff peaks[b] | Country | # tariff lines comprising 3%[a] | # tariff peaks[b] |
|---|---|---|---|---|---|
| *Bangladesh* | 17 | 114 | *Afghanistan* | 2 | 7 |
| *Nepal* | 13 | 77 | Congo DR | 2 | 0 |
| *Cambodia* | 10 | 89 | Lesotho | 1 | 0 |
| *Haiti* | 8 | 55 | Uganda | 1 | 0 |
| Madagascar | 6 | 3 | *Laos* | 1 | 21 |
| Sierra Leone | 4 | 1 | Malawi | 1 | 0 |
| Ethiopia | 3 | 2 | Mozambique | 1 | 0 |
| Mali | 3 | 0 | *Burkina Faso* | 1 | 2 |
| Tanzania | 2 | 1 | Zambia | 1 | 0 |
| Senegal | 2 | 2 | Somalia | 1 | 0 |
| Niger | 2 | 0 | Yemen | 1 | 0 |
| Guinea | 2 | 0 | | | |

[a]Rounded down to the nearest whole item
[b]Over 15% *ad valorem* or AVE, plus items for which the AVE could not be calculated (because export volumes are given as zero) or for which the tariff is unclear for any reason
*Source:* Derived from data obtained from USITC and UNCTAD TRAINS.

In the case of the seven countries italicised in Table 3.4 (Bangladesh, Nepal, Cambodia, Haiti, Afghanistan, Laos and Burkina Faso) the number of imports facing tariff peaks exceeds the total number of potential exclusions. For the rest it does not. The first group have been labelled 'more-sensitive' and the second 'less-sensitive' import sources. There is one country in each group that does not currently receive LDC treatment from the USA.

In the case of the 'more-sensitive' import sources the excess of tariff peaks over allowable exclusions (considerable in some cases) raises the question of which products will be excluded and which not. This section shows the results arising from three alternative assumptions on the selection of products to be excluded.

## The three assumptions

One approach is to assume that the USA will exclude the items with the highest tariffs. This has involved calculating *ad valorem* equivalents (AVEs) wherever possible for the

27 imports from Bangladesh, 24 from Nepal and 18 from Cambodia that face specific duties (or for which the duty is unknown).[10]

The second assumption made is that the USA excludes the items facing tariff peaks that are imported to the greatest value. It provides an answer to the question: what is the minimum share of imports that is likely to receive full DFQF during the transition phase?

The third assumption takes account of the possibility that the current pattern of trade has been distorted by current protection and that some imports into the USA are artificially depressed by the current tariffs. These may be even more sensitive than those items imported to large values. This is necessarily a very speculative area, and the approach adopted in the report is described below in relation to Bangladesh (and also applied to the other 'more-sensitive' import sources).

## Bangladesh

Bangladesh faces 120 tariff peaks, only 17 of which can be excluded from liberalisation under the 3 per cent rule. The broad conclusion, therefore is that even the minimal implementation of DFQF by the USA will have a significant effect on Bangladesh's terms of access to the US market.

The full list of US imports from Bangladesh facing tariff peaks is provided in Table A3.1. A very high proportion of these are clothing items. Hence, the USA will not be able to avoid liberalising on all clothing items even it were to concentrate its 3 per cent of exclusions solely on this product group.

On assumption 1 (that exclusions are concentrated on the items facing the highest tariffs), the USA could withhold DFQF from 5 per cent of its current imports from Bangladesh.[11] This is, of course, much lower than the share that could be excluded on assumption 2, since imports of the highest tariff items tend to be artificially restricted – but for precisely for this reason they are the items for which liberalisation would have the greatest impact.

On assumption 2 (that it is the highest-value items facing tariff peaks that are excluded),[12] the USA could withhold DFQF from half of its current total imports. If this were to happen, there might well be a redirection of trade into the other items that currently face tariff peaks and which, by definition, would not have been excluded. It is beyond the scope of this chapter to estimate the scope for substitutability between items in the clothing and other sensitive sectors listed in Appendix Table 1. But it would be surprising if there were not some scope. The figure of 50 per cent almost certainly overstates, therefore, the share of trade that would not receive DFQF treatment.

What if the USA were, instead, to focus on items that have lower imports – precisely because the current tariffs are a deliberate barrier to very sensitive goods? Making predictions in such a case is of course impossible, but the chapter provides one suggestive piece of information.

Appendix Table 1 shows for each product its share of imports by the USA from Bangladesh, and its average share of the imports of all Quad countries.[13] Appendix Table

1 is presented in ascending order of the figure in the right-hand column. This shows for each HS sub-head its share of total US imports from Bangladesh as a proportion of its average share of the other Quad countries' imports from Bangladesh. In the case of printed bed linen, for example, which is at the top of the table, this product accounted for 0.0001 per cent of US imports from Bangladesh, but 0.5 per cent on average into the Quad as a whole. Hence, the share in the USA was 0.02 per cent of the average share in Quad imports. In the case of footwear with rubber outer soles (HS 640419), the product's share of US imports from Bangladesh was 0.8 per cent of the average. In other words, these are products that are imported into both the USA and least one other Quad country, but where US imports are proportionally smaller than the average.

Does proportionate smallness provide an indicator of sensitivity? It may do. To the extent that it does, one can identify the products for which US imports were proportionately particularly small. In the case of Bangladesh this includes all items that account for less than half the average share of all Quad imports. This is shown in Table 3.5.[14] There are 20 such items, all of them clothing with the exception of three that are footwear and three that are textiles. Table 3.5 also gives the current tariff applied by the USA on imports from Bangladesh of this product. As the USA can exclude only 17 items, at least three of those in the table would need to be liberalised. But that will still leave some very high-tariff items that can be excluded. Three of the products face a combination of specific and *ad valorem* duties, normally a sure sign of major protection. A further nine have *ad valorem* tariffs in excess of 20 per cent. Indeed, only six have tariffs at the bottom end of the 'tariff peak' range, of 16 per cent or so.

## Cambodia

As with Bangladesh, the chapter provides information on what might be excluded from DFQF on three alternative assumptions about the USA's priorities. As indicated in Table 3.4, the USA could exclude ten items from Cambodia without breaching the 3 per cent rule. If these ten were the items facing the highest tariffs, the USA would withhold DFQF from 5 per cent of its imports from Cambodia. If they were the items facing tariff peaks that are imported to the greatest value, the proportionate exclusion would rise to 54 per cent. As with Bangladesh, though, some substitution of goods in all other categories (all of which would have had to be included in DFQF) is likely to take place. This figure therefore overstates the extent to which the 3 per cent option undermines DFQF.

As with Bangladesh an attempt has also been made to identify items imported in low values that may be very sensitive. Since there is a smaller number of imports from the other 'more-sensitive' sources than is the case with Bangladesh, the tables for Cambodia and the others provide information on the number of excludable items for which the US share is lowest relative to the Quad average.

In the case of Cambodia (Table 3.6) there are seven items (against the maximum excludable of ten) that have tariffs in excess of 27 per cent, and one of these has an 8-digit sub-code to which a combined specific and *ad valorem* duty applies. Just two are at the bottom of the tariff peak range. All except one are garments.

### Table 3.5. Bangladesh: Proportionately Low, High-tariff Products

| HS6 | Description | Value 2004 (US$000)[a] | Maximum tariff 2006[b] | Share of US imports (%)[c] | Avg. share of other Quad imports (%)[c] | US share as % of average Quad share |
|---|---|---|---|---|---|---|
| 630221 | Printed bed-linen of cotton (excl. knitted or crocheted) | 2.5 | 20.9% | 0.0001 | 0.5 | 0.02 |
| 621120 | ski suits (excl. knitted or crocheted) | 4.8 | 28.6% | 0.0002 | 0.1 | 0.1 |
| 640411 | sports footwear, incl. tennis shoes, basketball shoes, gym shoes, training shoes and the like, with outer soles of rubber or plastics and uppers of textile materials | 1.1 | 90 cents/pr+37.5% | 0 | 0.02 | 0.2 |
| 630231 | bed-linen of cotton (excl. printed, knitted or crocheted) | 18.5 | 20.9% | 0.001 | 0.1 | 0.6 |
| 640419 | footwear with outer soles of rubber or plastics and uppers of textile materials (excl. sports footwear, incl. tennis shoes, basketball shoes, gym shoes, training shoes and the like, and toy footwear) | 24.7 | 37.5% or 90 cents/ pr+20% | 0.001 | 0.1 | 0.8 |
| 640291 | footwear covering the ankle, with outer soles and uppers of rubber or plastics (excl. incorporating a protective metal toe-cap, waterproof footwear of heading 6401, sports footwear, orthopaedic footwear and toy footwear) | 5.3 | 90 cents/pr+20% | 0.0002 | 0.02 | 1 |
| 611011 | Jerseys, pullovers, cardigans, waistcoats and similar articles, of wool, knitted or crocheted (excl. wadded waistcoats) | 300.3 | 16% | 0.01 | 0.4 | 3 |
| 610342 | men's or boys' trousers, bib and brace overalls, breeches and shorts of cotton, knitted or crocheted (excl. swimwear and underpants) | 369.8 | 16.1% | 0.02 | 0.3 | 5 |
| 620193 | men's or boys' anoraks, windcheaters, wind jackets and similar articles, of man-made fibres (not knitted or crocheted and excl. suits, ensembles, jackets, blazers, trousers and tops of ski suits) | 5,133.8 | 27.7% | 0.2 | 2.0 | 11 |

**Table 3.5** (continued)

| HS6 | Description | Value 2004 (US$000)[a] | Maximum tariff 2006[b] | Share of US imports (%)[c] | Avg. share of other Quad imports (%)[c] | US share as % of average Quad share |
|---|---|---|---|---|---|---|
| 611120 | babies' garments and clothing accessories of cotton, knitted or crocheted (excl. hats) | 521.5 | 19.7 | 0.02 | 0.2 | 11 |
| 581091 | embroidery of cotton on a textile fabric ground, in the piece, in strips or as motifs (excl. burnt-out embroidery and embroidery with a cutaway ground) | 0.5 | Free, but in the case of embroidery in the piece not less than the rate which would apply to such product if not embroidered. | 0.0 | 0.0002 | 12 |
| 620722 | men's or boys' nightshirts and pyjamas of man-made fibres (excl. knitted or crocheted, vests, singlets and underpants) | 194.7 | 16% | 0.01 | 0.1 | 13 |
| 611019 | 'jerseys, pullovers, cardigans, waistcoats and similar articles, of fine animal hair, knitted or crocheted (excl. from hair of kashmir "cashmere" goats and quilted articles)' | 73.1 | 16% | 0.003 | 0.02 | 13 |
| 620293 | Women's or girls' anoraks, windcheaters, wind jackets and similar articles, of man-made fibres (not knitted or crocheted and excl. suits, ensembles, jackets, blazers, trousers and tops of ski suits) | 2,431.3 | 27.7% | 0.1 | 0.8 | 13 |
| 610910 | t-shirts, singlets and other vests of cotton, knitted or crocheted | 32,512.9 | 16.5% | 1.4 | 8.3 | 17 |
| 620113 | men's or boys' overcoats, raincoats, car-coats, capes, cloaks and similar, of man-made fibres (excl. knitted or crocheted) | 223.0 | 27.7% | 0.01 | 0.04 | 25 |

**Table 3.5** (continued)

| HS6 | Description | Value 2004 (US$000)[a] | Maximum tariff 2006[b] | Share of US imports (%)[c] | Avg. share of other Quad imports (%)[c] | US share as % of average Quad share |
|---|---|---|---|---|---|---|
| 611430 | special garments for professional, sporting or other purposes, n.e.s., of man-made fibres, knitted or crocheted | 795.7 | 32% | 0.03 | 0.1 | 29 |
| 621230 | corselettes of all types of textile materials, whether or not elasticated, incl. knitted or crocheted | 52.9 | 23.5% | 0.002 | 0.01 | 30 |
| 611519 | panty hose and tights of textile materials, knitted or crocheted (excl. of synthetic fibres and hosiery for babies) | 21.4 | 16% | 0.001 | 0.002 | 39 |
| 620333 | men's or boys' jackets and blazers of synthetic fibres (excl. knitted or crocheted, and wind-jackets and similar articles) | 380.3 | 27.3% | 0.02 | 0.04 | 41 |

[a]Total value of the 8-digit items within the HS6 aggregate
[b]Applicable to any of the items within the HS6 aggregate. Where more than one tariff is shown it is because it is not clear which is the higher
[c]Displayed to a maximum of four decimal places. '0' denotes that the share is less than one-ten-thousandth of 1 per cent
*Source:* Derived from data obtained from Statistics Canada, Eurostat, Japanese MoF, USITC and UNCTAD TRAINS.

**Table 3.6. Cambodia: Proportionately Low, High-tariff Products**

| HS6 | Description | Value 2004 (US$000)[a] | Maximum tariff 2006[b] | Share of US imports (%)[c] | Avg. share of other Quad imports (%)[c] | US share as % of average Quad share |
|---|---|---|---|---|---|---|
| 420292 | travel bags, toilet bags, rucksacks, shopping bags, map cases, tool bags, sports bags, make-up boxes, cutlery boxes, cases for binoculars, cameras, video cameras, musical instruments or arms and similar containers | 2.6 | 20% | 0.0002 | 0.01 | 2 |
| 620469 | women's or girls' trousers, bib and brace overalls, breeches and shorts of textile materials (excl. of wool, fine animal hair, cotton or synthetic fibres, knitted or crocheted, panties and swimwear) | 72.3 | 28.6% | 0.005 | 0.1 | 4 |
| 620113 | men's or boys' overcoats, raincoats, car-coats, capes, cloaks and similar, of man-made fibres (excl. knitted or crocheted) | 2.2 | 27.7% | 0.0001 | 0.003 | 5 |
| 620193 | men's or boys' anoraks, windcheaters, wind jackets and similar articles, of man-made fibres (not knitted or crocheted and excl. suits, ensembles, jackets, blazers, trousers and tops of ski suits) | 863.7 | 27.7% | 0.1 | 0.7 | 8 |
| 610230 | women's or girls' overcoats, car-coats, capes, cloaks, anoraks, incl. ski-jackets, wind-cheaters, wind-jackets and similar articles of man-made fibres, knitted or crocheted (excl. suits, ensembles, jackets, blazers, dresses, skirts, divide | 533.4 | 2% or 64.4 cents/ 28.kg + 18.8% | 0.04 | 0.2 | 17 |
| 620463 | women's or girls' trousers, bib and brace overalls, breeches and shorts of synthetic fibres (excl. knitted or crocheted, panties and swimwear) | 3,168.1 | 28.6% | 0.2 | 1.1 | 19 |

**Table 3.6** (continued)

| HS6 | Description | Value 2004 (US$000)[a] | Maximum tariff 2006[b] | Share of US imports (%)[c] | Avg. share of other Quad imports (%)[c] | US share as % of average Quad share |
|---|---|---|---|---|---|---|
| 620293 | women's or girls' anoraks, windcheaters, wind jackets and similar articles, of man-made fibres (not knitted or crocheted and excl. suits, ensembles, jackets, blazers, trousers and tops of ski suits) | 497.8 | 27.7% | 0.03 | 0.1 | 24 |
| 610822 | women's or girls' briefs and panties of man-made fibres, knitted or crocheted | 287.6 | 15.6% | 0.02 | 0.1 | 25 |
| 621133 | men's or boys' track suits and other garments n.e.s. of man-made fibres (excl. knitted or crocheted) | 714.8 | 16% | 0.05 | 0.1 | 42 |
| 610130 | overcoats, car-coats, capes, cloaks, anoraks, incl. ski-jackets, wind-cheaters, wind-jackets and similar articles of man-made fibres, for men or boys, knitted or crocheted (excl. suits, ensembles, jackets, blazers and trousers) | 48,135.5 | 32% | 0.2 | 0.4 | 50 |

[a]Total value of the 8-digit items within the HS6 aggregate
[b]Applicable to any of the items within the HS6 aggregate. Where more than one tariff is shown it is because it is not clear which is the higher
*Source:* Derived from data obtained from Statistics Canada, Eurostat, Japanese MoF, USITC and UNCTAD TRAINS.

## Haiti

In the case of Haiti, both assumptions 1 and 2 produce substantially higher proportionate exclusions than is the case with either Bangladesh or Cambodia. On assumption 1 (that the eight highest-tariff items will be excluded) the USA would withhold DFQF from 13 per cent of total import value.[15] On assumption 2 (with exclusions concentrated on the highest-value items facing tariff peaks), a staggering 74 per cent of current imports could be excluded from DFQF. The same caveat about substitution applies as above given that most are clothing items.

The alternative approach of identifying proportionately low imports does not work in the case of Haiti as there are just two of them, both with tariffs of less than 20 per cent (Table 3.7). In all other cases, the USA imports proportionately more than the Quad average. The other six items in Table 3.7 (included to make the total of seven items that the USA could exclude on the 3 per cent rule) face tariffs that are high – but so do many other imports from Haiti.

## Nepal

In the case of Nepal, assumption 1 removes only 0.2 per cent of US imports from DFQF.[16] The second assumption sees the USA excluding from DFQF 53 per cent of the current value of imports.

On the third assumption, eight of the possible exclusion basket of 13 items are goods with a low to very low proportionate share (Table 3.8). The tariffs that they face are, in the main, very high, and all except two items are clothing.

## Afghanistan, Laos and Burkina Faso

The US imports from Afghanistan facing tariff peaks are almost all clothing, textiles or leather goods. The highest tariff is 28.2 per cent (on one item of female trousers which is imported to only a small value – either because of the tariff or because of poor supply capacity). If the USA were simply to concentrate on the goods facing tariff peaks currently imported to the highest values, it could exclude T-shirts (tariff of 16.5 per cent on imports of US$28,900) and woven fabrics (15 per cent on imports of US$19,300). These two items between them account for only a small share of total imports from Afghanistan (less than 2 per cent).

In the case of Laos, predicting which product might be excluded is even more hit and miss: only one item could be excluded under the 3 per cent rule and there are 22 that face tariff peaks. However, knitted sweaters, which account for 51 per cent of US imports from Laos have a tariff of 16.5 per cent. This is far from the highest tariff (which is 32 per cent), but it is the only item facing a tariff peak that is imported to a substantial share of the total. In other words, were the USA to deploy its one-item exclusion on this product, over half of the value of the country's imports from Laos would not be covered by the DFQF initiative. But this finding is subject to the same caveat about substitution made above.

## Table 3.7. Haiti: Proportionately Low, High-tariff Products

| HS6 | Description | Value 2004 (US$000)[a] | Maximum tariff 2006[b] | Share of US imports (%)[c] | Avg. share of other Quad imports (%)[c] | US share as % of average Quad share |
|---|---|---|---|---|---|---|
| 420292 | travel bags, toilet bags, rucksacks, shopping bags, map cases, tool bags, sports bags, make-up boxes, cutlery boxes, cases for binoculars, cameras, video cameras, musical instruments or arms and similar containers | 1.0 | 17.6% | 0.0003 | 0.001 | 43 |
| 611120 | babies' garments and clothing accessories of cotton, knitted or crocheted (excl. hats) | 2.1 | 19.7% | 0.001 | 0.001 | 47 |
| 420222 | handbags, whether or not with shoulder straps, incl. those without handles, with an outer surface of plastic sheeting or textile materials | 0.5 | 17.6% | 0.0001 | 0 | 1082 |
| 620349 | men's or boys' trousers, bib and brace overalls, breeches and shorts of textile materials (excl. of wool, fine animal hair, cotton or synthetic fibres, knitted or crocheted, underpants and swimwear) | 2.0 | 27.9% | 0.001 | 0 | 1332 |
| 620520 | men's or boys' shirts of cotton (excl. knitted or crocheted, nightshirts, singlets and other vests) | 82.0 | 19.7% | 0.02 | 0.001 | 1857 |
| 610910 | t-shirts, singlets and other vests of cotton, knitted or crocheted | 90,059.5 | 16.5% | 24.6 | 0.6 | 3937 |
| 610610 | women's or girls' blouses, shirts and shirt-blouses of cotton, knitted or crocheted (excl. t-shirts and vests) | 171.8 | 19.7% | 0.05 | 0.001 | 4517 |
| 610822 | women's or girls' briefs and panties of man-made fibres, knitted or crocheted | 30.4 | 15.6% | 0.01 | 0.0002 | 5096 |

[a]Total value of the 8-digit items within the HS6 aggregate
[b]Applicable to any of the items within the HS6 aggregate
[c]Displayed to a maximum of four decimal places. '0' denotes that the share is less than one-ten-thousandth of 1 per cent
*Source:* Derived from data obtained from Statistics Canada, Eurostat, Japanese MoF, USITC and UNCTAD TRAINS.

**Table 3.8. Nepal: Proportionately Low, High-tariff Products**

| HS6 | Description | Value 2004 (US$000)[a] | Maximum tariff 2006[b] | Share of US imports (%)[c] | Avg. share of other Quad imports (%)[c] | US share as % of average Quad share |
|---|---|---|---|---|---|---|
| 640420 | footwear with outer soles of leather or composition leather and uppers of textile materials (excl. toy footwear) | 0.3 | 37.5% | 0.0002 | 0.02 | 1 |
| 420292 | travel bags, toilet bags, rucksacks, shopping bags, map cases, tool bags, sports bags, make-up boxes, cutlery boxes, cases for binoculars, cameras, video cameras, musical instruments or arms and similar containers, with an outer surface of | 44.3 | 20% | 0.03 | 0.1 | 21 |
| 610343 | men's or boys' trousers, bib and brace overalls, breeches and shorts of synthetic fibres, knitted or crocheted (excl. swimwear and underpants) | 0.4 | 58.5 cents/ kg + 15.2% | 0.0003 | 0.001 | 28 |
| 610431 | women's or girls' jackets and blazers, of wool or fine animal hair, knitted or crocheted (excl. wind-jackets and similar articles) | 2.4 | 54.8 cents/ kg + 16% | 0.002 | 0.01 | 31 |
| 611012 | 'jerseys, pullovers, cardigans, waistcoats and similar articles, of hair of kashmir "cashmere" goats, knitted or crocheted (excl. quilted articles)' | 9.7 | 16% | 0.01 | 0.02 | 32 |
| 620331 | men's or boys' jackets and blazers of wool or fine animal hair (excl. knitted or crocheted, and wind-jackets and similar articles) | 1.3 | 17.5% | 0.001 | 0.002 | 41 |
| 420229 | handbags, whether or not with shoulder strap, incl. those without handle, with outer surface of vulcanized fibre or paperboard, or wholly or mainly covered with such materials or with paper | 0.8 | 20% | 0.001 | 0.001 | 59 |

**Table 3.8** (continued)

| HS6 | Description | Value 2004 (US$000)[a] | Maximum tariff 2006[b] | Share of US imports (%)[c] | Avg. share of other Quad imports (%)[c] | US share as % of average Quad share |
|---|---|---|---|---|---|---|
| 620469 | women's or girls' trousers, bib and brace overalls, breeches and shorts of textile materials (excl. of wool, fine animal hair, cotton or synthetic fibres, knitted or crocheted, panties and swimwear) | 2.8 | 28.6% | 0.002 | 0.003 | 73 |
| 610990 | t-shirts, singlets and other vests of textile materials, knitted or crocheted (excl. cotton) | 8.0 | 16% | 0.01 | 0.01 | 95 |
| 640299 | footwear with outer soles and uppers of rubber or plastics (excl. covering the ankle or with upper straps or thongs assembled to the sole by means of plugs, waterproof footwear of heading 6401, sports footwear, orthopaedic footwear and toy | 1.4 | 48% | 0.001 | 0.001 | 98 |
| 650300 | felt hats and other felt headgear, made from the hat bodies, hoods or plateaux of heading 6501, whether or not lined or trimmed (excl. made by assembling strips or pieces of felt, and toy and carnival headgear) | 1.5 | 13.5 cents /kg+6.3%+ 1.9 cents/ article | 0.001 | 0.001 | 120 |
| 650590 | hats and other headgear, knitted or crocheted, or made up from pieces, but not strips, of lace, felt or other textile fabrics, whether or not lined or trimmed (excl. hair-nets, headgear for animals, and toy and fancy-dress headgear) | 351.7 | 18.7 cents/ kg + 6.8% to 20 cents/kg + 7% | 0.2 | 0.2 | 127 |
| 610120 | overcoats, car-coats, capes, cloaks, anoraks, incl. ski-jackets, wind-cheaters, wind-jackets and similar articles of cotton, for men or boys, knitted or crocheted (excl. suits, ensembles, jackets, blazers and trousers) | 7.4 | 15.9% | 0.01 | 0.003 | 175 |

[a]Total value of the 8-digit items within the HS6 aggregate [b]Applicable to any of the items within the HS6 aggregate
*Source:* Derived from data obtained from Statistics Canada, Eurostat, Japanese MoF, USITC and UNCTAD TRAINS.

Only two US imports from Burkina Faso face tariff peaks – both of 17.6 per cent. Only one could be excluded on the 3 per cent rule. Neither accounts for a significant share of the total. Moreover, the 'peak' is so low that it cannot plausibly explain the very low level of imports. Hence, in the case of this country, it seems unlikely that the application of the 3 per cent rule will significantly affect the implementation of DFQF in relation to current trade.

### Less-sensitive import sources

Tables 3.9 and 3.10 provide salient information on the less-sensitive countries. Table 3.9 indicates the tariff peaks that apply to US imports from them. If the USA were to decide to use the 3 per cent exclusion rule, and were to apply it to the items currently facing the highest tariffs, then Table 3.9 indicates which products would be excluded for which LDC. They are all textile products.

Some tariffs undermine competitiveness even though they are not set at peak levels, and these are covered in Table 3.10. This covers the incidence of all positive tariffs in respect of US imports from the five less-sensitive import sources. Just over one-third of these are in the 5–10 per cent tariff band and just under one-third are in the 0–5 per cent band.

Column 2 in Table 3.10 can be used to check how high any remaining tariffs would be if the USA were to concentrate its allowable 3 per cent exclusions on the highest-tariff items. For example, it could exclude six items from Madagascar – which would mean that all tariffs of less than 5 per cent would need to be abolished, as would five of those in the 5–10 per cent range. For Ethiopia, only one tariff above 10 per cent and two above 15 per cent could remain.

### Interpretation 2

The foregoing analysis has given us the material to make plausible assumptions about where the axe might fall if the DFQF tolerance were applied by the USA according to Interpretation 2, i.e. that it excludes 3 per cent of the total items imported from all LDCs. Obviously, Interpretation 2 will allow a larger number of exclusions than does Interpretation 1: the 'population' of items imported from all LDCs can never be smaller and will usually be larger than the number imported from a single LDC; in the case of the USA the number that can be excluded is much larger. The USA imported 1597 items from all the states on the UN list of LDCs in 2004, compared to just 569 from the largest single source, Bangladesh. Consequently, on Interpretation 2 the USA could exclude from DFQF during the transition phase up to 48 lines, which is almost three times as many as the highest figure in Table 3.3, Column 2, which deals with Interpretation 1.

Whether or not this increased total number of exclusions translates into more exclusions for any particular LDC depends on: (a) what the USA decides to exclude; and (b) whether the LDC in question exports any of those items. In other words, the assumptions made about the selection of products to exclude is even more central to the assessed impact of DFQF on Interpretation 2 than it is on Interpretation 1.

**Table 3.9. USA: Tariff Peaks Affecting Less Sensitive Import Sources**

| NTL | Description | Tariff | Imported from: | | | | | |
|---|---|---|---|---|---|---|---|---|
| | | | Madagascar | Ethiopia | Senegal | Sierra Leone | Tanzania | Total |
| 42022280 | Handbags with or without shoulder strap or without handle, with outer surface of textile materials, nesi | 17.6% | – | – | | – | | 3 |
| 42029230 | Travel, sports and similar bags with outer surface of textile materials other than of vegetable fibers | 17.6% | – | | – | | | 2 |
| 42029290 | Bags, cases and similar containers nesi, with outer surface of plastic sheeting or of textile materials, excl. cotton | 17.6% | | – | | | – | 2 |
| 58109100 | Embroidery of cotton, in the piece, in strips or in motifs, other than without visible ground | Free, but in the case of embroidery in the piece, not less than the rate which would apply to such product if not embroidered | | | – | | | 1 |
| 63023150 | Bed linen, not knit/croc, not printed, of cotton, cont any embroidery, lace, braid, edging, trimming, piping or applique work, not napped | 20.9% | – | | | | | 1 |

*Source:* UNCTAD TRAINS.

**Table 3.10. USA: Other Tariffs Affecting Less Sensitive Import Sources**

| Country | # tariff lines comprising 3% | Tariff band (%) | | | |
|---|---|---|---|---|---|
| | | >0–5 | >5–10 | >10–15 | >15[a] |
| Madagascar | 6 | 4 | 7 | 1 | 3 |
| Ethiopia | 3 | 2 | – | 3 | 2 |
| Senegal | 2 | 2 | 5 | 3 | 2 |
| Sierra Leone | 4 | 2 | 1 | 2 | 1 |
| Tanzania | 2 | 1 | 4 | – | 1 |

[a]Includes one item (for Senegal) for which the tariff is not known
*Source:* UNCTAD TRAINS.

This study has assumed that the USA will give priority to excluding the most sensitive items currently imported from Bangladesh. This is because Bangladesh is the dominant LDC supplier in terms of the range and value of its exports, and has a significant concentration of 'sensitive' products in its export basket.[17] In other words, we have assumed that the USA will use all 48 permitted exclusions to avoid giving full DFQF treatment to the highest-tariff items it imports from Bangladesh.[18]

If it were to decide otherwise, and use some of its exclusions to hit sensitive items imported from other LDCs, it would have to forgo restricting some of the items imported from Bangladesh – all of which face high tariff peaks. Moreover, there is a certain degree of overlap between the 48 'most sensitive' imports from Bangladesh and the most sensitive goods imported from Cambodia and, to a lesser extent, from Nepal and Haiti. Of the 48 most sensitive imports from Bangladesh, 58 per cent are also on the list of the 48 most sensitive imports from Cambodia (and the proportions for Nepal and Haiti are 35 and 40 per cent respectively).

The results are shown in the third column of Table 3.3, which gives the number of each country's exports that overlap with the '48 most sensitive' Bangladesh items. There is no change between Interpretations 1 and 2 for 23 of the 25 states at the foot of the table; under neither interpretation will any of the countries' exports to the USA be excluded from DFQF. Moreover, one of the two that would see a change, Cape Verde, is covered by duty free access under AGOA for all its exports that overlap with the list of 48. At the upper end of the table, eight states would face fewer exclusions under Interpretation 2 than under Interpretation 1, and nine of those that would see an increase have duty-free access under AGOA for those exports that overlap with the 48; a tenth (Senegal) has duty-free access for two out of the three overlapping exports.

The principal 'victims' of Interpretation 2 compared to Interpretation 1, therefore, are four Asian states plus Haiti. Bangladesh and Cambodia would see the greatest absolute increase in the number of possible exclusions (by 31 and 18 items respectively), and Laos the greatest proportional rise (up ninefold). Haiti would also face an increase of almost 140 per cent.

This suggests that the pattern of the exclusions would be rather similar under the two interpretations, with the same countries having the gains from DFQF restricted but to a greater extent. The scale of the increased dilution of DFQF can be gauged by comparing the share of imports that would be excluded under Interpretation 2 with the analogous figures under assumption 1 for Interpretation 1. The items assumed to be excluded under Interpretation 2 account for 15 per cent by value of US imports from Bangladesh (compared with 5 per cent under assumption 1 of Interpretation 1). The comparable shares for Cambodia are 8 per cent (and 5 per cent), for Nepal 4 per cent (and 0.2 per cent) and for Haiti 18 per cent (against 13%). This would dilute further the support of the Hong Kong Declaration for LDC export diversification into items in which there is every reason to suppose that they are very competitive – which is why they face the highest import barriers.

## Summary

There are two 'banner headlines' that could be written about the USA's scope for excluding important products from DFQF. They report diametrically opposite stories. And like all banner headlines the picture they present is oversimplified.

From one perspective, the Hong Kong provision allowing countries to defer implementation of DFQF on up to 3 per cent of tariff lines presents only a limited danger. Two-thirds of the LDCs from which the USA imports would not see even a single item excluded on Interpretation 2; for Interpretation 1 it would be half. And for the rest, the USA would not be able to exclude whole sectors. Hard choices would need to be made over which to exclude and which to liberalise.

The other banner headline story is very different. On Interpretation 1 the USA could exclude from DFQF 51 per cent of the value of its current imports from Bangladesh, 54 per cent of those from Cambodia, 53 per cent from Nepal and as much as 74 per cent from Haiti. If it were to start offering LDC access to Laos (which it does not at present) it could exclude over half current imports by value. If it were instead to exclude the items facing the highest tariffs, the figures do not look so dramatic – but the impact could be greater on the relatively small number of LDC states (mainly in Asia plus the hapless Haiti) that would be hit.[19] Although the USA would still be unable to exclude whole sectors from DFQF, it could retain restrictions on many of the most sensitive items.

Given the uncertainties that arise because the impact of DFQF will be determined by which items the USA chooses to exclude, the most important conclusion (apart from noting the range of possible outcomes) is to focus attention on the extent to which product substitution can take place. Unless countries attempt to bend the letter as well as the spirit of the Hong Kong Declaration (a possibility considered below), far more items will be liberalised than not. And often the liberalised and not liberalised items will be in the same sub-sector. To the extent that LDCs can shift their export basket in the light of any exclusions that the USA does make, then the 'shock horror' headline will overstate the limitations allowed by the 3 per cent rule. To the extent that they cannot diversify, the headline may not overstate the case.

## Japan

In 2004 Japan imported goods from 48 of the 50 countries on the UN's list of least developed countries and accorded LDC tariff treatment to 45 of them (Table 3.11).[20] But it imports a much smaller range of items than does the USA. On the one hand, this means that it can exclude fewer items and so the scope for watering down the impact of DFQF is reduced. On the other, it suggests that there may be factors outside the ambit of the Hong Kong Declaration that are limiting imports from LDCs and which, by definition, will not be addressed by DFQF.

**Table 3.11. Japan: The Potential for Exclusions**

| Country[a] | # tariff lines excluded on Interpretation 1 | Interpretation 2 | Country[a] | # tariff lines excluded on Interpretation 1 | Interpretation 2 |
|---|---|---|---|---|---|
| Bangladesh | 8.0 | 3 | Mozambique | 0.3 | – |
| Myanmar | 5.9 | 9 | Bhutan | 0.3 | – |
| Nepal | 5.6 | 1 | Ethiopia | 0.3 | – |
| Cambodia | 2.7 | – | Malawi | 0.3 | – |
| Madagascar | 2.7 | 1 | Togo | 0.2 | – |
| Laos | 2.5 | 1 | Kiribati | 0.2 | – |
| Tanzania | 1.2 | – | Liberia | 0.2 | – |
| Senegal | 0.9 | – | Sierra Leone | 0.2 | – |
| Mauritania | 0.8 | – | Somalia | 0.2 | – |
| Vanuatu | 0.7 | 7 | *Timor–Leste* | 0.2 | – |
| Uganda | 0.6 | – | Cape Verde | 0.2 | – |
| Zambia | 0.6 | – | Central African Rep. | 0.2 | – |
| Guinea | 0.5 | – | Gambia | 0.2 | – |
| Maldives | 0.5 | – | Samoa | 0.2 | 3 |
| Mali | 0.5 | – | Congo DR | 0.1 | – |
| Niger | 0.5 | – | Eritrea | 0.1 | – |
| Burkina Faso | 0.5 | – | Benin | 0.1 | – |
| Haiti | 0.5 | – | *Comoros* | 0.1 | – |
| Solomon Is | 0.5 | – | Guinea–Bissau | 0.1 | – |
| Sudan | 0.5 | – | Burundi | 0.1 | – |
| Afghanistan | 0.4 | 1 | Chad | 0.1 | – |
| Yemen | 0.4 | – | Rwanda | 0.1 | – |
| Angola | 0.3 | – | *Djibouti* | 0.03 | – |
| Lesotho | 0.3 | – | Equatorial Guinea | 0.03 | – |

[a]The countries in italics are not eligible for LDC (or GSP) treatment in Japan. No imports were recorded from São Tomé or Tuvalu.
*Source:* Derived from data obtained from the Japanese MoF.

### Interpretation 1

On Interpretation 1, there are only seven cases where the product breadth of imports is sufficiently wide for Japan to be able to exclude one or more items (since a single tariff line represents less than 3 per cent of the total). Imports from these seven countries have been analysed further to identify tariff peaks (defined as an *ad valorem* tariff of 15 per cent or more or any specific duty). In each case a count has been made of the number of items facing a tariff peak and the result compared to the total number of permissible exclusions under the 3 per cent rule (Table 3.12). All the countries in the table currently receive LDC treatment from Japan.

In the case of the two countries at the top of the table (Bangladesh and Myanmar), the number of imports facing tariff peaks exceeds, or is the same as, the total number of potential exclusions. For the rest it does not. The first group have been labelled 'more-sensitive' and the second 'less-sensitive' import sources.

**Table 3.12. Japan: Tariff Peaks**

| Country | # tariff lines comprising 3%[a] | # tariff peaks[b] | Country | # tariff lines comprising 3%[a] | # tariff peaks[b] |
|---|---|---|---|---|---|
| Bangladesh | 8 | 3 | Madagascar | 2 | 0 |
| Myanmar | 5 | 5 | Laos | 2 | 0 |
| Nepal | 5 | 0 | Tanzania | 1 | 0 |
| Cambodia | 2 | 0 | | | |

[a]Rounded down to the nearest whole item
[b]Over 15 per cent *ad valorem* or with specific duties/other notes which mean that the *ad valorem* equivalent is unknown
*Source:* Derived from data obtained from the Japanese MoF and UNCTAD TRAINS.

## Tariff peaks

Table 13.3 provides salient information on the tariff peaks facing imports from the two more-sensitive countries. If Japan were to decide to use the 3 per cent exclusion rule, and were to apply it to the items currently facing highest *ad valorem tariffs* or specific duties, then Table 3.13 indicates which products would be excluded. They accounted for just 0.2 per cent (Bangladesh) and 0.1 per cent (Myanmar) of the total value of Japanese imports from each country. All are agricultural or livestock products. Half face only specific duties and so further work is desirable to check whether or not all of these are actually significant access barriers. Of the four *ad valorem* tariffs, two are very high and the others are in the 15–20 per cent band.

## Non-peak tariffs

Table 3.14 shows the incidence of all positive tariffs in respect of US imports from all seven states for which the 3 per cent rule would allow Japan to exclude one or more items from DFQF treatment. For Bangladesh, apart from the three peak tariffs, most of the items on which there is any tariff to pay are in the up to 5 per cent range. Laos faces one tariff in the 10–15 per cent range but for the others (apart from Myanmar) most are in the 5–10 per cent range.

**Table 3.13. Japan: Tariff peaks affecting more sensitive import sources**

| NTL | Description | Tariff | Imported from: | | |
|---|---|---|---|---|---|
| | | | Bangladesh | Myanmar | Total |
| 100630090 | Semi-milled or wholly milled rice, n.e.s. | 49 yen/kg | – | | 1 |
| 121299110 | Tubers of konnyaku (Amorphophalus), whether or not cut, dried or powdered, for 'the Pooled Quota' | 40 | | – | 1 |
| 121299190 | Tubers of konnyaku (Amorphophalus), whether or not cut, dried or powdered, n.e.s. | 2,796 yen/kg | | – | 1 |
| 151590520 | Other fixed vegetable fats and oils its fractions, not chemically modified, n.e.s. | 10.4 yen/kg | | – | 1 |
| 200490212 | Leguminous vegetables, prepared or preserved, not containing added sugar, frozen | 17 | | – | 1 |
| 200980123 | Juice of any other single fruit, not containing added sugar, not more than 10% by weight of sucrose, excluding prune juice | 19.1 | | – | 1 |
| 250100010 | Salt and pure sodium chloride, of which at least 70 per cent by weight passes through a woven metal wire cloth sieve with an aperture of 2.8mm, or agglomerated, other than those in aqueous solution | 2.9 yen/kg | – | | 1 |
| 410449122 | Tanned or crust hides and skins of bovine (including buffalo) or equine animals (in the dry state (crust) (excluding full grains (unsplit) and grain splits), of tanned but not chrome tanned leather, n.e.s. | 30 | – | | 1 |

*Source:* UNCTAD TRAINS.

**Table 3.14. Japan: Other Tariffs Affecting More and Less Sensitive Import Sources**

| Country | # tariff lines comprising 3% | Tariff band (%) | | | |
|---|---|---|---|---|---|
| | | >0–5 | >5–10 | >10–15 | >15 |
| Madagascar | 6 | 4 | 7 | 1 | 3 |
| Bangladesh | 8 | 4 | 1 | – | 3 |
| Myanmar | 5 | 1 | – | – | 4 |
| Nepal | 5 | – | 3 | – | – |
| Cambodia | 2 | 1 | 3 | – | – |
| Madagascar | 2 | – | 1 | – | – |
| Laos | 2 | – | – | 1 | – |
| Tanzania | 1 | 1 | 1 | – | – |

*Source:* UNCTAD TRAINS.

### Interpretation 2

As with the USA, Interpretation 2 (which sets the number of exclusions at 3 per cent of the items imported from all LDCs) would allow a large proportional increase in the total – to 24 products. And, as with the USA, an assumption must be made on which items Japan would choose to exclude before the potential impact can be calculated. Bangladesh is also the dominant supplier to Japan but, unlike in the USA, its exports are not sufficiently sensitive to make it the plausible principal target. Only eight of its exports to Japan in 2004 were dutiable. In the absence of a clear 'target country' against which to apply the exclusions, the assumption made in this study is that Japan will seek to exclude the 24 items facing the highest tariffs imported from any LDC.[21]

The results are shown in Column 3 of Table 3.11. Some 39 of the 41 countries that would face no exclusion under Interpretation 1 also survive unscathed under Interpretation 2. Vanuatu, though, would see seven exclusions instead of zero, while Afghanistan would face just one. Of the remaining seven states at the top of the table, six would see fewer exclusions under Interpretation 2 than 1. This leaves just Myanmar with Vanuatu and Afghanistan facing increased exclusions.

### Summary

In the case of Japan, there is only one of the two obvious 'banner headlines' that could have applied to the USA. This is the one that finds that for most LDCs the Hong Kong tolerance of 3 per cent is unlikely to affect substantially the effect of DFQF *on current imports*.

The reason for the emphasis on current imports is that this difference with the USA arises mainly because Japan currently imports a much narrower range of goods. Whereas the USA bought sufficient items from half of the LDCs from which it imported to allow one or more to be excluded under the 3 per cent rule, for Japan the figure is only 15 per cent.

The critical question for Japan, therefore, is whether there are other items in which LDCs have a supply capacity but which are not imported because tariffs are currently very high – and whether it will choose to exclude these. As explained above, given the assumptions made in the first section of this chapter, the Hong Kong Declaration gives developed Members only a finite number of possible exclusions from DFQF treatment. Any exclusion of an item that is not imported (precisely because it is very sensitive) must be at the 'expense' of another item that would otherwise have been excluded. To the extent that a country chooses this route, therefore, the immediate impact of DFQF may be higher than it otherwise would be, although the potential for future LDC export diversification may be reduced. Although this is the conclusion for 'most LDCs', it does not apply to Myanmar and Vanuatu. Myanmar could see, on both Interpretations 1 and 2, the exclusion from DFQF of half of its current dutiable exports to Japan under Interpretation 1, and 90 per cent under Interpretation 2. Vanuatu would escape unscathed under Interpretation 1 but could see excluded from DFQF all of its current exports that face tariff peaks.

## Conclusions

This chapter has assessed whether or not the DFQF initiative is likely to result in the removal of significant barriers to Quad imports from LDCs. It has noted two completely different legitimate reasons why the initiative might not remove significant barriers in a specific market, to which may be added a third, illegitimate reason. These are:

- There are few barriers to be removed;
- Barriers exist but there is scope in the small print to continue restricting some significant sensitive items;
- Developed countries flout the letter of the Declaration as well as exploiting loopholes in its provisions.

### Limitations to the Hong Kong Declaration

#### Prevalence of access barriers

Implementation of the Hong Kong Declaration will have a significant impact only if it alters substantially the *status quo*, which it will not do if developed countries are already committed to offering DFQF to around 97 per cent of imports from LDCs. The EU and Canada are already so committed. This does not mean that their import regimes are perfect for LDCs (let alone for other poor countries) – far from it. What it means, though, is that the constraints to LDC exports to these countries are not to be found in their border taxes; if they are to be addressed it will be through means other than those covered by the Hong Kong Declaration. One principal positive effect of the Declaration will be to 'lock in' the current 'voluntary' commitments of the EU and Canada – provided that it is binding and actionable within the WTO, a point to which we return below.

Another would be the requirement that DFQF is offered to all 50 countries on the UN list of LDCs, since neither Quad currently makes its autonomous regime available to all of these.

In relation to Japan and, especially, the USA, the Hong Kong Declaration could make a difference. There exist significant imports from LDCs that pay positive tariffs, plus many more items that are not imported and for which the group has a 'revealed supply capacity'. When fully implemented, DFQF will alter in a significantly favourable way the market access terms of LDCs to these two markets and, by the same token, adversely affect the relative position of their competitors if it is not accompanied by parallel, broader liberalisation. As with the EU and Canada, though, DFQF will do nothing directly to remove any non-border constraints on market entry for exports from LDCs. In the case of Japan, the limited range of current imports, despite quite low tariffs, on a range of goods suggests that such non-border constraints may be binding. As with the EU and Canada, an additional effect would be the requirement to offer DFQF to all 50 UN-listed LDCs, some of which do not currently receive preferential access.

## The small print

### The obvious loophole

For the USA and Japan the main issue assessed in this chapter is whether 'the small print' could allow the impact of DFQF to be substantially diluted. The small print in question is the possibility of temporarily excluding 3 per cent of imports during the implementation phase.

For the USA there are two possible 'banner headlines' which report diametrically opposite (and of course oversimplified) stories. From one perspective, the 3 per cent tolerance presents only a limited danger. A majority of the LDCs from which the USA imports might not see even a single item excluded. For the rest, the USA would not be able to exclude whole sectors. Hard choices would need to be made over which to exclude and which to liberalise.

The other, very different, banner headline is that the USA could exclude from DFQF a high proportion of its imports from a small group of mainly Asian LDCs. If its exclusions were concentrated on the sensitive items imported to the largest value, it could avoid granting DFQF to 50 per cent of the value of its current imports from Bangladesh, 54 per cent of those from Cambodia, 74 per cent of those from Haiti and 53 per cent of those from Nepal. If it were to start offering LDC access to Laos (which it does not at present) it could exclude over half current imports by value. If, instead, it concentrated on the most sensitive items (even those imported to low values, probably because of the high tariffs) the figures would be less dramatic, but the impact in stymieing LDC export diversification could be even greater.

Only one of these banner headlines applies to Japan: the Hong Kong tolerance of 3 per cent is unlikely to affect substantially the effect of DFQF *on current imports*. The reason for emphasising the effect on current imports is that this difference with the USA arises mainly because Japan currently imports a much narrower range of goods. Whereas the USA bought sufficient items from half of the LDCs from which it imported to allow one or more to be excluded under the 3 per cent rule, for Japan the figure is only 15 per cent.

**Creative thinking**

The assumption made in this report is that the choice of the term 'the tariff line level' in the Hong Kong Declaration (Annex F 36(a)(ii)) rather than, say, 'the HS 6 level' means that implementation will be by reference to a level of product disaggregation that is set at the discretion of each state and not by international agreement. This opens up the possibility that states could manipulate their product nomenclature in order to alter their scope for excluding items.

Since countries are able to set their own 8–10 digit product codes, they have available to them the possibility of creating more codes on goods that are imported from LDCs. The larger the number of NTLs imported, the more that can be excluded under the 3 per cent rule. Since the extent of such action is wholly unpredictable, it is beyond the scope of this chapter to tackle it. But it should be borne in mind, and we return to the issue below.

## Illegitimate restrictions

It has been suggested that developed countries might use the ambiguity in the Hong Kong Declaration to flout not only its spirit (for example by creating new 8-digit items) but also its letter (for example, by setting its exclusions in relation to HS 6 sub-heads or in relation to value). There is certainly plenty of evidence from past practice (thrown up not least by successful challenges to developed country practice in the WTO's dispute settlement facility) that members use any vagueness in commitments, deliberately or unwittingly, to do things that are subsequently demonstrated to be contrary to the commitments they have made. Will they do the same with DFQF?

The answer must be that they almost certainly will, but since the range of possible abuses is infinite, it is not something that can be measured in this chapter. If, for example, countries were to interpret 'tariff line level' in a different way from current practice, they could just as easily claim that it meant the 4-digit as the 6-digit level of the Harmonised System. Yet the impact of these two similar abuses would be quite different.

What the report can do is to draw readers' attention to what might be done to limit the abuse. And the key question that needs to be addressed is whether or not the DFQF commitment is actionable and enforceable within the WTO. No definitive answer to this question is given *within* the text of the Ministerial Declaration; it needs to be clarified during the rest of the Doha negotiations. If the commitment is not actionable, there is little that LDCs or their supporters can do to prevent DFQF being diluted other than lobbying.

If the commitment is enforceable, it will be the first time that a tariff regime other than the MFN level has been binding on WTO members. It would allow any LDC that felt its access had been infringed to take the errant Quad state to dispute settlement. The task of defining any vagueness in the phraseology of the Hong Kong Declaration would then lie ultimately with the Appellate Body. This might throw up some interesting cases. At present, for example, Myanmar is denied GSP treatment by three of the four Quad states. This is possible because the GSP is an autonomous voluntary regime.[22] If the requirement to provide DFQF to countries which are listed as LDCs by the UN becomes a binding requirement on developed country members, this latitude will disappear.

## Impact on Other Poor Countries

### Non-LDC developing countries

The terms of reference specifically ask us to consider the impact of full DFQF implementation on non-LDC developing countries. Clearly, in general terms the implementation of DFQF will erode some developing country preferences and, in other cases, place LDCs at a competitive advantage to other developing countries.

To go beyond such generalities, however, it is necessary to know:

- Which items currently exported by LDCs to each Quad market currently pay a tariff (which will be removed by DFQF);
- What future exports from LDCs might be stimulated by DFQF;
- Which other developing countries exports these items;
- The terms under which non-LDC developing countries export.

This chapter has provided information only on the first of these. As can be seen from the analysis above, there are a large number of LDC exports to the USA that currently face positive (and often high) tariffs, and there is potential for non-LDC developing countries to lose their competitive position as a result of DFQF. But this list needs to be further elaborated to identify precisely which developing countries export the items in question and to assess their terms of access under existing agreements. In the case of Japan, too, DFQF will tend to remove tariffs on some imports from LDCs. The list is shorter than for the USA, possibly because other non-tariff barriers limit market entry. For the EU and Canada there seems little prospect of the Hong Kong initiative adversely affecting developing countries – because the improvement in the access terms of LDCs has largely been completed already.

### Impact on AGOA

Analyses of AGOA indicate that by far and away the most substantial impact has been in the area of clothing exports, particularly by lesser developed countries. And a critical element in the growth of exports has been the derogation on the rules of origin that allows them to use non-originating cloth. While exports from South Africa and Mauritius (which do not benefit from the derogation) have increased, they have not done so to the same extent as those from lesser developed countries.

DFQF will not affect the relative preference given to lesser developed African countries through the derogation on the rules of origin. But it will reduce the tariff advantage that African countries receive over non-African LDCs. It will tend to reduce Africa's relative attraction, therefore, as a location for clothing exports to the USA – but only to the extent that non-African countries can compete successfully using originating cloth. If they fail to use originating cloth they will not benefit from any DFQF tariff cuts.

The major problem of DFQF for African exporters is that it may be implemented during the same period that their clothing industries are being hit, first, by the expiry of the Multifibre Arrangement (MFA) and, second, by the buoyancy of Chinese exports. All three changes need to be taken into consideration at the same time. Since some non-African LDCs are also being hit by the MFA expiry and Chinese competitiveness (for example Bangladesh) the interplay of factors affecting relative competitiveness will be complex. Clearly, DFQF cannot help African countries to cope with the difficult situation in which they find themselves. Whether it will contribute significantly to a further decline in their exports remains to be seen. These exports may collapse anyway regardless of DFQF. Or, if they do not, the remaining advantage of AGOA for lesser developed countries of the rules of origin may be sufficient to allow them to maintain their position relative to non-beneficiary LDCs.

### What Next?

The analysis in this chapter suggests that while the 3 per cent tolerance built into the Hong Kong Declaration must dilute its impact to some extent, it does not make it a nugatory gesture. There is reason, therefore, to build on it both within the remainder of the Doha Round and outside. Such 'building' should focus on:

- Removing vagueness in the Hong Kong Declaration in order to close off possible 'escape routes' for developed countries wishing to evade their commitments; and
- Dealing with the many other aspects of market entry that limit poor country exports to rich countries.

#### Closing escape routes

The two most obvious required measures are to make implementation of DFQF independent of the Doha Round's conclusion, and to make it a binding requirement for developed country Members. As the Hong Kong Declaration stands, DFQF need not be put into effect until the start of the implementation period for the Doha Round. This means that if the Doha Round does not reach a conclusion in the near future, DFQF will be deferred indefinitely.

It also means that LDCs may be under an obligation to approve an otherwise unsatisfactory Doha text in order to secure DFQF. Whereas this report concludes that DFQF is better than nothing, it does not necessarily make a case that it is sufficiently good to warrant LDCs agreeing to a Doha text that they might otherwise oppose. There will be no significant improvement in access to the EU and Canadian markets; there may be other, more powerful barriers to the Japanese market; and the outlook for a group of Asian exporters to the USA is for only a limited improvement in market access.

So long as DFQF remains a voluntary commitment, LDCs must expect that developed countries will find many imaginative ways to avoid liberalising on sensitive items. To be worthwhile (and especially to make it worth compromising in other negotiating areas) it must be a binding commitment against which errant members can be taken to dispute settlement. To avoid any doubt on this matter (especially since at present only MFN tariffs are binding) there needs to be an explicit agreement to this effect.

One area in which negotiation might be worthwhile, and which is therefore worthy of further consideration, concerns the extent to which the application of anti-surge safeguard measures (whether within the DFQF initiative or elsewhere in the eventual Doha text) could give developed countries the confidence to move to 100 per cent duty-free coverage immediately on implementation. This chapter has shown that if exclusions were to be concentrated on the most sensitive items (which seems likely, if only for reasons of practicality in implementation) the items concerned would in the main be imported to small values at present. The use of an anti-surge device, or the application of country-specific TQs, would provide Quad states with an insurance against rapid increases in imports from LDCs.

## Extending DFQF

A binding DFQF commitment is sufficiently attractive to make it a no-cost option for LDCs (i.e. one for which they do not need to make concessions elsewhere). Whether or not it is worth making compromises to acquire it depends partly on the nature of what is sought in return (which is unpredictable), and partly on whether or not the start made in the Hong Kong Declaration can be reinforced by ancillary measures; it also depends on how far LDCs can alter practice to evade restrictions.

For the EU and Canada, the impact of DFQF will depend on how far it builds on the current regimes. Apart from increasing the certainty of the current autonomous preferences, the main avenues through which conditions for LDC exports might be improved lie in the commitments other than DFQF, for example on rules of origin. These are mentioned in the Hong Kong Declaration, but in an unspecific form. The task of specifying required changes more concretely could be seen as a matter for the agenda when the Doha negotiations resume.

A critical question for Japan is over the interpretation of what the Hong Kong Declaration requires during the implementation phase in respect of goods not currently imported from LDCs. Are there other items in which LDCs have a supply capacity but which are not imported because tariffs are currently very high? If so, will Japan choose to exclude these? We have assumed that any exclusion of a non-imported item would be at the 'expense' of another item that would otherwise have been excluded. This assumption makes it unlikely that the exclusion of non-traded products would reduce the immediate impact of DFQF, although it might reduce the potential for future LDC export diversification. But the Hong Kong text is somewhat ambiguous on this point, and further clarification during the Doha negotiations is desirable.

In the case of the USA, the key to determining whether reality is closer to the benign or the adverse banner headline is in forecasting the extent of product substitution that can take place. Far more items will be liberalised than not. And often the liberalised and not liberalised items will be in the same sub-sector. To the extent that LDCs can shift their export basket *in the light of* any exclusions that the USA does make, the second 'shock horror' headline will overstate the limitations allowed by the 3 per cent rule. To the extent that they cannot diversify, the headline may not overstate the case.

These conclusions point to the next research steps required to obtain a greater understanding of the potential impact of a Doha agreement on LDC exports to each of the Quad. For the EU and Canada the next step is to identify more clearly other changes to import regimes (such as on the rules of origin and cumulation within them) that are needed if Doha is to result in any significant improvement on the *status quo*. For the USA, the key research task is to assess the scope for substitution between 8-digit items within product groups. If it is great, the impact of DFQF is likely to be substantial. If it is limited, the impact could be heavily diluted. And for Japan the task is the same as for the EU and Canada – but writ large. Why does the country import so few items from LDCs, and are there additional barriers to effective access that could be tackled under Doha?

# Appendix Tables

## Appendix A3.1. USA: Relative Importance of Imports from Bangladesh Compared to Quad Average (HS6)

| HS6 | Description | Share of US imports (%)[a] | Avg. share of other Quad imports (%)[a] | US share as percentage of average Quad share |
|---|---|---|---|---|
| 630221 | printed bed-linen of cotton (excl. knitted or crocheted) | 0.0001 | 0.5 | 0.02 |
| 621120 | ski suits (excl. knitted or crocheted) | 0.0002 | 0.1 | 0.1 |
| 640411 | sports footwear, incl. tennis shoes, basketball shoes, gym shoes, training shoes and the like, with outer soles of rubber or plastics and uppers of textile materials | 0 | 0.02 | 0.2 |
| 630231 | bed-linen of cotton (excl. printed, knitted or crocheted) | 0.001 | 0.1 | 0.6 |
| 640419 | footwear with outer soles of rubber or plastics and uppers of textile materials (excl. sports footwear, incl. tennis shoes, basketball shoes, gym shoes, training shoes and the like, and toy footwear) | 0.001 | 0.1 | 0.8 |
| 640291 | footwear covering the ankle, with outer soles and uppers of rubber or plastics (excl. incorporating a protective metal toe-cap, waterproof footwear of heading 6401, sports footwear, orthopaedic footwear and toy footwear) | 0.0002 | 0.02 | 1 |
| 611011 | jerseys, pullovers, cardigans, waistcoats and similar articles, of wool, knitted or crocheted (excl. wadded waistcoats) | 0.01 | 0.4 | 3 |
| 610342 | men's or boys' trousers, bib and brace overalls, breeches and shorts of cotton, knitted or crocheted (excl. swimwear and underpants) | 0.02 | 0.3 | 5 |
| 620193 | men's or boys' anoraks, windcheaters, wind jackets and similar articles, of man-made fibres (not knitted or crocheted and excl. suits, ensembles, jackets, blazers, trousers and tops of ski suits) | 0.2 | 2.0 | 11 |
| 611120 | babies' garments and clothing accessories of cotton, knitted or crocheted (excl. hats) | 0.02 | 0.2 | 11 |
| 581091 | embroidery of cotton on a textile fabric ground, in the piece, in strips or as motifs (excl. burnt-out embroidery and embroidery with a cutaway ground) | 0 | 0.0002 | 12 |

**Appendix A3.1** (continued)

| HS6 | Description | Share of US imports (%)[a] | Avg. share of other Quad imports (%)[a] | US share as percentage of average Quad share |
|---|---|---|---|---|
| 630221 | printed bed-linen of cotton (excl. knitted or crocheted) | 0.0001 | 0.5 | 0.02 |
| 620722 | men's or boys' nightshirts and pyjamas of man-made fibres (excl. knitted or crocheted, vests, singlets and underpants) | 0.01 | 0.1 | 13 |
| 611019 | 'jerseys, pullovers, cardigans, waistcoats and similar articles, of fine animal hair, knitted or crocheted (excl. from hair of kashmir "cashmere" goats and quilted articles)' | 0.003 | 0.02 | 13 |
| 620293 | women's or girls' anoraks, windcheaters, wind jackets and similar articles, of man-made fibres (not knitted or crocheted and excl. suits, ensembles, jackets, blazers, trousers and tops of ski suits) | 0.1 | 0.8 | 13 |
| 610910 | t-shirts, singlets and other vests of cotton, knitted or crocheted | 1.4 | 8.3 | 17 |
| 620113 | men's or boys' overcoats, raincoats, car-coats, capes, cloaks and similar, of man-made fibres (excl. knitted or crocheted) | 0.01 | 0.04 | 25 |
| 611430 | special garments for professional, sporting or other purposes, n.e.s., of man-made fibres, knitted or crocheted | 0.03 | 0.1 | 29 |
| 621230 | corselettes of all types of textile materials, whether or not elasticated, incl. knitted or crocheted | 0.002 | 0.01 | 30 |
| 611519 | panty hose and tights of textile materials, knitted or crocheted (excl. of synthetic fibres and hosiery for babies) | 0.001 | 0.002 | 39 |
| 620333 | men's or boys' jackets and blazers of synthetic fibres (excl. knitted or crocheted, and wind-jackets and similar articles) | 0.02 | 0.04 | 41 |
| 610510 | men's or boys' shirts of cotton, knitted or crocheted (excl. nightshirts, t-shirts, singlets and other vests) | 0.7 | 1.3 | 52 |

**Appendix A3.1** (continued)

| HS6 | Description | Share of US imports (%)[a] | Avg. share of other Quad imports (%)[a] | US share as percentage of average Quad share |
|---|---|---|---|---|
| 420292 | travel bags, toilet bags, rucksacks, shopping bags, map cases, tool bags, sports bags, make-up boxes, cutlery boxes, cases for binoculars, cameras, video cameras, musical instruments or arms and similar containers, with an outer surface of | 0.03 | 0.1 | 55 |
| 611030 | jerseys, pullovers, cardigans, waistcoats and similar articles, of man-made fibres, knitted or crocheted (excl. wadded waistcoats) | 4.0 | 7.2 | 55 |
| 620469 | women's or girls' trousers, bib and brace overalls, breeches and shorts of textile materials (excl. of wool, fine animal hair, cotton or synthetic fibres, knitted or crocheted, panties and swimwear) | 0.1 | 0.1 | 59 |
| 620463 | women's or girls' trousers, bib and brace overalls, breeches and shorts of synthetic fibres (excl. knitted or crocheted, panties and swimwear) | 0.7 | 1.1 | 60 |
| 620291 | women's or girls' anoraks, incl. ski-jackets, windcheaters, wind-jackets and similar articles, of wool or fine animal hair (excl. knitted or crocheted, suits, ensembles, jackets, blazers and trousers) | 0.1 | 0.1 | 61 |
| 620530 | men's or boys' shirts of man-made fibres (excl. knitted or crocheted, nightshirts, singlets and other vests) | 1.7 | 2.6 | 64 |
| 610230 | women's or girls' overcoats, car-coats, capes, cloaks, anoraks, incl. ski-jackets, windcheaters, wind-jackets and similar articles of man-made fibres, knitted or crocheted (excl. suits, ensembles, jackets, blazers, dresses, skirts, divide | 0.4 | 0.6 | 65 |
| 620462 | women's or girls' trousers, bib and brace overalls, breeches and shorts of cotton (excl. knitted or crocheted, panties and swimwear) | 5.1 | 7.9 | 65 |
| 610990 | t-shirts, singlets and other vests of textile materials, knitted or crocheted (excl. cotton) | 0.3 | 0.4 | 70 |
| 611212 | track-suits of synthetic fibres, knitted or crocheted | 0.03 | 0.04 | 72 |

**Appendix A3.1** (continued)

| HS6 | Description | Share of US imports (%)[a] | Avg. share of other Quad imports (%)[a] | US share as percentage of average Quad share |
|---|---|---|---|---|
| 610610 | women's or girls' blouses, shirts and shirt-blouses of cotton, knitted or crocheted (excl. t-shirts and vests) | 0.3 | 0.4 | 77 |
| 621600 | gloves, mittens and mitts of all types of textile materials (excl. knitted or crocheted and for babies) | 0.0003 | 0.0004 | 78 |
| 621133 | men's or boys' track suits and other garments n.e.s. of man-made fibres (excl. knitted or crocheted) | 0.2 | 0.2 | 88 |
| 620342 | men's or boys' trousers, bib and brace overalls, breeches and shorts, of cotton (excl. knitted or crocheted, underpants and swimwear) | 7.7 | 8.6 | 90 |
| 611130 | babies' garments and clothing accessories of synthetic fibres, knitted or crocheted (excl. hats) | 0.1 | 0.1 | 90 |
| 620892 | women's or girls' vests, briefs, panties, negliges, bathrobes, dressing gowns, housecoats and similar articles of man-made fibres (excl. knitted or crocheted, slips, petticoats, nightdresses and pyjamas, brassieres, girdles, corsets and singlets | 0.03 | 0.04 | 90 |
| 620343 | men's or boys' trousers, bib and brace overalls, breeches and shorts of synthetic fibres (excl. knitted or crocheted, underpants and swimwear) | 1.2 | 1.3 | 92 |
| 620213 | women's or girls' overcoats, raincoats, car-coats, capes, cloaks and similar, of man-made fibres (excl. knitted or crocheted) | 0.04 | 0.04 | 96 |
| 610822 | women's or girls' briefs and panties of man-made fibres, knitted or crocheted | 0.7 | 0.6 | 106 |
| 610130 | overcoats, car-coats, capes, cloaks, anoraks, incl. ski-jackets, windcheaters, wind-jackets and similar articles of man-made fibres, for men or boys, knitted or crocheted (excl. suits, ensembles, jackets, blazers and trousers) | 0.4 | 0.4 | 107 |

**Appendix A3.1** (continued)

| HS6 | Description | Share of US imports (%)[a] | Avg. share of other Quad imports (%)[a] | US share as percentage of average Quad share |
|---|---|---|---|---|
| 611020 | jerseys, pullovers, cardigans, waistcoats and similar articles, of cotton, knitted or crocheted (excl. wadded waistcoats) | 4.2 | 3.6 | 117 |
| 620423 | women's or girls' ensembles of synthetic fibres (excl. knitted or crocheted, ski overalls and swimwear) | 0.01 | 0.01 | 123 |
| 610520 | men's or boys' shirts of man-made fibres, knitted or crocheted (excl. nightshirts, t-shirts, singlets and other vests) | 0.3 | 0.2 | 133 |
| 620349 | men's or boys' trousers, bib and brace overalls, breeches and shorts of textile materials (excl. of wool, fine animal hair, cotton or synthetic fibres, knitted or crocheted, underpants and swimwear) | 0.1 | 0.04 | 136 |
| 621143 | women's or girls' track suits and other garments n.e.s. of man-made fibres (excl. knitted or crocheted) | 0.2 | 0.2 | 142 |
| 621210 | brassieres of all types of textile materials, whether or not elasticated, incl. knitted or crocheted | 1.0 | 0.7 | 148 |
| 610463 | women's or girls' trousers, bib and brace overalls, breeches and shorts of synthetic fibres, knitted or crocheted (excl. panties and swimwear) | 0.2 | 0.1 | 150 |
| 611692 | gloves, mittens and mitts, of cotton, knitted or crocheted (excl. impregnated, coated or covered with plastics or rubber, and for babies) | 0.03 | 0.02 | 152 |
| 611220 | ski-suits, knitted or crocheted | 0.001 | 0.001 | 170 |
| 610220 | women's or girls' overcoats, car-coats, capes, cloaks, anoraks, incl. ski-jackets, windcheaters, wind-jackets and similar articles of cotton, knitted or crocheted (excl. suits, ensembles, jackets, blazers, dresses, skirts, divided skirts | 0.2 | 0.1 | 184 |

**Appendix A3.1** (continued)

| HS6 | Description | Share of US imports (%)[a] | Avg. share of other Quad imports (%)[a] | US share as percentage of average Quad share |
|---|---|---|---|---|
| 420299 | travel, shopping & tool bags, jewellery or cutlery boxes and similar containers, with outer surface of vulcanized fibre or paperboard; cases for binoculars, cameras, musical instruments or arms, and similar containers (with outer surface o | 0.0003 | 0.0001 | 186 |
| 620191 | men's or boys' anoraks, incl. ski-jackets, windcheaters, wind-jackets and similar articles, of wool or fine animal hair (excl. knitted or crocheted, suits, ensembles, jackets, blazers and trousers) | 0.1 | 0.04 | 193 |
| 420222 | handbags, whether or not with shoulder straps, incl. those without handles, with an outer surface of plastic sheeting or textile materials | 0.004 | 0.002 | 200 |
| 620323 | men's or boys' ensembles of synthetic fibres (excl. knitted or crocheted, ski ensembles and swimwear) | 0.02 | 0.01 | 214 |
| 610620 | women's or girls' blouses, shirts and shirt-blouses of man-made fibres, knitted or crocheted (excl. t-shirts and vests) | 0.2 | 0.1 | 226 |
| 620453 | women's or girls' skirts and divided skirts of synthetic fibres (excl. knitted or crocheted and petticoats) | 0.2 | 0.1 | 267 |
| 611231 | men's or boys' swimwear of synthetic fibres, knitted or crocheted | 0.02 | 0.01 | 273 |
| 610892 | women's or girls' negliges, bathrobes, dressing gowns, housejackets and similar articles of man-made fibres, knitted or crocheted (excl. vests, slips, petticoats, briefs and panties, nightdresses, pyjamas, brassieres, girdles, corsets and | 0.2 | 0.1 | 275 |
| 620459 | women's or girls' skirts and divided skirts of textile materials (excl. of wool, fine animal hair, cotton or synthetic fibres, knitted or crocheted and petticoats) | 0.1 | 0.02 | 302 |
| 620439 | women's or girls' jackets and blazers of textile materials (excl. of wool, fine animal hair, cotton or synthetic fibres, knitted or crocheted, wind-jackets and similar articles) | 0.03 | 0.01 | 320 |

**Appendix A3.1** (continued)

| HS6 | Description | Share of US imports (%)[a] | Avg. share of other Quad imports (%)[a] | US share as percentage of average Quad share |
|---|---|---|---|---|
| 610120 | overcoats, car-coats, capes, cloaks, anoraks, incl. ski-jackets, windcheaters, wind-jackets and similar articles of cotton, for men or boys, knitted or crocheted (excl. suits, ensembles, jackets, blazers and trousers) | 0.2 | 0.05 | 328 |
| 610832 | women's or girls' nightdresses and pyjamas of man-made fibres, knitted or crocheted (excl. t-shirts, vests and negliges) | 0.3 | 0.1 | 342 |
| 610443 | women's or girls' dresses of synthetic fibres, knitted or crocheted (excl. petticoats) | 0.03 | 0.01 | 343 |
| 610453 | women's or girls' skirts and divided skirts of synthetic fibres, knitted or crocheted (excl. petticoats) | 0.01 | 0.003 | 348 |
| 620520 | men's or boys' shirts of cotton (excl. knitted or crocheted, nightshirts, singlets and other vests) | 11.5 | 3.1 | 372 |
| 610343 | men's or boys' trousers, bib and brace overalls, breeches and shorts of synthetic fibres, knitted or crocheted (excl. swimwear and underpants) | 1.4 | 0.3 | 456 |
| 620211 | women's or girls' overcoats, raincoats, car-coats, capes, cloaks and similar, of wool or fine animal hair (excl. knitted or crocheted) | 0.1 | 0.02 | 480 |
| 620640 | women's or girls' blouses, shirts and shirt-blouses of man-made fibres (excl. knitted or crocheted and vests) | 1.8 | 0.4 | 483 |
| 620822 | women's or girls' nightdresses and pyjamas of man-made fibres (excl. knitted or crocheted, vests and negliges) | 0.1 | 0.01 | 724 |
| 620930 | babies' garments and clothing accessories of synthetic fibres (excl. knitted or crocheted and hats) | 0.3 | 0.05 | 725 |
| 621111 | men's or boys' swimwear (excl. knitted or crocheted) | 1.5 | 0.2 | 810 |

**Appendix A3.1** (continued)

| HS6 | Description | Share of US imports (%)[a] | Avg. share of other Quad imports (%)[a] | US share as percentage of average Quad share |
|---|---|---|---|---|
| 620630 | women's or girls' blouses, shirts and shirt-blouses of cotton (excl. knitted or crocheted and vests) | 4.8 | 0.5 | 915 |
| 620312 | men's or boys' suits of synthetic fibres (excl. knitted or crocheted, track suits, ski suits and swimwear) | 0.04 | 0.004 | 924 |
| 620433 | women's or girls' jackets and blazers of synthetic fibres (excl. knitted or crocheted, wind-jackets and similar articles) | 0.3 | 0.03 | 1116 |
| 620444 | women's or girls' dresses of artificial fibres (excl. knitted or crocheted and petticoats) | 0.1 | 0.01 | 1356 |
| 610722 | men's or boys' nightshirts and pyjamas of man-made fibres, knitted or crocheted (excl. vests and singlets) | 0.1 | 0.005 | 1517 |
| 620341 | men's or boys' trousers, bib and brace overalls, breeches and shorts, of wool or fine animal hair (excl. knitted or crocheted, underpants and swimwear) | 0.2 | 0.01 | 1531 |
| 620443 | women's or girls' dresses of synthetic fibres (excl. knitted or crocheted and petticoats) | 0.4 | 0.02 | 1628 |
| 611241 | women's or girls' swimwear of synthetic fibres, knitted or crocheted | 0.6 | 0.03 | 2145 |
| 611219 | track-suits of textile materials, knitted or crocheted (excl. cotton or synthetic fibres) | 0.001 | 0 | 2254 |
| 620331 | men's or boys' jackets and blazers of wool or fine animal hair (excl. knitted or crocheted, and wind-jackets and similar articles) | 0.03 | 0.0004 | 7176 |
| 611693 | gloves, mittens and mitts, of synthetic fibres, knitted or crocheted (excl. impregnated, coated or covered with plastics or rubber, and for babies) | 0.04 | 0.001 | 7226 |
| 620413 | women's or girls' suits of synthetic fibres (excl. knitted or crocheted, ski overalls and swimwear) | 0.03 | 0.0004 | 9039 |

**Appendix A3.1** (continued)

| HS6 | Description | Share of US imports (%)[a] | Avg. share of other Quad imports (%)[a] | US share as percentage of average Quad share |
|---|---|---|---|---|
| 620311 | men's or boys' suits of wool or fine animal hair (excl. knitted or crocheted, track suits, ski suits and swimwear) | 0.2 | 0.002 | 10768 |
| 611511 | panty hose and tights of synthetic fibres, knitted or crocheted, measuring per single yarn < 67 decitex | 0.001 | 0 | 31035 |
| 620419 | women's or girls' suits of textile materials (excl. of wool, fine animal hair, cotton or synthetic fibres, knitted or crocheted, ski overalls and swimwear) | 0.003 | 0 | 79172 |
| 620431 | women's or girls' jackets and blazers of wool or fine animal hair (excl. knitted or crocheted, wind-jackets and similar articles) | 0.1 | 0.0001 | 165354 |
| 040510 | butter (excl. dehydrated butter and ghee) | 0.0003 | | (b) |
| 521041 | plain woven fabrics of cotton, containing > 50 % to < 85 % cotton by weight, mixed principally or solely with man-made fibres and weighing =< 200 g per m2, made of yarn of different colours | 0.0005 | | (b) |
| 521049 | woven fabrics of cotton, containing > 50 % to < 85 % cotton by weight, mixed principally or solely with man-made fibres and weighing =< 200 g per m2, made from yarn of different colours (excl. those in three-thread or four-thread twill, in | 0.003 | | (b) |

[a]Displayed to a maximum of four decimal places. '0' denotes that the share is less than one-ten-thousandth of 1 per cent
[b]HS6 sub-head not imported from Bangladesh by other Quad markets
*Source:* Statistics Canada, Eurostat, Japanese Ministry of Finance and USITC.

## Appendix A3.2. USA: Relative Importance of Imports from Cambodia Compared to Quad Average (HS6)

| HS6 | Description | Share of US imports (%)[a] | Avg. share of other Quad imports (%)[a] | US share as percentage of average Quad share |
|---|---|---|---|---|
| 420292 | travel bags, toilet bags, rucksacks, shopping bags, map cases, tool bags, sports bags, make-up boxes, cutlery boxes, cases for binoculars, cameras, video cameras, musical instruments or arms and similar containers, with an outer surface of | 0.0002 | 0.01 | 2 |
| 620469 | women's or girls' trousers, bib and brace overalls, breeches and shorts of textile materials (excl. of wool, fine animal hair, cotton or synthetic fibres, knitted or crocheted, panties and swimwear) | 0.005 | 0.1 | 4 |
| 620113 | men's or boys' overcoats, raincoats, car-coats, capes, cloaks and similar, of man-made fibres (excl. knitted or crocheted) | 0.0001 | 0.003 | 5 |
| 620193 | men's or boys' anoraks, windcheaters, wind jackets and similar articles, of man-made fibres (not knitted or crocheted and excl. suits, ensembles, jackets, blazers, trousers and tops of ski suits) | 0.1 | 0.7 | 8 |
| 610230 | women's or girls' overcoats, car-coats, capes, cloaks, anoraks, incl. ski-jackets, windcheaters, wind-jackets and similar articles of man-made fibres, knitted or crocheted (excl. suits, ensembles, jackets, blazers, dresses, skirts, divide | 0.04 | 0.2 | 17 |
| 620463 | women's or girls' trousers, bib and brace overalls, breeches and shorts of synthetic fibres (excl. knitted or crocheted, panties and swimwear) | 0.2 | 1.1 | 19 |
| 620293 | women's or girls' anoraks, windcheaters, wind jackets and similar articles, of man-made fibres (not knitted or crocheted and excl. suits, ensembles, jackets, blazers, trousers and tops of ski suits) | 0.03 | 0.1 | 24 |
| 610822 | women's or girls' briefs and panties of man-made fibres, knitted or crocheted | 0.02 | 0.1 | 25 |
| 621133 | men's or boys' track suits and other garments n.e.s. of man-made fibres (excl. knitted or crocheted) | 0.05 | 0.1 | 42 |

**Appendix A3.2** (continued)

| HS6 | Description | Share of US imports (%)[a] | Avg. share of other Quad imports (%)[a] | US share as percentage of average Quad share |
|---|---|---|---|---|
| 610130 | overcoats, car-coats, capes, cloaks, anoraks, incl. ski-jackets, windcheaters, wind-jackets and similar articles of man-made fibres, for men or boys, knitted or crocheted (excl. suits, ensembles, jackets, blazers and trousers) | 0.2 | 0.4 | 50 |
| 611120 | babies' garments and clothing accessories of cotton, knitted or crocheted (excl. hats) | 0.04 | 0.1 | 54 |
| 611430 | special garments for professional, sporting or other purposes, n.e.s., of man-made fibres, knitted or crocheted | 0.1 | 0.1 | 68 |
| 611231 | men's or boys' swimwear of synthetic fibres, knitted or crocheted | 0.002 | 0.003 | 73 |
| 460210 | basketwork and other articles made directly from vegetable plaiting materials or from goods of heading 4601, plus articles of loofah (excl. wall coverings of heading 4814; twine, cord and rope; footware and headgear and parts thereof | 0.0001 | 0.0001 | 75 |
| 610990 | t-shirts, singlets and other vests of textile materials, knitted or crocheted (excl. cotton) | 0.2 | 0.2 | 76 |
| 620433 | women's or girls' jackets and blazers of synthetic fibres (excl. knitted or crocheted, wind-jackets and similar articles) | 0.03 | 0.03 | 109 |
| 610520 | men's or boys' shirts of man-made fibres, knitted or crocheted (excl. nightshirts, t-shirts, singlets and other vests) | 0.2 | 0.1 | 110 |
| 620213 | women's or girls' overcoats, raincoats, car-coats, capes, cloaks and similar, of man-made fibres (excl. knitted or crocheted) | 0.01 | 0.01 | 141 |
| 620343 | men's or boys' trousers, bib and brace overalls, breeches and shorts of synthetic fibres (excl. knitted or crocheted, underpants and swimwear) | 0.2 | 0.1 | 143 |
| 610463 | women's or girls' trousers, bib and brace overalls, breeches and shorts of synthetic fibres, knitted or crocheted (excl. panties and swimwear) | 0.2 | 0.1 | 155 |

**Appendix A3.2** (continued)

| HS6 | Description | Share of US imports (%)[a] | Avg. share of other Quad imports (%)[a] | US share as percentage of average Quad share |
|---|---|---|---|---|
| 611019 | 'jerseys, pullovers, cardigans, waistcoats and similar articles, of fine animal hair, knitted or crocheted (excl. from hair of kashmir "cashmere" goats and quilted articles)' | 0.002 | 0.001 | 156 |
| 610910 | t-shirts, singlets and other vests of cotton, knitted or crocheted | 1.0 | 0.6 | 167 |
| 611030 | jerseys, pullovers, cardigans, waistcoats and similar articles, of man-made fibres, knitted or crocheted (excl. wadded waistcoats) | 3.2 | 1.8 | 181 |
| 611011 | jerseys, pullovers, cardigans, waistcoats and similar articles, of wool, knitted or crocheted (excl. wadded waistcoats) | 0.2 | 0.1 | 193 |
| 610220 | women's or girls' overcoats, car-coats, capes, cloaks, anoraks, incl. ski-jackets, windcheaters, wind-jackets and similar articles of cotton, knitted or crocheted (excl. suits, ensembles, jackets, blazers, dresses, skirts, divided skirts | 0.2 | 0.1 | 202 |
| 621210 | brassieres of all types of textile materials, whether or not elasticated, incl. knitted or crocheted | 0.4 | 0.2 | 213 |
| 610343 | men's or boys' trousers, bib and brace overalls, breeches and shorts of synthetic fibres, knitted or crocheted (excl. swimwear and underpants) | 0.1 | 0.05 | 214 |
| 620722 | men's or boys' nightshirts and pyjamas of man-made fibres (excl. knitted or crocheted, vests, singlets and underpants) | 0.01 | 0.002 | 340 |
| 620930 | babies' garments and clothing accessories of synthetic fibres (excl. knitted or crocheted and hats) | 0.03 | 0.01 | 369 |
| 611020 | jerseys, pullovers, cardigans, waistcoats and similar articles, of cotton, knitted or crocheted (excl. wadded waistcoats) | 10.9 | 2.2 | 507 |
| 610443 | women's or girls' dresses of synthetic fibres, knitted or crocheted (excl. petticoats) | 0.1 | 0.03 | 517 |

**Appendix A3.2** (continued)

| HS6 | Description | Share of US imports (%)[a] | Avg. share of other Quad imports (%)[a] | US share as percentage of average Quad share |
|---|---|---|---|---|
| 610510 | men's or boys' shirts of cotton, knitted or crocheted (excl. nightshirts, t-shirts, singlets and other vests) | 2.4 | 0.4 | 616 |
| 610433 | women's or girls' jackets and blazers, of synthetic fibres, knitted or crocheted (excl. wind-jackets and similar articles) | 0.001 | 0.0001 | 635 |
| 610610 | women's or girls' blouses, shirts and shirt-blouses of cotton, knitted or crocheted (excl. t-shirts and vests) | 1.7 | 0.3 | 670 |
| 610120 | overcoats, car-coats, capes, cloaks, anoraks, incl. ski-jackets, windcheaters, wind-jackets and similar articles of cotton, for men or boys, knitted or crocheted (excl. suits, ensembles, jackets, blazers and trousers) | 0.3 | 0.04 | 726 |
| 620342 | men's or boys' trousers, bib and brace overalls, breeches and shorts, of cotton (excl. knitted or crocheted, underpants and swimwear) | 7.2 | 0.9 | 786 |
| 621143 | women's or girls' track suits and other garments n.e.s. of man-made fibres (excl. knitted or crocheted) | 0.2 | 0.03 | 813 |
| 620462 | women's or girls' trousers, bib and brace overalls, breeches and shorts of cotton (excl. knitted or crocheted, panties and swimwear) | 17.2 | 2.0 | 842 |
| 610342 | men's or boys' trousers, bib and brace overalls, breeches and shorts of cotton, knitted or crocheted (excl. swimwear and underpants) | 0.2 | 0.02 | 883 |
| 620459 | women's or girls' skirts and divided skirts of textile materials (excl. of wool, fine animal hair, cotton or synthetic fibres, knitted or crocheted and petticoats) | 0.2 | 0.02 | 898 |
| 610620 | women's or girls' blouses, shirts and shirt-blouses of man-made fibres, knitted or crocheted (excl. t-shirts and vests) | 0.8 | 0.1 | 1120 |

**Appendix A3.2** (continued)

| HS6 | Description | Share of US imports (%)[a] | Avg. share of other Quad imports (%)[a] | US share as percentage of average Quad share |
|---|---|---|---|---|
| 620640 | women's or girls' blouses, shirts and shirt-blouses of man-made fibres (excl. knitted or crocheted and vests) | 1.0 | 0.1 | 1173 |
| 620822 | women's or girls' nightdresses and pyjamas of man-made fibres (excl. knitted or crocheted, vests and negliges) | 1.1 | 0.1 | 1187 |
| 620530 | men's or boys' shirts of man-made fibres (excl. knitted or crocheted, nightshirts, singlets and other vests) | 0.4 | 0.03 | 1258 |
| 620319 | men's or boys' suits of textile materials (excl. of wool, fine animal hair or synthetic fibres, knitted or crocheted, track suits, ski suits and swimwear) | 0.0003 | 0 | 1416 |
| 621111 | men's or boys' swimwear (excl. knitted or crocheted) | 1.1 | 0.1 | 1429 |
| 620191 | men's or boys' anoraks, incl. ski-jackets, windcheaters, wind-jackets and similar articles, of wool or fine animal hair (excl. knitted or crocheted, suits, ensembles, jackets, blazers and trousers) | 0.1 | 0.004 | 1441 |
| 620520 | men's or boys' shirts of cotton (excl. knitted or crocheted, nightshirts, singlets and other vests) | 3.1 | 0.2 | 1606 |
| 620892 | women's or girls' vests, briefs, panties, negliges, bathrobes, dressing gowns, housecoats and similar articles of man-made fibres (excl. knitted or crocheted, slips, petticoats, nightdresses and pyjamas, brassieres, girdles, corsets and singlets | 0.1 | 0.01 | 1700 |
| 610453 | women's or girls' skirts and divided skirts of synthetic fibres, knitted or crocheted (excl. petticoats) | 0.5 | 0.03 | 1781 |
| 611130 | babies' garments and clothing accessories of synthetic fibres, knitted or crocheted (excl. hats) | 0.4 | 0.02 | 1817 |

**Appendix A3.2** (continued)

| HS6 | Description | Share of US imports (%)[a] | Avg. share of other Quad imports (%)[a] | US share as percentage of average Quad share |
|---|---|---|---|---|
| 610892 | women's or girls' negliges, bathrobes, dressing gowns, housejackets and similar articles of man-made fibres, knitted or crocheted (excl. vests, slips, petticoats, briefs and panties, nightdresses, pyjamas, brassieres, girdles, corsets and | 0.3 | 0.02 | 1893 |
| 620453 | women's or girls' skirts and divided skirts of synthetic fibres (excl. knitted or crocheted and petticoats) | 1.6 | 0.1 | 2030 |
| 620443 | women's or girls' dresses of synthetic fibres (excl. knitted or crocheted and petticoats) | 0.3 | 0.01 | 2120 |
| 611241 | women's or girls' swimwear of synthetic fibres, knitted or crocheted | 1.1 | 0.05 | 2353 |
| 620630 | women's or girls' blouses, shirts and shirt-blouses of cotton (excl. knitted or crocheted and vests) | 2.8 | 0.1 | 3481 |
| 620444 | women's or girls' dresses of artificial fibres (excl. knitted or crocheted and petticoats) | 0.1 | 0.001 | 5722 |
| 620211 | women's or girls' overcoats, raincoats, car-coats, capes, cloaks and similar, of wool or fine animal hair (excl. knitted or crocheted) | 0.04 | 0.001 | 6607 |
| 620339 | men's or boys' jackets and blazers of textile materials (excl. of wool, fine animal hair, cotton or synthetic fibres, knitted or crocheted, and wind-jackets and similar articles) | 0.001 | 0 | 7632 |
| 610832 | women's or girls' nightdresses and pyjamas of man-made fibres, knitted or crocheted (excl. t-shirts, vests and negliges) | 3.8 | 0.04 | 8477 |
| 620419 | women's or girls' suits of textile materials (excl. of wool, fine animal hair, cotton or synthetic fibres, knitted or crocheted, ski overalls and swimwear) | 0.02 | 0.0002 | 8551 |
| 620312 | men's or boys' suits of synthetic fibres (excl. knitted or crocheted, track suits, ski suits and swimwear) | 0.1 | 0.0004 | 27880 |

**Appendix A3.2** (continued)

| HS6 | Description | Share of US imports (%)[a] | Avg. share of other Quad imports (%)[a] | US share as percentage of average Quad share |
|---|---|---|---|---|
| 610210 | women's or girls' overcoats, car-coats, capes, cloaks, anoraks, incl. ski-jackets, windcheaters, wind-jackets and similar articles, of wool or fine animal hair, knitted or crocheted (excl. suits, ensembles, jackets, blazers, dresses, skirts | 0.1 | 0.0003 | 31424 |
| 610469 | women's or girls' trousers, bib and brace overalls, breeches and shorts of textile materials, knitted or crocheted (excl. of wool, fine animal hair, cotton or synthetic fibres, panties and swimwear) | 0.01 | 0 | 33485 |
| 620333 | men's or boys' jackets and blazers of synthetic fibres (excl. knitted or crocheted, and wind-jackets and similar articles) | 0.1 | 0.0003 | 35468 |
| 620413 | women's or girls' suits of synthetic fibres (excl. knitted or crocheted, ski overalls and swimwear) | 0.5 | 0.001 | 74065 |
| 610722 | men's or boys' nightshirts and pyjamas of man-made fibres, knitted or crocheted (excl. vests and singlets) | 2.0 | 0.003 | 74763 |
| 420212 | trunks, suitcases, vanity cases, attache-cases, briefcases, school satchels and similar containers, with an outer surface of plastics or textile materials | 0.0001 | 0 | (b) |
| 610431 | women's or girls' jackets and blazers, of wool or fine animal hair, knitted or crocheted (excl. wind-jackets and similar articles) | 0.004 | 0 | (b) |
| 620111 | men's or boys' overcoats, raincoats, car-coats, capes, cloaks and similar, of wool or fine animal hair (excl. knitted or crocheted) | 0.003 | 0 | (b) |
| 620311 | men's or boys' suits of wool or fine animal hair (excl. knitted or crocheted, track suits, ski suits and swimwear) | 0.2 | 0 | (b) |
| 620331 | men's or boys' jackets and blazers of wool or fine animal hair (excl. knitted or crocheted, and wind-jackets and similar articles) | 0.003 | 0 | (b) |

**Appendix A3.2** (continued)

| HS6 | Description | Share of US imports (%)[a] | Avg. share of other Quad imports (%)[a] | US share as percentage of average Quad share |
|---|---|---|---|---|
| 620341 | men's or boys' trousers, bib and brace overalls, breeches and shorts, of wool or fine animal hair (excl. knitted or crocheted, underpants and swimwear) | 0.01 | 0 | (b) |
| 630221 | printed bed-linen of cotton (excl. knitted or crocheted) | 0.001 | 0 | (b) |

[a]Displayed to a maximum of four decimal places. '0' denotes that the share is less than one-ten-thousandth of 1 per cent
[b]HS6 sub-head not imported from Cambodia by other Quad markets
*Source:* Statistics Canada, Eurostat, Japanese Ministry of Finance and USITC.

## Appendix A3.3. USA: Relative Importance of Imports from Haiti Compared to Quad Average (HS6)

| HS6 | Description | Share of US imports (%)[a] | Avg. share of other Quad imports (%)[a] | US share as percentage of average Quad share |
|---|---|---|---|---|
| 420292 | travel bags, toilet bags, rucksacks, shopping bags, map cases, tool bags, sports bags, make-up boxes, cutlery boxes, cases for binoculars, cameras, video cameras, musical instruments r arms and similar containers, with an outer surface of | 0.0003 | 0.001 | 43 |
| 611120 | babies' garments and clothing accessories of cotton, knitted or crocheted (excl. hats) | 0.001 | 0.001 | 47 |
| 420222 | handbags, whether or not with shoulder straps, incl. those without handles, with an outer surface of plastic sheeting or textile materials | 0.0001 | 0 | 1082 |
| 620349 | men's or boys' trousers, bib and brace overalls, breeches and shorts of textile materials (excl. of wool, fine animal hair, cotton or synthetic fibres, knitted or crocheted, underpants and swimwear) | 0.001 | 0 | 1332 |
| 620520 | men's or boys' shirts of cotton (excl. knitted or crocheted, nightshirts, singlets and other vests) | 0.02 | 0.001 | 1857 |
| 610910 | t-shirts, singlets and other vests of cotton, knitted or crocheted | 24.6 | 0.6 | 3937 |
| 610610 | women's or girls' blouses, shirts and shirt-blouses of cotton, knitted or crocheted (excl. t-shirts and vests) | 0.05 | 0.001 | 4517 |
| 610822 | women's or girls' briefs and panties of man-made fibres, knitted or crocheted | 0.01 | 0.0002 | 5096 |
| 620630 | women's or girls' blouses, shirts and shirt-blouses of cotton (excl. knitted or crocheted and vests) | 0.004 | 0.0001 | 5112 |
| 610510 | men's or boys' shirts of cotton, knitted or crocheted (excl. nightshirts, t-shirts, singlets and other vests) | 1.0 | 0.02 | 6151 |
| 611610 | gloves, mittens and mitts, impregnated, coated or covered with plastics or rubber, knitted or crocheted | 0.2 | 0.003 | 6167 |

**Appendix A3.3** (continued)

| HS6 | Description | Share of US imports (%)[a] | Avg. share of other Quad imports (%)[a] | US share as percentage of average Quad share |
|---|---|---|---|---|
| 620463 | women's or girls' trousers, bib and brace overalls, breeches and shorts of synthetic fibres (excl. knitted or crocheted, panties and swimwear) | 0.2 | 0.004 | 6597 |
| 620443 | women's or girls' dresses of synthetic fibres (excl. knitted or crocheted and petticoats) | 0.001 | 0 | 10316 |
| 620530 | men's or boys' shirts of man-made fibres (excl. knitted or crocheted, nightshirts, singlets and other vests) | 0.3 | 0.003 | 10476 |
| 610832 | women's or girls' nightdresses and pyjamas of man-made fibres, knitted or crocheted (excl. t-shirts, vests and negliges) | 0.2 | 0.001 | 18551 |
| 611030 | jerseys, pullovers, cardigans, waistcoats and similar articles, of man-made fibres, knitted or crocheted (excl. wadded waistcoats) | 2.3 | 0.01 | 35787 |
| 620343 | men's or boys' trousers, bib and brace overalls, breeches and shorts of synthetic fibres (excl. knitted or crocheted, underpants and swimwear) | 2.5 | 0.005 | 51886 |
| 620640 | women's or girls' blouses, shirts and shirt-blouses of man-made fibres (excl. knitted or crocheted and vests) | 0.03 | 0 | 67185 |
| 610990 | t-shirts, singlets and other vests of textile materials, knitted or crocheted (excl. cotton) | 6.0 | 0.004 | 142127 |
| 611430 | special garments for professional, sporting or other purposes, n.e.s., of man-made fibres, knitted or crocheted | 1.1 | 0.001 | 147103 |
| 611020 | jerseys, pullovers, cardigans, waistcoats and similar articles, of cotton, knitted or crocheted (excl. wadded waistcoats) | 31.2 | 0.01 | 261176 |
| 610520 | men's or boys' shirts of man-made fibres, knitted or crocheted (excl. nightshirts, t-shirts, singlets and other vests) | 1.1 | 0.0004 | 262240 |
| 621143 | women's or girls' track suits and other garments n.e.s. of man-made fibres (excl. knitted or crocheted) | 0.6 | 0.0001 | 404827 |

**Appendix A3.3** (continued)

| HS6 | Description | Share of US imports (%)[a] | Avg. share of other Quad imports (%)[a] | US share as percentage of average Quad share |
|---|---|---|---|---|
| 621210 | brassieres of all types of textile materials, whether or not elasticated, incl. knitted or crocheted | 0.1 | 0 | 437098 |
| 610342 | men's or boys' trousers, bib and brace overalls, breeches and shorts of cotton, knitted or crocheted (excl. swimwear and underpants) | 1.8 | 0.0002 | 1106039 |
| 610463 | women's or girls' trousers, bib and brace overalls, breeches and shorts of synthetic fibres, knitted or crocheted (excl. panties and swimwear) | 1.7 | 0.0001 | 1179274 |
| 621133 | men's or boys' track suits and other garments n.e.s. of man-made fibres (excl. knitted or crocheted) | 0.1 | 0 | 2667878 |
| 610230 | women's or girls' overcoats, car-coats, capes, cloaks, anoraks, incl. ski-jackets, windcheaters, wind-jackets and similar articles of man-made fibres, knitted or crocheted (excl. suits, ensembles, jackets, blazers, dresses, skirts, divide | 0.1 | 0 | 3479933 |
| 620462 | women's or girls' trousers, bib and brace overalls, breeches and shorts of cotton (excl. knitted or crocheted, panties and swimwear) | 0.6 | 0 | 7183245 |
| 610453 | women's or girls' skirts and divided skirts of synthetic fibres, knitted or crocheted (excl. petticoats) | 0.2 | 0 | 10223023 |
| 610343 | men's or boys' trousers, bib and brace overalls, breeches and shorts of synthetic fibres, knitted or crocheted (excl. swimwear and underpants) | 0.1 | 0 | 13671784 |
| 620342 | men's or boys' trousers, bib and brace overalls, breeches and shorts, of cotton (excl. knitted or crocheted, underpants and swimwear) | 3.3 | 0 | 22703115 |
| 581092 | embroidery of man-made fibres on a textile fabric base, in the piece, in strips or as motifs (excl. burnt-out embroidery and embroidery with a cutaway ground) | 0.1 | 0 | (b) |

**Appendix A3.3** (continued)

| HS6 | Description | Share of US imports (%)[a] | Avg. share of other Quad imports (%)[a] | US share as percentage of average Quad share |
|---|---|---|---|---|
| 610130 | overcoats, car-coats, capes, cloaks, anoraks, incl. ski-jackets, windcheaters, wind-jackets and similar articles of man-made fibres, for men or boys, knitted or crocheted (excl. suits, ensembles, jackets, blazers and trousers) | 2.4 | 0 | (b) |
| 610220 | women's or girls' overcoats, car-coats, capes, cloaks, anoraks, incl. ski-jackets, windcheaters, wind-jackets and similar articles of cotton, knitted or crocheted (excl. suits, ensembles, jackets, blazers, dresses, skirts, divided skirts | 0.2 | 0 | (b) |
| 610722 | men's or boys' nightshirts and pyjamas of man-made fibres, knitted or crocheted (excl. vests and singlets) | 0.04 | 0 | (b) |
| 610892 | women's or girls' negliges, bathrobes, dressing gowns, housejackets and similar articles of man-made fibres, knitted or crocheted (excl. vests, slips, petticoats, briefs and panties, nightdresses, pyjamas, brassieres, girdles, corsets and | 0.002 | 0 | (b) |
| 611219 | track-suits of textile materials, knitted or crocheted (excl. cotton or synthetic fibres) | 0.0001 | 0 | (b) |
| 611241 | women's or girls' swimwear of synthetic fibres, knitted or crocheted | 0.02 | 0 | (b) |
| 611692 | gloves, mittens and mitts, of cotton, knitted or crocheted (excl. impregnated, coated or covered with plastics or rubber, and for babies) | 0.4 | 0 | (b) |
| 611693 | gloves, mittens and mitts, of synthetic fibres, knitted or crocheted (excl. impregnated, coated or covered with plastics or rubber, and for babies) | 0.1 | 0 | (b) |
| 620193 | men's or boys' anoraks, windcheaters, wind jackets and similar articles, of man-made fibres (not knitted or crocheted and excl. suits, ensembles, jackets, blazers, trousers and tops of ski suits) | 0.1 | 0 | (b) |
| 620213 | women's or girls' overcoats, raincoats, car-coats, capes, cloaks and similar, of man-made fibres (excl. knitted or crocheted) | 0.01 | 0 | (b) |

**Appendix A3.3** (continued)

| HS6 | Description | Share of US imports (%)[a] | Avg. share of other Quad imports (%)[a] | US share as percentage of average Quad share |
|---|---|---|---|---|
| 620333 | men's or boys' jackets and blazers of synthetic fibres (excl. knitted or crocheted, and wind-jackets and similar articles) | 0.001 | 0 | (b) |
| 620433 | women's or girls' jackets and blazers of synthetic fibres (excl. knitted or crocheted, wind-jackets and similar articles) | 0.0004 | 0 | (b) |
| 620444 | women's or girls' dresses of artificial fibres (excl. knitted or crocheted and petticoats) | 0.001 | 0 | (b) |
| 620453 | women's or girls' skirts and divided skirts of synthetic fibres (excl. knitted or crocheted and petticoats) | 0.01 | 0 | (b) |
| 620822 | women's or girls' nightdresses and pyjamas of man-made fibres (excl. knitted or crocheted, vests and negliges) | 0.02 | 0 | (b) |
| 620892 | women's or girls' vests, briefs, panties, negliges, bathrobes, dressing gowns, housecoats and similar articles of man-made fibres (excl. knitted or crocheted, slips, petticoats, nightdresses and pyjamas, brassieres, girdles, corsets and singlets | 0.003 | 0 | (b) |
| 621010 | garments made up of felt or nonwovens, whether or not impregnated, coated, covered or laminated (excl. babies' garments and clothing accessories) | 0.02 | 0 | (b) |
| 621220 | girdles and panty girdles of all types of textile materials, whether or not elasticated, incl. knitted or crocheted (excl. belts and corselets made entirely of rubber) | 0.03 | 0 | (b) |
| 621600 | gloves, mittens and mitts of all types of textile materials (excl. knitted or crocheted and for babies) | 0.01 | 0 | (b) |

[a]Displayed to a maximum of four decimal places. '0' denotes that the share is less than one-ten-thousandth of 1 per cent
[b]HS6 sub-head not imported from Haiti by other Quad markets
*Source:* Statistics Canada, Eurostat, Japanese Ministry of Finance and USITC.

## Appendix A3.4. USA: Relative Importance of Imports from Nepal Compared to Quad Average (HS6)

| HS6 | Description | Share of US imports (%)[a] | Avg. share of other Quad imports (%)[a] | US share as percentage of average Quad share |
|---|---|---|---|---|
| 640420 | footwear with outer soles of leather or composition leather and uppers of textile materials (excl. toy footwear) | 0.0002 | 0.02 | 1 |
| 420292 | travel bags, toilet bags, rucksacks, shopping bags, map cases, tool bags, sports bags, make-up boxes, cutlery boxes, cases for binoculars, cameras, video cameras, musical instruments or arms and similar containers, with an outer surface of | 0.03 | 0.1 | 21 |
| 610343 | men's or boys' trousers, bib and brace overalls, breeches and shorts of synthetic fibres, knitted or crocheted (excl. swimwear and underpants) | 0.0003 | 0.001 | 28 |
| 610431 | women's or girls' jackets and blazers, of wool or fine animal hair, knitted or crocheted (excl. wind-jackets and similar articles) | 0.002 | 0.01 | 31 |
| 611012 | 'jerseys, pullovers, cardigans, waistcoats and similar articles, of hair of kashmir "cashmere" goats, knitted or crocheted (excl. quilted articles)' | 0.01 | 0.02 | 32 |
| 620331 | men's or boys' jackets and blazers of wool or fine animal hair (excl. knitted or crocheted, and wind-jackets and similar articles) | 0.001 | 0.002 | 41 |
| 420229 | handbags, whether or not with shoulder strap, incl. those without handle, with outer surface of vulcanized fibre or paperboard, or wholly or mainly covered with such materials or with paper | 0.001 | 0.001 | 59 |
| 620469 | women's or girls' trousers, bib and brace overalls, breeches and shorts of textile materials (excl. of wool, fine animal hair, cotton or synthetic fibres, knitted or crocheted, panties and swimwear) | 0.002 | 0.003 | 73 |
| 610990 | t-shirts, singlets and other vests of textile materials, knitted or crocheted (excl. cotton) | 0.01 | 0.01 | 95 |

**Appendix A3.4** (continued)

| HS6 | Description | Share of US imports (%)[a] | Avg. share of other Quad imports (%)[a] | US share as percentage of average Quad share |
|---|---|---|---|---|
| 640299 | footwear with outer soles and uppers of rubber or plastics (excl. covering the ankle or with upper straps or thongs assembled to the sole by means of plugs, waterproof footwear of heading 6401, sports footwear, orthopaedic footwear and toy | 0.001 | 0.001 | 98 |
| 650300 | felt hats and other felt headgear, made from the hat bodies, hoods or plateaux of heading 6501, whether or not lined or trimmed (excl. made by assembling strips or pieces of felt, and toy and carnival headgear) | 0.001 | 0.001 | 120 |
| 650590 | hats and other headgear, knitted or crocheted, or made up from pieces, but not strips, of lace, felt or other textile fabrics, whether or not lined or trimmed (excl. hair-nets, headgear for animals, and toy and fancy-dress headgear) | 0.2 | 0.2 | 127 |
| 610120 | overcoats, car-coats, capes, cloaks, anoraks, incl. ski-jackets, windcheaters, wind-jackets and similar articles of cotton, for men or boys, knitted or crocheted (excl. suits, ensembles, jackets, blazers and trousers) | 0.01 | 0.003 | 175 |
| 610110 | overcoats, car-coats, capes, cloaks, anoraks, incl. ski-jackets, windcheaters, wind-jackets and similar articles of wool or fine animal hair, for men or boys, knitted or crocheted (excl. suits, ensembles, jackets, blazers and trousers) | 0.01 | 0.003 | 198 |
| 420232 | wallets, purses, key pouches, cigarette cases, tobacco pouches and similar articles carried in the pocket or handbag, with an outer surface of plastic sheeting or textile materials | 0.04 | 0.02 | 234 |
| 611011 | jerseys, pullovers, cardigans, waistcoats and similar articles, of wool, knitted or crocheted (excl. wadded waistcoats) | 0.1 | 0.1 | 244 |
| 620349 | men's or boys' trousers, bib and brace overalls, breeches and shorts of textile materials (excl. of wool, fine animal hair, cotton or synthetic fibres, knitted or crocheted, underpants and swimwear) | 0.02 | 0.01 | 264 |

**Appendix A3.4** (continued)

| HS6 | Description | Share of US imports (%)[a] | Avg. share of other Quad imports (%)[a] | US share as percentage of average Quad share |
|---|---|---|---|---|
| 640419 | footwear with outer soles of rubber or plastics and uppers of textile materials (excl. sports footwear, incl. tennis shoes, basketball shoes, gym shoes, training shoes and the like, and toy footwear) | 0.005 | 0.002 | 274 |
| 620431 | women's or girls' jackets and blazers of wool or fine animal hair (excl. knitted or crocheted, wind-jackets and similar articles) | 0.001 | 0.0004 | 374 |
| 620422 | women's or girls' ensembles of cotton (excl. knitted or crocheted, ski overalls and swimwear) | 0.004 | 0.001 | 377 |
| 420299 | travel, shopping & tool bags, jewellery or cutlery boxes and similar containers, with outer surface of vulcanized fibre or paperboard; cases for binoculars, cameras, musical instruments or arms, and similar containers | 0.003 | 0.001 | 385 |
| 610130 | overcoats, car-coats, capes, cloaks, anoraks, incl. ski-jackets, windcheaters, wind-jackets and similar articles of man-made fibres, for men or boys, knitted or crocheted (excl. suits, ensembles, jackets, blazers and trousers) | 0.03 | 0.01 | 397 |
| 620193 | men's or boys' anoraks, windcheaters, wind jackets and similar articles, of man-made fibres (not knitted or crocheted and excl. suits, ensembles, jackets, blazers, trousers and tops of ski suits) | 0.001 | 0.0002 | 434 |
| 620510 | men's or boys' shirts of wool or fine animal hair (excl. knitted or crocheted, nightshirts, singlets and other vests) | 0.001 | 0.0002 | 478 |
| 610210 | women's or girls' overcoats, car-coats, capes, cloaks, anoraks, incl. ski-jackets, windcheaters, wind-jackets and similar articles, of wool or fine animal hair, knitted or crocheted (excl. suits, ensembles, jackets, blazers, dresses, skirts | 0.03 | 0.01 | 485 |
| 620343 | men's or boys' trousers, bib and brace overalls, breeches and shorts of synthetic fibres (excl. knitted or crocheted, underpants and swimwear) | 0.2 | 0.04 | 506 |

**Appendix A3.4** (continued)

| HS6 | Description | Share of US imports (%)[a] | Avg. share of other Quad imports (%)[a] | US share as percentage of average Quad share |
|---|---|---|---|---|
| 620111 | men's or boys' overcoats, raincoats, car-coats, capes, cloaks and similar, of wool or fine animal hair (excl. knitted or crocheted) | 0.001 | 0.0002 | 534 |
| 420212 | trunks, suitcases, vanity cases, attache-cases, briefcases, school satchels and similar containers, with an outer surface of plastics or textile materials | 0.003 | 0.0005 | 542 |
| 611019 | 'jerseys, pullovers, cardigans, waistcoats and similar articles, of fine animal hair, knitted or crocheted (excl. from hair of kashmir "cashmere" goats and quilted articles)' | 0.02 | 0.004 | 546 |
| 620463 | women's or girls' trousers, bib and brace overalls, breeches and shorts of synthetic fibres (excl. knitted or crocheted, panties and swimwear) | 0.1 | 0.02 | 632 |
| 620291 | women's or girls' anoraks, incl. ski-jackets, windcheaters, wind-jackets and similar articles, of wool or fine animal hair (excl. knitted or crocheted, suits, ensembles, jackets, blazers and trousers) | 0.01 | 0.001 | 938 |
| 620211 | women's or girls' overcoats, raincoats, car-coats, capes, cloaks and similar, of wool or fine animal hair (excl. knitted or crocheted) | 0.02 | 0.002 | 1205 |
| 420222 | handbags, whether or not with shoulder straps, incl. those without handles, with an outer surface of plastic sheeting or textile materials | 0.1 | 0.01 | 1245 |
| 611120 | babies' garments and clothing accessories of cotton, knitted or crocheted (excl. hats) | 0.1 | 0.005 | 1254 |
| 620113 | men's or boys' overcoats, raincoats, car-coats, capes, cloaks and similar, of man-made fibres (excl. knitted or crocheted) | 0.001 | 0.0001 | 1546 |
| 620439 | women's or girls' jackets and blazers of textile materials (excl. of wool, fine animal hair, cotton or synthetic fibres, knitted or crocheted, wind-jackets and similar articles) | 0.03 | 0.002 | 1614 |
| 620459 | women's or girls' skirts and divided skirts of textile materials (excl. of wool, fine animal hair, cotton or synthetic fibres, knitted or crocheted and petticoats) | 0.01 | 0.001 | 1815 |

**Appendix A3.4** (continued)

| HS6 | Description | Share of US imports (%)[a] | Avg. share of other Quad imports (%)[a] | US share as percentage of average Quad share |
|---|---|---|---|---|
| 620191 | men's or boys' anoraks, incl. ski-jackets, windcheaters, wind-jackets and similar articles, of wool or fine animal hair (excl. knitted or crocheted, suits, ensembles, jackets, blazers and trousers) | 0.01 | 0.0003 | 1862 |
| 620910 | babies' garments and clothing accessories of wool or fine animal hair (excl. knitted or crocheted and hats) | 0.0002 | 0 | 3102 |
| 610610 | women's or girls' blouses, shirts and shirt-blouses of cotton, knitted or crocheted (excl. t-shirts and vests) | 0.7 | 0.02 | 4044 |
| 620453 | women's or girls' skirts and divided skirts of synthetic fibres (excl. knitted or crocheted and petticoats) | 0.3 | 0.01 | 4476 |
| 610910 | t-shirts, singlets and other vests of cotton, knitted or crocheted | 1.7 | 0.04 | 4594 |
| 611693 | gloves, mittens and mitts, of synthetic fibres, knitted or crocheted (excl. impregnated, coated or covered with plastics or rubber, and for babies) | 0.01 | 0.0002 | 5139 |
| 621210 | brassieres of all types of textile materials, whether or not elasticated, incl. knitted or crocheted | 0.001 | 0 | 5772 |
| 560221 | felt, not impregnated, coated, covered or laminated, of wool or fine animal hair, n.e.s. (excl. needleloom felt and stitch-bonded fibre fabrics) | 0.0005 | 0 | 6007 |
| 620630 | women's or girls' blouses, shirts and shirt-blouses of cotton (excl. knitted or crocheted and vests) | 3.3 | 0.04 | 7950 |
| 611030 | jerseys, pullovers, cardigans, waistcoats and similar articles, of man-made fibres, knitted or crocheted (excl. wadded waistcoats) | 1.1 | 0.01 | 8331 |
| 610342 | men's or boys' trousers, bib and brace overalls, breeches and shorts of cotton, knitted or crocheted (excl. swimwear and underpants) | 0.1 | 0.002 | 8398 |

**Appendix A3.4** (continued)

| HS6 | Description | Share of US imports (%)[a] | Avg. share of other Quad imports (%)[a] | US share as percentage of average Quad share |
|---|---|---|---|---|
| 610510 | men's or boys' shirts of cotton, knitted or crocheted (excl. nightshirts, t-shirts, singlets and other vests) | 3.3 | 0.04 | 8473 |
| 620462 | women's or girls' trousers, bib and brace overalls, breeches and shorts of cotton (excl. knitted or crocheted, panties and swimwear) | 13.1 | 0.2 | 8593 |
| 620443 | women's or girls' dresses of synthetic fibres (excl. knitted or crocheted and petticoats) | 0.2 | 0.002 | 9260 |
| 610463 | women's or girls' trousers, bib and brace overalls, breeches and shorts of synthetic fibres, knitted or crocheted (excl. panties and swimwear) | 0.1 | 0.001 | 10640 |
| 620342 | men's or boys' trousers, bib and brace overalls, breeches and shorts, of cotton (excl. knitted or crocheted, underpants and swimwear) | 15.0 | 0.1 | 13642 |
| 611020 | jerseys, pullovers, cardigans, waistcoats and similar articles, of cotton, knitted or crocheted (excl. wadded waistcoats) | 10.0 | 0.1 | 14243 |
| 620520 | men's or boys' shirts of cotton (excl. knitted or crocheted, nightshirts, singlets and other vests) | 2.3 | 0.01 | 16557 |
| 620293 | women's or girls' anoraks, windcheaters, wind jackets and similar articles, of man-made fibres (not knitted or crocheted and excl. suits, ensembles, jackets, blazers, trousers and tops of ski suits) | 0.1 | 0.001 | 19197 |
| 610220 | women's or girls' overcoats, car-coats, capes, cloaks, anoraks, incl. ski-jackets, windcheaters, wind-jackets and similar articles of cotton, knitted or crocheted (excl. suits, ensembles, jackets, blazers, dresses, skirts, divided skirts | 0.1 | 0.0005 | 23498 |
| 620444 | women's or girls' dresses of artificial fibres (excl. knitted or crocheted and petticoats) | 0.3 | 0.001 | 30821 |
| 620433 | women's or girls' jackets and blazers of synthetic fibres (excl. knitted or crocheted, wind-jackets and similar articles) | 1.1 | 0.003 | 32522 |

**Appendix A3.4** (continued)

| HS6 | Description | Share of US imports (%)[a] | Avg. share of other Quad imports (%)[a] | US share as percentage of average Quad share |
|---|---|---|---|---|
| 620640 | women's or girls' blouses, shirts and shirt-blouses of man-made fibres (excl. knitted or crocheted and vests) | 0.4 | 0.001 | 38235 |
| 610620 | women's or girls' blouses, shirts and shirt-blouses of man-made fibres, knitted or crocheted (excl. t-shirts and vests) | 0.02 | 0 | 45751 |
| 621143 | women's or girls' track suits and other garments n.e.s. of man-made fibres (excl. knitted or crocheted) | 0.3 | 0.001 | 48089 |
| 610230 | women's or girls' overcoats, car-coats, capes, cloaks, anoraks, incl. ski-jackets, windcheaters, wind-jackets and similar articles of man-made fibres, knitted or crocheted (excl. suits, ensembles, jackets, blazers, dresses, skirts, divide | 0.1 | 0.0002 | 64078 |
| 620620 | women's or girls' blouses, shirts and shirt-blouses of wool or fine animal hair (excl. knitted or crocheted and vests) | 0.02 | 0 | 431091 |
| 610422 | women's or girls' ensembles of cotton, knitted or crocheted (excl. ski ensembles and swimwear) | 0.2 | 0 | 4539419 |
| 620530 | men's or boys' shirts of man-made fibres (excl. knitted or crocheted, nightshirts, singlets and other vests) | 1.0 | 0 | 5287676 |
| 580390 | gauze (excl. that of cotton and narrow woven fabrics of heading 5806) | 0.0002 | 0 | (b) |
| 611519 | panty hose and tights of textile materials, knitted or crocheted (excl. of synthetic fibres and hosiery for babies) | 0.001 | 0 | (b) |
| 620413 | women's or girls' suits of synthetic fibres (excl. knitted or crocheted, ski overalls and swimwear) | 0.0004 | 0 | (b) |
| 621120 | ski suits (excl. knitted or crocheted) | 0.0002 | 0 | (b) |

[a]Displayed to a maximum of four decimal places. '0' denotes that the share is less than one-ten-thousandth of 1 per cent
[b]HS6 sub-head not imported from Nepal by other Quad markets
*Source:* Statistics Canada, Eurostat, Japanese Ministry of Finance and USITC

# Annex 1

## Annex F

## Special and Differential Treatment

### LDC Agreement-specific Proposals

#### 23) Understanding in Respect of Waivers of Obligations under the GATT 1994

(i) We agree that requests for waivers by least-developed country Members under Article IX of the WTO Agreement and the Understanding in respect of Waivers of Obligations under the GATT 1994 shall be given positive consideration and a decision taken within 60 days.

(ii) When considering requests for waivers by other Members exclusively in favour of least-developed country Members, we agree that a decision shall be taken within 60 days, or in exceptional circumstances as expeditiously as possible thereafter, without prejudice to the rights of other Members.

#### 36) Decision on Measures in Favour of Least-Developed Countries

We agree that developed-country Members shall, and developing-country Members declaring themselves in a position to do so should:

(a) (i) Provide duty-free and quota-free market access on a lasting basis, for all products originating from all LDCs by 2008 or no later than the start of the implementation period in a manner that ensures stability, security and predictability.

(ii) Members facing difficulties at this time to provide market access as set out above shall provide duty-free and quota-free market access for at least 97 per cent of products originating from LDCs, defined at the tariff line level, by 2008 or no later than the start of the implementation period. In addition, these Members shall take steps to progressively achieve compliance with the obligations set out above, taking into account the impact on other developing countries at similar levels of development, and, as appropriate, by incrementally building on the initial list of covered products.

(iii) Developing-country Members shall be permitted to phase in their commitments and shall enjoy appropriate flexibility in coverage.

(b) Ensure that preferential rules of origin applicable to imports from LDCs are transparent and simple, and contribute to facilitating market access.

Members shall notify the implementation of the schemes adopted under this decision every year to the Committee on Trade and Development. The Committee on Trade and

Development shall annually review the steps taken to provide duty-free and quota-free market access to the LDCs and report to the General Council for appropriate action.

We urge all donors and relevant international institutions to increase financial and technical support aimed at the diversification of LDC economies, while providing additional financial and technical assistance through appropriate delivery mechanisms to meet their implementation obligations, including fulfilling SPS and TBT requirements, and to assist them in managing their adjustment processes, including those necessary to face the results of MFN multilateral trade liberalisation.

### 38) Decision on Measures in Favour of Least-Developed Countries

It is reaffirmed that least-developed country Members will only be required to undertake commitments and concessions to the extent consistent with their individual development, financial or trade needs, or their administrative and institutional capacities.

Within the context of coherence arrangements with other international institutions, we urge donors, multilateral agencies and international financial institutions to coordinate their work to ensure that LDCs are not subjected to conditionalities on loans, grants and official development assistance that are inconsistent with their rights and obligations under the WTO Agreements.

### 84) Agreement on Trade-Related Investment Measures

LDCs shall be allowed to maintain on a temporary basis existing measures that deviate from their obligations under the TRIMs Agreement. For this purpose, LDCs shall notify the Council for Trade in Goods (CTG) of such measures within two years, starting 30 days after the date of this declaration. LDCs will be allowed to maintain these existing measures until the end of a new transition period, lasting seven years. This transition period may be extended by the CTG under the existing procedures set out in the TRIMs Agreement, taking into account the individual financial, trade, and development needs of the Member in question.

LDCs shall also be allowed to introduce new measures that deviate from their obligations under the TRIMs Agreement. These new TRIMs shall be notified to the CTG no later than six months after their adoption. The CTG shall give positive consideration to such notifications, taking into account the individual financial, trade, and development needs of the Member in question. The duration of these measures will not exceed five years, renewable subject to review and decision by the CTG.

Any measures incompatible with the TRIMs Agreement and adopted under this decision shall be phased out by year 2020.

### 88) Decision on Measures in Favour of Least-Developed Countries – Paragraph 1

Least-developed country Members, whilst reaffirming their commitment to the fundamental principles of the WTO and relevant provisions of GATT 1994, and while complying with the general rules set out in the aforesaid instruments, will only be required to undertake commitments and concessions to the extent consistent with their individual development, financial and trade needs, and their administrative and institutional capabilities. Should a least-developed country Member find that it is not in a position to comply with a specific obligation or commitment on these grounds, it shall bring the matter to the attention of the General Council for examination and appropriate action.

We agree that the implementation by LDCs of their obligations or commitments will require further technical and financial support directly related to the nature and scope of such obligations or commitments, and direct the WTO to coordinate its efforts with donors and relevant agencies to significantly increase aid for trade-related technical assistance and capacity building.

## Notes

1 *User Guide: TradeMap*, Geneva: International Trade Centre, Market Analysis Section, November 2005, p. 8.
2 *http://www.wto.org/english/docs_e/legal_e/itadec_e.doc*
3 To a minimum value of US$1 million and, necessarily, at the HS6 level of aggregation because countries do not apply identical nomenclatures at the 8- and 10-digit levels.
4 The data for Japan and USA are freely available from the websites listed in the references for this chapter. Those for Canada, by contrast, had to be specifically ordered and purchased for this study.
5 The tariff data for Canada are downloadable in machine-readable form from the website listed in the references. Access to tariff data in UNCTAD's TRAINS database is by subscription only.
6 Or any item for which the notes given in the source used for the tariff data are not sufficient to establish the tariff applicable.
7 They are: Burkina Faso, Central African Republic, Chad, Comoros, Djibouti, Equatorial Guinea, Guinea, Guinea Bissau, Liberia, Mali, Mauritania, Niger, Rwanda, São Tomé and Principe, Seychelles, the Solomon Islands, Somalia, and Tuvalu (*UK Tariff 2006*, Volume 1, pp. 62 and 61).
8 It also accords LDC treatment to the two countries from which it did not import anything in 2004.
9 A superior tranche of the General Preferential Tariff (GPT), which is the Canadian equivalent of the GSP.
10 No AVE could be calculated from the data obtained for eight imports from Bangladesh and 12 from Nepal. Since the existence of a specific duty tends to denote that the item is sensitive, all these unknowns have been assumed to be highly sensitive.
11 This assumes that the 17 excluded items are the eight 'unknown' tariffs plus the nine known highest AVs or AVEs (all of which are AVs of 30 per cent or more; no AVEs are this high).
12 I.e. the 17 highest-value items among the 114 exports which have a specific/unknown duty or an AV/AVE of 15 per cent or more
13 In order to make the comparison with other Quad countries, the table has had to aggregate the 8-digit items imported by the USA from Bangladesh into 6-digit groups. It has then compared the relative importance of these 6-digit groups in the total imports of each Quad country. Of course, each Quad country may be importing different 8-, 9- or 10-digit items within these 6-digit groups, but this is an unavoidable simplification. The 'average Quad share' is obtained by calculating for each HS6 group its share in the imports of each Quad country and then averaging these shares.
14 Which is a summary of Table A3.1 – as are Tables 3.6–3.8 of Tables A3.2–A3.4.
15 These are the two items for which the tariff applicable cannot be ascertained.
16 In this case the calculation of the highest tariffs is especially problematic because of data gaps. The 13 'highest-tariff items' comprise the 12 'unknown' tariffs plus the one known highest AV
17 We have not included the other two alternative assumptions on product selection made for Interpretation 1. Assumption 3 is necessarily country specific and so unsuitable for Interpretation 2. Assumption 2 is less plausible under Interpretation 2.The highest tariff peaks are much higher than the lowest. Given that the exclusions selected in relation to Bangladesh will, on the assumption in the report, apply to all other LDCs it seems less likely that the USA would choose items with lower tariff peaks, some of which may be much less substantial imports from other LDCs, whilst allowing full DFQF to all LDCs on items facing higher tariffs.
18 The eight specific-duty items exported by Bangladesh for which it has not been possible to calculate AVEs are assumed to be high-tariff, and are included among the 48.
19 These results are influenced by the high number of specific duties (in the case of Interpretation 1 they exceed the maximum number of items the USA could exclude from the most sensitive import sources). All AVEs need to be treated with caution. Nonetheless, they provide the best approximation to what the USA's exclusion list would look like if it were concentrated exclusively on the items that apparently face the highest tariffs.
20 Japan also grants LDC treatment to the two countries from which it did not import anything in 2004.
21 In practice this means that the exclusions are all items facing an ad valorem or AVE tariff of over 10 per cent plus the highest-value imports facing a 10 per cent tariff.
22 Although Myanmar could, presumably, bring a case of discrimination in relation to one of its LDC competitors being treated more favourably.

## References

Canadian Border Services Agency, *http://www.cbsa-asfc.gc.ca/general/publications/customs _ tariff-e.html*

Eurostat. *Intra- and Extra-EU Trade*, Supplement 5/2003 (DVD). Luxembourg: Office for Official Publications of the European Communities.

Japanese Ministry of Finance. Trade Statistics of Japan, *http://www.customs.go.jp/toukei/info/index_e.htm*, data downloaded February 2006.

Statistics Canada. Data on Canadian Imports Statistics 2004, supplied on request, February 2006, Ottawa: Statistics Canada.

UNCTAD. Trade Analysis and Information System (TRAINS), powered by the World Integrated Trade Solution (WITS), Geneva: United Nations Conference on Trade and Development, *http://wits.worldbank.org*, data downloaded February 2006).

UK Tariff (2006). *Integrated Tariff of the United Kingdom*, 2006 edition, London: TSO.

USITC. Interactive Tariff and Trade DataWeb. Washington, DC: United States International Trade Commission, *http://dataweb.usitc.gov/scripts/user_set.asp*, data downloaded February 2006).

# 4

# Addressing Global Cotton Subsidies: Uprooting the Seeds of Poverty

David Primack

## Introduction

International trade in cotton came to the fore in trade and development debates in 2002, with the Brazilian request for consultations on US cotton subsidies. This was followed by the 2003 WTO proposal by Benin, Burkina Faso, Chad and Mali for a 'Sectoral Initiative on Cotton'. The trade exemplifies the way in which the playing field is tilted against developing countries in agriculture. On the one hand, some of the poorest developing countries (in West and Central Africa) and some of the largest (Brazil, China and India) hold a competitive advantage in the production of raw cotton; on the other, the USA and the EU spend billions of dollars annually in subsidies to prop up an otherwise inefficient and high-cost sector. The pernicious impacts of these continued subsidies are now well established: they result in depressed world cotton prices, lost market share for otherwise competitive producers and the concomitant loss of hundreds of millions of dollars in forgone export earnings. What remains a matter of intense debate, however, is exactly how, when and where the impact of these subsidies should be addressed.

One of the key problems at the heart of the battle to address the problem of global cotton subsidies is whether those countries whose support to the cotton sector is most distorting (i.e. the USA and the EU) will pursue meaningful domestic reform to mitigate the harm caused to otherwise competitive cotton producers, or whether they will seek to avoid such reform by, for example, offering an attractive financial package aimed at generating support for effectively carrying on with 'business as usual'. If the seeds of the poverty caused by the subsidies are to be uprooted, the issue of compensation (especially for those least capable of mitigating the damage caused), pending the needed reforms, must also be addressed.

The debate surrounding trade and development has been reinvigorated in recent years, as evidenced by the latest round of multilateral trade negotiations launched in Doha in 2001. At Doha the international community – and in particular the major OECD trading powers – made a commitment to place development at the centre of the trade agenda. However, what has been termed by some the 'Doha Development Agenda' has now passed its original 1 January 2005 completion date, and there has so far been only slow progress. This includes the failure in September 2003 to reach consensus at the

The author would like to thank Roman Grynberg for his guidance and input, and Ivan Mbirimi and Alex Werth for their helpful comments. Any errors or omissions remain the author's sole responsibility.

Cancun Ministerial Meeting[1] and sluggish progress since, including at the recently concluded Ministerial Meeting in Hong Kong.[2] As with the Uruguay Round negotiations (which lasted seven and a half years – twice as long as envisaged), the area of agriculture has proved particularly troublesome.

Since the lead-up to Cancun, the cotton sector has received particular attention on the WTO agenda. Indeed, with the persistence of such a clear imbalance in the sector, many observers have viewed cotton as a litmus test of the ability of the multilateral trading system to focus its attention on the needs of its most vulnerable members. As was the case with Cancun, these observers looked to the Sixth WTO Ministerial Meeting in Hong Kong to see what, if anything, the major trading powers were prepared to deliver on cotton in the context of the Doha Development Agenda. Like most items on the agenda in Hong Kong however, low ambitions resulted in little change.

With the 'trade aspects' of cotton having been subsumed into the broader agricultural talks, meaningful progress is now predicated on making significant progress in the achievement of across the board reform – as part of which deeper cuts in cotton subsidies can be pursued. However, with the most difficult decisions left unresolved in Hong Kong, and negotiators facing the extremely ambitious (if not impossible) deadline of end-April 2006 to finalise the agricultural modalities, a realistic assessment would indicate that significant support to inefficient cotton producers (and the associated injury to competitive producers) will continue for some time to come.

While the successful Brazilian challenge to US subsidies means that it may be possible to achieve some of the objectives sought through the Cotton Initiative, no reforms are scheduled prior to mid-2006, and these are not directed at the domestic support measures that constitute the bulk of the US support programme. The latter appears to be an issue on which no progress can be made until after the passage of the 2007 US Farm Bill, and even after that the pre-2008 election political landscape in the USA could derail potential reforms until some time into 2009 when the next administration takes over. As for the EU's support programme, some time will be required to assess the recent reforms and determine their real impact; initial assessments do not bode well.

With these probable delays in the achievement of meaningful reforms in the cotton sector, the complementary issue of transitional compensation should return to the WTO agenda. The issue is important both in terms of compensation for continued injury to those producers least capable of coping with the harm resulting from depressed cotton prices and lost market share, and as an additional reminder of the responsibility of the offending subsidisers to reform their distorting ways. While the proposed 'financial assistance' from the donor community is an important part of the broader support to cotton-producing countries from the international community (irrespective of existing distortions in the cotton market), it cannot serve as a substitute for compensation.

This is in no way intended to absolve the USA and the EU of responsibility for confronting their domestic cotton interests and undertaking the often difficult domestic reforms that developing country WTO Members are well versed in. While a range of international technical and financial efforts – both to compensate injured cotton producers and support export diversification – must form some part of the solution, the reduction of the distortionary effects of US and EU cotton subsidies are a *sine qua non* of effectively mitigating the damage. Without this, developing country cotton producers will not be able to maximise the benefits of their competitive advantage in cotton.

Should the required reforms seem unattainable in a reasonable time-frame through negotiations, the LDC net exporters may wish to consider taking the offending parties to a dispute panel. Barring that, while waiting for the deeper reforms to take effect, a range of other elements in the reform package could potentially be pursued. They include a structure to ensure that the elimination of all trade-distorting cotton support measures occurs more rapidly, and agreement (at least in principle) on the development of mechanisms to ensure that the reduction is meaningful and not simply an exercise in 'box-shifting'. In parallel, WTO Members must accept responsibility for the injury that will be caused to competitive cotton producers pending the elimination of distortions in the cotton trade and should agree to recommence discussions under the auspices of the WTO. (They should do this even if it was agreed *ex ante* that such compensation would be delivered outside the WTO framework.) Indeed, the passage on cotton's 'development dimension' in the Hong Kong Declaration (2005f) refers to some as yet undefined mechanism outside the WTO aimed at addressing the decline in incomes in the cotton sector.

If the international community wishes to maintain or bolster the legitimacy of the multilateral trading system, distortions as flagrant as those in the cotton sector must be addressed in a timely, effective and fair manner. While the issue may have not impeded consensus in Hong Kong, as the proponents held it might, the challenge it poses for the legitimacy of the system (to say nothing of potential direct challenges to the US cotton and other support programmes) calls for urgent action.

The structure of this chapter is as follows. The next section presents background information on cotton production, highlighting its importance in developing countries and reviewing the existing literature, which confirms the link between cotton subsidies, recent price trends and the loss of export earnings by competitive producers. The chapter then enquires into what is currently being done to address distortions in the trade in cotton, including a review of the West and Central African (WCA) Cotton Initiative and the WTO dispute ruling, as well as the financial assistance initiative outside the WTO. Following on from the discussion on the unsatisfactory progress made so far, the next section considers areas for potential improvements within existing initiatives, as well as touching on other systemic difficulties related to commodity dependence that require attention. The chapter concludes with recommendations for reforms in the aftermath of the Hong Kong WTO Ministerial Meeting.

## Cotton in the Developing World: Why Distortions Matter

Two-thirds of global cotton production occurs in developing countries, and the importance of the cotton trade to their growth and poverty reduction prospects cannot be overstated. By extension, neither can the damage done by subsidies and domestic support.

Indeed, alongside the magnitude of the support given to Northern cotton farmers, one of the key reasons that so much attention has been focused on the sector is the essential role it plays in many developing country producers. This chapter reviews production and price trends before turning to recent studies linking subsidies to depressed cotton prices and lost export earnings. With the clear linkage between US and EU subsidies and significant injury to competitive producers, and the fact that many of these producers are some of the lowest-income countries in the world, for which cotton is a vital cash crop, this chapter emphasises that the unique nature of the problem facing the global cotton sector warrants short-term practical action.

## The Importance of Cotton

Despite fairly stagnant global demand for cotton (due partly to synthetic substitutes and partly to the rising productivity of some producers), global cotton production has grown at almost 2 per cent annually over the past 40 years, doubling from just over 10 million tonnes in 1960 to 20 million in 2001 (Baffes, 2004). In terms of value, both relative to other agricultural activities and as a source of income in developing countries, it is the highest earning non-food crop globally and has been estimated to employ 7 per cent of all labour in developing countries, mostly in smallholder farms (Clay, 2004). Indeed, much of the growth in global production is attributable to large increases in production in developing countries, including traditional producers such as India, China and Pakistan, as well as new entrants such as WCA (Baffes, 2004).[3]

For example, in the latter group, which include some of the lowest-income countries in the world, cotton production rose from just over 100,000 tonnes in the early 1960s to over 1.1 million tonnes in 2002 (Gillson *et al.*, 2004). Based on production volume, WCA has become the sixth largest producer after China, the USA, India, Pakistan and Uzbekistan. Accounting for 13 per cent of world exports in 2001/02, the region is on a par with Uzbekistan as the second largest exporter after the USA (which accounts for 37 per cent of total exports) (Goreux, 2004b). This figure is somewhat misleading in absolute terms, however, as WCA ranks high in terms of exports due to the fact that a number of the larger cotton producers tend not to export their production, but rather consume it in domestic textile industries (for example China, India and Pakistan). Thus, in absolute terms of production volume, they are still a marginal player, accounting for between 10–15 per cent of global cotton production (Gillson *et al.*, 2004).

However, WCA's low proportion of global production does not diminish the importance of cotton domestically. On the contrary, its relative economic importance is far greater than in most other cotton producers, accounting for between 5 to 10 per cent of GDP, more than a third of the value of export earnings and over two-thirds of the value of agricultural exports (Gillson *et al.*, 2004). It has been estimated that 6 million people in the region are employed in cotton production (UNCTAD, 2005). Because of the use of manual harvesting techniques, WCA produces good quality fibre delivered at highly competitive costs.[4] Because of their low labour costs, WCA countries are believed to hold a comparative advantage in cotton production (Goreux, 2004a). Expanded cotton production from 1993–98 has also been attributed to significant health and poverty reduction improvements in WCA cotton growing areas, where incidences of poverty declined from 50 to 42 per cent, as opposed to a two percentage point increase in non-cotton-producing rural areas (Goreux, 2004b). With such a fundamental role in livelihoods and well-being, it comes as no surprise that these countries are pushing for an expedited track in the negotiations to address specific distortions.

Cotton production also plays an important role in other areas of the developing world. India, for example, accounted for approximately 10 per cent of global cotton production in 2002 (ranking third globally with 1.9 million tonnes) (Gillson *et al.*, 2004). Due, however, to its large textile sector, exports were negligible – and thus the depression of global cotton prices is of smaller significance. In the case of Pakistan, on the other hand, which accounted for 9 per cent of global production in 2002 (ranking fourth globally with 1.7 million tonnes), cotton exports amounted to almost 15 per cent of the value of all agricultural exports (Fortucci, 2002).

Cotton production and export is a significant economic activity elsewhere in Africa, in countries such as Tanzania, Zambia, Mozambique and Uganda – although it is declining in importance in some regions, while increasing in others. Despite a decline in relative importance since the 1980s in Tanzania and Zambia, raw cotton exports still accounted for 6 per cent and 27 per cent, respectively, of the value of all agricultural exports in 2000 (Fortucci, 2002). For other countries in the region, the trend ran in the other direction, with cotton exports taking on relatively greater importance over the 20-year period, rising as a share of the value of all agricultural exports in 2000 from 5 to 14 per cent in Mozambique and from 1 to 7 per cent in Uganda.

## Recent Trends in Cotton Prices and Subsidies

Looking at historical price trends,[5] Baffes (2004) notes that real cotton prices (i.e. cotton prices in constant dollar terms) in 2003/04 were one fifth of their 1950 level.[6] Taking into account various price data sources and previous studies on commodity price trends, Razzaque *et al.* (2004) find a declining price trend rate of approximately 2.5 per cent over the 1960–2002 period, with greater volatility in the last two decades. Echoing the latter point, Baffes (2004) points out that cotton price volatility has been twice as high since 1985 compared to the period before 1973; he finds a structural break at the start of the recent period of increased volatility which coincided with the 1985 change in the US support programme from stockholding (i.e. supply management) to price support. Indeed, this latter observation foreshadows the relationship found in recent literature between the US cotton support programme and price movements. Figure 4.1, showing annual A Index prices in both nominal terms (current US$) and real terms (constant 2000 US$),[7] presents a picture of both the downward trend and the heightened post-1985 volatility.

**Figure 4.1. Cotlook A Index Annual**

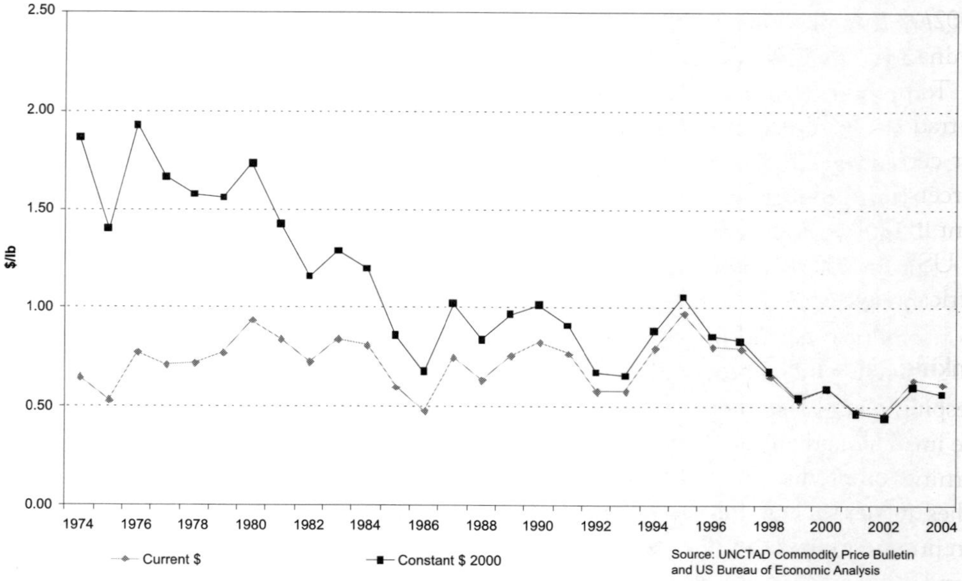


Numerous factors lie behind recent price movements. They include erratic changes in production and exports from India, Pakistan and China (where high levels of production, usually bound for domestic textile sectors, have at times found their way onto export markets); reductions in the cost of production (a combination of technological innovations resulting in yield improvements and decreased transportation costs, as well as sectoral reforms); and competition from synthetic substitutes (where declining prices in the late 1990s, resulting in part from the impact of the Asian financial crisis on producers in the region, placed downward pressure on demand for and the price of cotton (Baffes, 2004; Gillson *et al.*, 2004). Another key factor placing downward pressure on cotton prices in recent years has been the large increase in subsidies[8] to cotton producers, which, as discussed below, facilitated levels of production and exports that did not reflect their real cost, thereby inducing excess supply and helping to lower global prices (Sumner, 2003; Goreux, 2004b; Gillson *et al.*, 2004).

Depending on what is taken to constitute a subsidy, estimates of annual government support to the cotton industry worldwide have ranged from US$3.8 to US$6 billion for the 1997/98 to 2001/02 period (Baffes, 2004; ICAC, 2005). In terms of absolute support, the USA provides the highest level (averaging US$2.5 billion annually in the period 1997/98–2001/02), followed by China (US$1.2 billion in 2001/02) and the EU (US$0.8 billion in 2001/02) (Baffes, 2004). As the USA is by far the largest exporter, US subsidies exert the strongest influence on world prices, followed by the EU, which offers the highest per unit support (nearly twice that of the A Index price in 1995/96–1999/2000). The impact of Chinese subsidies on world prices depends largely on whether China is a net importer (pushing prices higher) or net exporter (depressing prices); since the 1980s, it has been slightly more often the former than the latter. Indeed, as noted above, the 2002/03 price rise was largely attributed to a poor Chinese crop, which meant that China increased its imports to meet the demands of its textile sector).

To put these figures (and their recent growth) into perspective: whereas 50 per cent of traded cotton was already subject to subsidies in 1997/98, this figure increased to 75 per cent in 20001/02 (Goreux, 2004b). By 2001/02, direct annual support alone as a percentage of the A Index price reached 75 per cent in the USA, and 187 and 253 per cent in Greece and Spain respectively (Baffes, 2004). US support that season, estimated at US$3.9 billion, totalled three times the amount of the entire USAID budget for Africa in the same year (Oxfam, 2002).

### Linking Subsidies, Declining Prices and Lost Earnings

Despite important differences in their conclusions,[9] numerous recent studies estimating the impact of cotton subsidies (primarily US and EU) on cotton prices and/or the export earnings of other cotton producers have confirmed the relationship between cotton subsidies, depressed cotton prices and lost export earnings. With respect to increases in cotton prices resulting from the removal of subsidies, the estimates generally range between 3 and 30 per cent. In the more limited subset of studies directly addressing lost export earnings, the injury to WCA producers (the group most commonly treated) tends to fall within a US$30–260 million range.[10] While estimation techniques are fraught with subjective judgements and parameter values that prevent definitive results (for example the difficult task of judging the capacity of producers to change supplies in response to global price changes, i.e. their price elasticity of supply), the studies offer a sense of the scale on which cotton subsidies distort global cotton markets and harm other producers.

An exhaustive review of the literature lies outside the remit of this chapter – and has been well covered in FAO (2004).[11] Here, therefore, we briefly consider three influential and important studies. The first, which was used by Brazil to support its WTO dispute case, is that by Sumner (2003), who estimates the impact of various elements of the US cotton support programme on world cotton prices. The other two, offering estimates of both price changes and forgone earnings, are by Goreux (2003; 2004b), which underpinned the WCA WTO proposal and by Gillson *et al.* (2004), building on the Goreux model but allowing for scenarios based on different market segmentation and elasticity assumptions. The latter is particularly interesting, both in its attempts to better approximate the conditions and dynamics of global and domestic cotton markets, and because it offers estimates of forgone earnings for countries outside WCA.

In his 2003 study, Sumner considers the production and price effects of the removal of all US subsidies. He bases his work largely on the Food and Agricultural Policy Research Institute (FAPRI) policy modelling framework, which is a multi-market, world agricultural model widely employed by governmental and international researchers to model the impacts of trade liberalisation. Notably, this framework forms the basis of work undertaken by the US Department of Agriculture (USDA) to determine (and market) the beneficial impact of the 2002 US Farm Bill on the domestic cotton industry. Of interest to the Brazilian WTO challenge (to which we return in more detail below), Sumner's disaggregated approach allows him to identify the specific distortionary effects of the various elements within the complex US support programme (Table 4.1). On aggregate however, for the marketing period 1999–2002, Sumner finds that the removal of all US production and export subsidies would have resulted in an average 12.6 per cent increase in the world A Index price. Over the longer period of 1999–2007, the price increase would have been slightly lower, averaging 11.6 per cent.

**Table 4.1. Impact of Eliminating Elements of the US Cotton Support Programme on World Cotton Prices (% change from baseline, average 1999/2000–2007/08)**

| Programme type | % Increase in world price | Type of support measure |
|---|---|---|
| Marketing loan payments | 3.61 | Price-contingent domestic support |
| User marketing (Step 2) payments | 2.95 | Price-contingent export subsidy |
| Market loss assistance/counter-cyclical payments | 1.46 | Price-contingent domestic support |
| Crop insurance payments | 1.27 | Non price-contingent domestic support |
| Export credit guarantees | 1.03 | Non price-contingent export subsidy |
| Production flexibility contracts/direct payments | 0.60 | Non price-contingent domestic support |
| Interaction between programmes | 0.66 | |
| All subsidies | 11.58 | |

*Source:* Table 1.4, Sumner (2003) and Table 5, Goreux (2004a).

This estimate is broadly in line with that derived by Goreux (2003), which serves as a background document to the WCA WTO submission. In it, Goreux employs a partial equilibrium model to simulate prices that would have prevailed over the 1997/98–2001/02 period in the absence of subsidies in the USA, China, Greece and Spain (the latter two taken to represent EU cotton support). In his initial paper (based on the demand and supply elasticities commonly employed in ICAC analysis), Goreux (2003) estimated an average 12 per cent increase in cotton prices over the five-year period. While his initial study saw an annual peak of 15.2 per cent in 1999/2000 during that period, his revised 2004 paper (based on newly available subsidy data) estimated a 17.6 per cent price increase in 2001/02 in the absence of subsidies (as opposed to the 13.3 per cent estimated for that season in the original study).

In terms of translating this into estimates of lost export earnings, despite similar shortcomings to those noted above in estimating price changes, Goreux (2003) estimated lost export earnings to WCA cotton producers at US$250 million in 2001/02 and an average annual loss of US$200 million over the previous five years. The losses from US subsidies alone, he calculates, represent between 30 and 40 per cent more than the US overseas development assistance (ODA) received by these four LDCs combined (Goreux, 2004a). However, the estimated losses are based on the initial subsidy data available and not the higher levels which were noted in the revised 2004 version of his paper (Goreux, 2004b). As such, it should be taken as a conservative estimate.

Gillson *et al.* (2004) attempt to better approximate different real world market conditions by developing four scenarios which distinguish between a single world cotton market and a perfectly fragmented market, as well as between uniform and differentiated supply elasticities between producers. By taking such an approach, the study is able to account for the heterogeneity in the quality of raw cotton supplied to the international market (and thus the different price dynamics), as well as the varying capacity of different countries/producers to respond to price changes. Subjective assumptions notwithstanding, they estimate that the removal of all cotton subsidies globally in 2001 would increase world cotton prices in the range of 18–28 per cent, with the low end coming under a single world cotton market with homogeneous supply elasticities across countries (as used in most other studies) and the upper figure arising in a world where cotton users cannot switch between suppliers (i.e. a perfectly fragmented market), and where different producers are capable of different supply responses to global price changes. Based on their qualitative assessment of both the demand conditions for cotton importers (i.e. the 'stickiness' of cotton trade flows) and the factors affecting the supply capacity of different cotton-producing countries, they conclude that of the four scenarios, 'the cotton market is probably more fragmented in the short term than in the long term, so our preferred simulation of the final impact would be ... [that of] a single market but with higher supply elasticities for WCA' (p. 65).

In terms of direct earnings forgone from subsidies in 2001, Gillson *et al.* find that WCA would have gained between 10 and 37 per cent of additional earnings that year, with the preferred scenario highlighted above suggesting the upper end of the spectrum. This would translate into additional export earnings in the range of US$94–360 million dollars for this group of countries. They posit a gain of 5–36 per cent for India and 3–36 per cent for Pakistan. Along with these two countries, the bulk of the gains from subsidy removal would be captured by Australia, Brazil and Turkey, ranging on aggregate from 68–73 per cent of the total available gains. With such gains potentially available to these non-WCA countries, they would be well placed to actively support the efforts of these small African producers to elicit a meaningful package of reform from the major subsidising countries.

Another noteworthy outcome of the Gillson *et al.* study relates to their estimates of the influence on global prices of individual subsidising countries. By virtue of their size alone, it has long been perceived that US cotton subsidies impose the greatest injury on other cotton producers. However, by disaggregating the impact of individual country subsidies, the study posits that EU subsidies, relative to their absolute level of support, cause disproportionate harm to WCA producers in terms of lost earnings. We note, however, the sensitivity of these results to the assumptions of market segmentation, with the losses attributable to EU subsidies jumping at least 30 per cent when it is assumed that cotton users cannot easily change suppliers. While the assumption of perfect market segmentation is clearly unrealistic and serves illustrative purposes in the study, the implication that EU subsidies cannot be overlooked when considering what is needed to reform the global cotton market still holds.

**Table 4.2.Estimated Impact of Developed Country Subsidy Removal on World Prices, EU and US Production Levels, and the Resulting Increase in WCA Export Earnings**

| | Estimated price without subsidies (US$/lb) | Effect on price (%) | Production fall in the USA | Production fall in the EU | Prejudice to WCA farmers (US$million)[e] |
|---|---|---|---|---|---|
| ODI (2004)[a] | | | | | |
| S/U | 0.675 | 18–28 | 15.2 | 26.6 | 266.5 |
| F/U | 0.688 | 20 | 8.3 | 19.8 | 93.8 |
| S/D | 0.70 | 22 | 13.6 | 25.2 | 354.6 |
| F/D | 0.732 | 28 | 1.5 | 8.9 | 133.5 |
| Goreux (2003) | 0.589–0.649 | 2.9–13.4 | 2.2–14.7 | 10–48 | 37–254 |
| ICAC (2002 | 0.742 | 29.7 | – | – | 274 |
| ICAC (2003)[b] | | | | | |
| 2000/01 | 0.742 | 21 | – | – | – |
| 2001/02 | 0.738 | 72.4[d] | – | – | 504 |
| FAO (2004) | 0.591–0.60 | 2.3–5.0 | 7.4–14.2 | 16.1–31.7 | 30 |
| FAPRI (2002) | – | 11.4 | 6.7 | 70.5 | 90.37 |
| Reeves *et al.* (2001)[b] | 0.474 | 10.7 | 15.9 | n.a. | 76 |
| Sumner (2003)[c] | 0.644 | 12.6 | 29.1 | n.a. | 116 |
| Tokarick (2003) | 0.588 | 2.8 | 8.6 | n.a. | 26 |

[a]The ODI studies run four model scenarios: S = Single; F = Fragmented market; U = Uniform elasticity; D = Differentiated elasticity. For the segmented world market assumption, the world price is an average across segments.

[b]All studies use 2000/01 as the simulation year data except ICAC (2003) and Reeves *et al.* (2001) which use 2001/02 data. Actual world price in 2000/01 = US$0.572/lb. Actual world price in 2001/02 = US$0.418/lb.

[c]Removal of US support only.

[d]The value of 72 per cent reported in ICAC is considered by many to be an outlier due to the very low world price during the simulation year. See discussion of base year below.

[e]Where the prejudice to WCA farmers is not explicitly stated in a study, the value in the table is estimated by using a cotton supply equation for WCA to determine additional export earnings generated by the increase in world price.

*Source:* Table 1, FAO (2004)

**Table 4.3. Key Assumptions Made in the Studies Reviewed**

| | Demand elasticity | Supply elasticity | Simulation from base year | Market segmentation assumed | Model includes stocks |
|---|---|---|---|---|---|
| ODI (2004) | –0.1 | 0.36 to 0.6 | 2000/01 | Yes | No |
| Goreux (2003) | –0.1 to –0.5 | 0.15 to 0.90 | 2000/01[a] | No | No |
| ICAC (2002) | –0.1 | 0.47 | 2000/01 | No | No |
| FAO (2004) | –0.75 to –1.25 | 0.2 to 1.25 | 2000/01 | No | No |
| FAPRI (2002) | Not specified | Not specified | Average 2002/03–2011/12 | No | No |
| Reeves *et al.*l (2001) | –0.3 | 0.8 | 2001/02 | No | No |
| Sumner (2003) | –0.2 to –0.47 | 0.14 to 0.6 | 2001/01 | No | Yes |
| Tokarick (2003) | –0.56[b] | 0.41[b] | 2001/01 | No | No |

[a]Goreux uses a five-year average for the base period
[b]Tokarik's elasticities are for the USA only
*Source:* Table 2, FAO (2004)

It is also important to note that the above estimates are exclusively direct losses resulting from forgone cotton trade and do not account for indirect impacts in other sectors of the economy. Such effects would be particularly important for those countries most dependent on cotton production – such as the WCA producers. Due to difficulties in estimating indirect impacts (resulting from insufficiently disaggregated consumption data), few studies have attempted it. One exception is a study by Minot and Daniels (2002) on the poverty impacts of cotton subsidies on Benin. The study attempts to estimate the indirect effects of a 40 per cent price fall on non-cotton producers by calculating the marginal propensity of cotton producers to consume tradable goods (i.e. their reduced domestic demand). They conclude that for every $1 reduction in cotton producers' income, there is a $3.3 contraction in overall demand. As noted by Goreux (2004b), in the WTO context, both in terms of dispute settlement and calculations for compensation, only direct losses are relevant. This is especially so with the latter, where compensation (assuming it was fully transmitted to cotton producers) would have similar indirect effects.

This discussion highlights the fact that cotton remains an essential component of the development trajectory for many developing countries. As such, the relative impacts resulting from distortions in the market are disproportionately borne by developing countries, many of which are among the lowest-income countries in the world; at the same time they are some of the most competitive cotton producers. Despite important methodological differences between the numerous studies estimating the impact of US and EU cotton subsidies, there appears to be consensus that they have depressed prices, resulting in meaningful income losses, exacerbated incidences of poverty and diminished developing countries' capacity to maximise the benefits of their comparative advantage. In sum, the combination of these factors should place cotton at the top of the global agricultural trade reform agenda. The reality on the ground, however, indicates that outside the realm of rhetoric, this is not taking place. It is to a consideration of what is currently being done to address this heavily distorted sector that we now turn.

## What Is Being Done?

To date, specific efforts to address distortions in the global cotton trade have occurred along two main tracks – one within the WTO and one outside. The former includes what has been termed the 'trade aspects' of the Cotton Initiative (i.e. the subsidy elimination elements), as well as the successful Brazilian challenge to US cotton subsidies. Outside the WTO, efforts have focused on the 'development assistance aspects', which have been equated, erroneously, with the compensation dimension of the Cotton Initiative and have largely been conducted as a discussion between African cotton producers and the development/donor community. A review of each of the prongs below helps to elucidate their respective objectives, consider the progress achieved to date and assess the potential of the current trajectory to effectively address the key challenges.

Specifically, while the successful challenge to US subsidies may help deliver on some of the reform objectives highlighted in the Cotton Initiative, neither of the current paths of negotiation or litigation are poised to deliver meaningful reductions in support to inefficient producers in the short term. While financial assistance is welcome, both to enhance the competitiveness of low-cost producers and assist in their efforts at export diversification, it would not be helpful if it gets in the way of the needed reforms – on the contrary, it could then exacerbate the harm. Nor for that matter should it be viewed as a substitute for transitional compensation pending reforms.

### The Cotton Initiative

The Cotton Initiative was brought to the WTO in April 2003 by Benin, Burkina Faso, Chad and Mali as part of the lead-up to the WTO Cancun Ministerial Meeting. It arose from a sense by its WCA proponents that the circumstances surrounding the cotton trade deserved a separate and expedited track in the latest 'development' round of trade negotiations. As noted above, this view was based on the fact that their comparative advantage in cotton – a commodity that is paramount in the welfare of a small group of some of the lowest-income countries in the world – was being undermined by the subsidies provided by two of the greatest champions of the fruits of comparative advantage-based trade liberalisation, the USA and the EU. With such an stark imbalance, a specific intervention on cotton, like the intervention on TRIPs and the public health issue that surfaced in Doha,[12] seemed to have a good prospect of making the major trading powers take the 'development agenda' seriously.

Citing the elimination of cotton subsidies as 'the only specific interest of WCA cotton-producing countries in the Doha round' (WTO, 2003a), the proponents called for: (a) a mechanism to phase out, with a view to eliminating, all support for cotton production; and (b) transitional financial compensation to offset the resulting injury (i.e. forgone earnings) during the period of elimination. As detailed in their August 2003 submission (WTO, 2003b), the specifics of the proposal (the 'modalities') outlined a three-year implementation period for the elimination of all production and export support to cotton, which was initially envisaged to begin in 2004. More recent proposals (for example WTO (2005a) by the Africa Group) differentiated between domestic support and export subsidies, calling for a slightly longer phase-out period for the former (which are more politically sensitive, especially in the USA where they form the bulk of expenditures).

With regard to compensation, the proposed 'stop-gap' emergency measure was intended as a temporary mechanism both to offset the injury caused by continued cotton support in the main subsidising countries and to provide an additional incentive to those countries to reduce their support expeditiously. The amount of compensation requested was based on the estimated direct losses suffered by LDC net exporters in the 1999/2000 to 2001/02 seasons; on the basis of the initial study by Goreux (2003), the proponents requested approximately US$250 million per annum.[13] Contributions would be based on a country's respective share in the total amount of global cotton subsidies and would decrease proportionately with the reduction of support. The allocation of compensation would be determined on the basis of shares of total cotton production within the group of recipient countries. It would be disbursed, wherever possible, via local producer associations so as to help ensure it enabled producers to maintain production in the face of depressed world prices and encourage competitiveness-enhancing investment. This was later repackaged in the April 2005 Africa Group proposal (WTO, 2005a) as an emergency support fund equivalent to 20 per cent of the value of cotton production in each beneficiary, linked directly to the pace of subsidy removal.

Structured in this way, the proposals seemed to address effectively the two core problems of continued subsidisation of uncompetitive cotton producers in the USA and the EU, and the resulting injury to the most vulnerable, yet competitive, LDC net exporting producers. Responses from the major trading powers in Cancun, however, were lukewarm at best (Oxfam, 2004b), especially with regard to compensation. As opposed to accepting the need for domestic adjustment and compensation for injury, the subsidising countries (led mostly prominently by the USA) called for LDC producers to diversify their economies. This was taken as an affront to both the LDC producers, as well as to the principles of trade liberalisation which the WTO ostensibly aimed to promote.

Despite the fact that the issue remained high on the post-Cancun agenda and on that of the Hong Kong Ministerial Meeting, very limited progress has been achieved on cotton reforms to date. Although this was initially opposed by the proponents, the 2004 'July Package' (WTO, 2004a) split the Initiative into two elements. This included those 'trade aspects' related to subsidy reduction, which would be 'addressed ambitiously, expeditiously, and specifically, within the agriculture negotiations' – or in other words, not on a separate and expedited track as requested. On those aspects of the Initiative said to be related to 'development assistance', the WTO Director-General would consult with the development community so as to 'direct effectively existing programmes and any additional resources towards development of the economies where cotton has vital importance'. Work in all three pillars of market access, domestic support and export competition, together with the coherence between the trade and development aspects, was to be the remit of a new sub-committee on cotton, formed under the auspices of the Special (negotiating) Session of the Committee on Agriculture.

In Hong Kong, despite continued expressions of sympathy with the plight of WCA cotton producers, only minor advances were made. On the 'trade dimension' aspect, apart from an ambiguously enhanced commitment to treat cotton reforms more ambitiously and expeditiously, developed country Members agreed to eliminate all forms of cotton export subsidies in 2006 and provide duty-free and quota-free access for LDC cotton exports at the start of the implementation period (WTO, 2005f). However, neither of these pledges confers much benefit. The USA is the only developed country to use export subsidies for cotton, and even then they constitute a small and declining percentage of their overall cotton support (averaging 14 per cent for 1999–2002 and less than 10 per cent in 2002 itself). As is shown below, while making up 4 per cent of an estimated 11.6 per cent gain in cotton prices stemming from US subsidy removal (1999–2001), these subsidies have already been marked for removal as a result of Brazil's successful dispute challenge. In addition, in the face of continued domestic subsidies to high-cost producers, commitments to provide greater access to the US cotton market are largely meaningless. This is true also of the EU, where LDCs already enjoy duty-free and quota-free access for cotton. No commitments were made where they really matter, namely on the key area where cotton distortions continue – domestic support.

Similarly, no commitments were made with respect to transitional compensation, although some language was included that could lead to a form of financial support mechanism linked to lost incomes (which as noted above have been shown to be due, in part, to cotton subsidies). In particular, the WTO Director-General, as part of his activities with the donor community under the 'development dimension', is urged to explore the possibility of establishing through the donor institutions a mechanism to address declining incomes in the cotton sector (WTO, 2005f). Although not on a par with the mid-2005 Africa Group proposal (WTO, 2005a), the language appears to allow for some kind of similar mechanism to operate outside the auspices of the WTO. Whether it will be tied to subsidy reduction remains to be determined. It should be emphasised, however, that to maintain maximum effectiveness, compensation should be explicitly tied to the reduction of distorting subsidies. The reason for this lies in the importance of ensuring that the mechanism serves as redress for continued injury and, at least in principle, as an additional incentive to reform. Moreover, compensation without subsidy reduction carries the potential to promote greater aggregate cotton production, thereby depressing cotton prices even more and leading to further injury.

The trajectory of the July Framework in relation to cotton, reinforced by the recent Hong Kong Declaration, does not effectively address the underlying objectives of the

Initiative. In particular, by failing to address the areas most in need of attention – namely reforms to domestic support measures in the USA and the EU, and refusing to commit to any specifics on implementing the mandate to address cotton 'ambitiously, expeditiously and specifically' within the agriculture negotiations, the international community has so far failed to prioritise the needs of its most vulnerable Members.

While the subsidy reduction negotiations appear to offer scope for delivering, to some extent, much-needed reform in the sector, the fact that this is now predicated on the achievement of much more complex and sensitive across the board agricultural reforms implies a much slower timeline (along with the potential for 'trade-offs' with other areas of the negotiations). Indeed, with Members having demonstrated an inability to agree on modalities for agriculture in Hong Kong, the view that there is likely in the short term to be little progress on cotton reform in the broader negotiations is reinforced. Recognising the likely slow progress of the negotiations, some observers are already pointing to the successful Brazilian challenge to US subsidies as an alternative avenue for pursuing more expeditious reforms in the sector. We turn now to consider this argument.

### Dispute Settlement – Brazil versus the USA

The successful Brazilian challenge to elements of the US cotton support programme stands as one of the most important challenges to the agricultural policies of developed countries in the history of the WTO. It offers an additional avenue, albeit somewhat limited in scope, to elicit significant reforms to the trade in cotton in the short term. In the medium term it may address some of the more egregious distortions in the US programme (for example Step 2 payments and distortions stemming from export credit guarantees). However, the extent and speed to which these and other reforms emanating from the decision may occur is likely to be tempered by political economy considerations in Brazil over pushing the USA to overcome entrenched domestic resistance. In addition, because it focuses on US subsidies, the ruling does little to address EU distortions, which also cause injury to competitive producers, especially those in WCA. These caveats notwithstanding, the case offers both a floor for the outcome of the forthcoming negotiations, as evidenced by the Hong Kong decision to eliminate export subsidies in 2006, as well as a template for possible additional challenges to US and EU subsidies from competitive producing countries such as WCA, India, Pakistan and Australia.

With this in mind, we review *United States – Subsidies on Upland Cotton* (hereafter 'the case'), as well as the findings of the Dispute Settlement Body Panel (hereafter 'the Panel' (WTO, 2005b), and the subsequent upholding of the decisions by the Appellate Body (AB) (WTO, 2005c). We highlight specific areas of relevance for addressing distortions via the negotiations, and their limitations.

After the passage of the 2002 US Farm Bill,[14] which authorised an additional US$51 billion in support to US farmers in the period 2002–2007 (Becker, 2002), Brazil requested consultations with the USA on its cotton support programme in September 2002. Brazil alleged that various elements of US farm legislation constituted prohibited[15] and actionable[16] subsidies in violation of WTO rules on agriculture and subsidies (i.e. the Agreement on Agriculture (AoA), GATT 1994 and the Agreement on Subsidies and Countervailing Measures (ASCM)) (WTO, 2002). Brazil held that these subsidies caused (for marketing year (MY) 1999–2001) and/or threatened to cause (for MY 2002–2007) adverse effects, in the sense of 'serious prejudice',[17] to its interests.

Based on the extensive evidence provided by the two main parties (as well as numerous third parties),[18] the Panel ruled on two key issues:[19] whether or not the subsidies were allowed or prohibited and, irrespective of this, whether they caused[20] 'serious prejudice' to Brazilian interests (Josling, 2005). As the USA is both the largest exporter and the largest absolute subsidiser of cotton, both questions clearly have important implications for the objective of reforming global cotton trade, even if the responses are restricted to the US context.

Listing the seven programmes of US support to cotton included in Brazil's challenge, ordered from most to least distortionary as cited in Sumner (2003),[21] Table 4.4 highlights the key elements of the ruling.

On the issue of whether subsidies were allowed or prohibited, the Panel found that the user marketing payments – or Step 2 payments,[22] were contingent on export performance and thus prohibited under the ASCM. Payments to exporters were found to constitute prohibited export subsidies not included in the US Schedule of subsidies,[23] while those to mills using US cotton were deemed prohibited import substitution subsidies. For this, the Panel instructed the USA to remove the prohibited subsidies 'without delay' and not later than 1 July 2005.

In addition, with the Step 2 payments being contingent on cotton prices, the Panel found that they were causally related to depressed and suppressed world cotton prices, and thus in part responsible for serious prejudice to Brazilian interests. Similarly, by maintaining higher US cotton production (and export) levels in the face of lower world prices (effectively shielding US cotton farmers from world price trends), the other two price-contingent programmes – the marketing loan payments[24] and the market loss assistance/counter cyclical payments[25] – were also found to be responsible for depressing and suppressing global cotton prices and thus causing serious prejudice. For this group of programmes, the USA was to remove the adverse effects (causing serious prejudice) or withdraw the subsidies; based on ASCM Article 7.9, this should occur 'within six months from the date when the WTO Dispute Settlement Body (DSB) adopts the panel report or the Appellate Body report' (WTO, 1995). With the latter having occurred on 21 March 2005, this implied a 21 September 2005 deadline.

Of note, however, was that the Panel did not feel it was necessary to quantify the degree to which expenditures in these price-contingent programmes needed to be reduced or changed to comply with the adverse effects ruling. In doing so, it opened a degree of ambiguity over exactly what is required for compliance with this finding, and as such, to what degree such compliance might contribute to the broader objectives of meaningful reform of the US cotton sector.

**Table 4.4. US Cotton Programmes and Summary of Panel/Appellate Body Report** (US – Subsidies for Upland Cotton: WT/DS267/R & WT/DS267/AB/R)

| Programme | Expenditure, US$ annual average 1999–2002 | Classification (as notified) | Panel/AB ruling on classification and/or serious prejudice | WTO discipline(s) under which ruling made | Remedy |
|---|---|---|---|---|---|
| 1. Marketing Loan (gain/deficiency) Payments | $1.4 billion | Amber box | • Amber box<br>• Caused significant price suppression on world market | SCM 6.3(c); 5(c) | Remove the adverse effects or withdraw the subsidy |
| 2. User Marketing (Step 2) Payments (to (i) users of domestic cotton; and (ii) cotton exporters) | $161 million | Amber box | • Caused significant price suppression on world market<br>• Payments constituted prohibited subsidy (i.e. not Amber box):<br>– import substitution subsidy (domestic);<br>– export subsidy not included in the US schedule (export) | SCM 6.3(c); 5(c)<br><br>SCM 3.1(b); 3.2<br><br>AoA 3.3; 8;<br>SCM 3.1(a); 3.2 | Remove the adverse effects or withdraw prohibited subsidies by 1 July 2005 |
| 3. Market Loss Assistance Payments (1999–2001)/ Counte-Cyclical Payments (2002–2007) | combined $797 million | Amber box | • Amber box<br>• Caused significant price suppression on world market | SCM 6.3(c), 5(c) | Remove the adverse effects or withdraw the subsidy |
| 4. Crop Insurance Payments | $197 million | Amber box | • Do not cause significant price suppression on world markets | SCM 6.3(c); 5(c) | None |

**Table 4.4** (continued)

| **Programme** | **Expenditure, US$ annual average 1999–2002** | **Classification (as notified)** | **Panel/AB ruling on classification and/or serious prejudice** | **WTO discipline(s) under which ruling made** | **Remedy** |
|---|---|---|---|---|---|
| 5. Export Credit Guarantees | $324 million (cotton products;[a] Fiscal Year) | Not notified | • Credit guarantees for cotton (and other products) are export subsidies not included in the US Schedule (rice export subsidy exceeded its scheduled level) | AoA 10.1<br>SCM Annex I, item (j); 3.1(a); 3.2 | Withdraw prohibited export subsidies by 1 July 2005 |
| 6. Production Flexibility Contract Payments 1999–2001)/Direct Payments (2002–2007) | combined $570 million | Green box | • Amber box – not eligible for green box due to land use restrictions<br>• Do not cause significant price suppression on world markets | AoA 13(a);<br>Annex 2, para. 6(b)<br>SCM 6.3(c); 5(c) | Re-notify domestic support |
| 7. Cottonseed Payments | $78 million | Amber box | • Do not cause significant price suppression on world markets (only 2000 considered) | SCM 6.3(c); 5(c) | None |

[a]As noted by Brazil in the case, this amount includes only those guarantee applications received for cotton specific allocations and not those (which possibly also included cotton) listed

*Source:* This table is based on information extracted from Josling (2005), Halverson-Cross (2005), WT/DS267/R and USDA (various).

For the three programmes not contingent on cotton prices, but aimed at income support, the Panel did not find causal evidence of price depression and suppression. These include crop insurance subsidies and cottonseed payments, despite the fact that the former was found by Sumner (2003) to cause downward pressure on global prices similar in magnitude to the market loss assistance/counter cyclical payments programme (see Table 4.1).

The third non price-contingent programme, the production flexibility contract (PFC) payments (which were in use from 1996 to mid-2002) and the subsequent direct payments (DP), brought in by the 2002 Farm Bill to cover the period to September 2007, were also not deemed to be prohibited subsidies. However, they were found to have been erroneously notified by the USA as 'green box' measures.[26] While not being strictly based on production targets, the Panel ruled that in keeping eligibility for the programmes related to certain types of agricultural production (i.e. by maintaining restrictions on current land usage), they were insufficiently decoupled from production and so should have been notified as 'amber box' measures.[27] Importantly, as discussed below with respect to the Peace Clause, by ruling in this manner the USA was deemed to put itself in violation of subsidy disciplines in the AoA, thus exposing its entire domestic support regime to challenge under the SCM for causing adverse effects.

On export credit guarantees,[28] the Panel ruled that due to the premiums not covering the long-term net operating costs of the programmes, they constituted export subsidies as defined in the ASCM's *Illustrative List of Export Subsidies* (Annex I, item (j)). Furthermore, the ruling (upheld by the AB in a majority decision) found that the subsidies were not exempt from export subsidy disciplines in the AoA. For those products not listed in the US Schedule of Subsidies, which include cotton,[29] they constituted prohibited export subsidies. It was also found that for rice, which is included in the Schedule, the USA had exceeded its commitments. These prohibited subsidies were also to be removed 'without delay', and not later than July 2005.

The ruling has far-reaching implications. Two legal implications have been highlighted (Josling, 2005; Halverson-Cross, 2005), relating to the Peace Clause and the determination of serious prejudice. The Peace Clause (AoA Article 13), which expired at the end of 2003, protected certain developed country agricultural support measures from challenges under WTO rules on subsidies. Measures protected included permitted export subsidies, 'green box' subsidies and domestic support measures below MY 1992 levels. While the case did not challenge the Peace Clause *per se* (it ruled that the USA had effectively disqualified itself from Peace Clause protection by erroneously classifying green box support and surpassing its 1992 levels), it did offer an indication on how to apply the ASCM to agriculture (Halverson-Cross, 2005). In particular, it did so with respect to the ability to challenge domestic support measures under the ASCM, irrespective of whether they are deemed allowable by the AoA.[30] By extension, this would more easily expose such domestic support to claims of serious prejudice. Indeed, due in part to the difficulties of demonstrating serious prejudice, this case is only the second to successfully do so with respect to domestic support measures (Halverson-Cross, 2005).[31] The way in which it occurred in this case also demonstrates the importance of econometric work such as that reviewed above in supporting Members' ability to show the causal impacts of domestic policies.

The case also has significant implications for the negotiations aimed at addressing global distortions in the cotton trade, . The ruling itself clearly has the potential to elicit many of the objectives sought by the Cotton Initiative. As demonstrated by Goreux (2004a), US compliance, by removing the prohibited export subsidies and withdrawing or removing the adverse effects of those found to cause serious prejudice, could (based on Sumner's estimates) achieve just over 9 per cent of the 11.6 per cent gain in cotton prices stemming from subsidy removal over the 1999–2001 period. As it currently stands, the Hong Kong commitment to remove cotton export subsidies would achieve 4 per cent of this gain.

In addition, the ruling on alleged green box measures and the clarification of criteria for eligibility could prove valuable in a discussion over mechanisms to ensure that the reduction or elimination of trade-distorting cotton subsidies does not occur simply by re-classifying them under the green box – which currently has a fairly open definition and does not have an expenditure limit (see below).

Despite a deadline of 1 July 2005 for the elimination of prohibited subsidies, and the instruction to remove the adverse effects (causing serious prejudice) or withdraw the relevant actionable subsidies as of 21 September 2005, the USA has as yet done little to comply. On 30 June, USDA announced the elimination of the 1 per cent cap on fees in the remaining export credit guarantee programmes, GSM-102 and SCGP,[32] thus, in its view, addressing the Panel's concern that the schemes' fees were insufficiently risk-based. Legislation was also sent to the US Congress on 5 July recommending the repeal of the Step 2 payments; however they were not scheduled to be removed before 31 July 2006.

Concerned that compliance on prohibited subsidies came over a year after the deadline, and wishing to safeguard its rights to retaliate under the AGSM and the Dispute Settlement Understanding (DSU), on 5 July Brazil requested authorisation to impose a $US3 billion penalty in retaliation for failure to repeal the measures in the allotted time. This included requests for the suspension of tariff concessions under the GATT 1994, as well as cross-retaliation in the form of suspended concessions in TRIPs and GATS. At the same time, however, recognising the amendment to the export credit programme and the proposed repeal of the Step 2 programme, the two Members came to an understanding that the retaliation authorisation request would be suspended, and because of a US challenge on the level and appropriateness of Brazil's request, this was to be sent to arbitration. Arbitration proceedings have thus been suspended, pending a possible compliance panel ruling on whether the measures taken by the USA constituted compliance (highlighting again the difficulties posed by the Panel's failure to specify the degree of expenditure amendment required). However, implicit in the Hong Kong commitment by developed countries (i.e. the USA) to remove cotton export subsidies in 2006, would appear to be Brazil's acceptance of this timeline. Future action on these measures is thus contingent on whether or not Brazil is satisfied with US implementation, as and when it is finalised.

On the issue of serious prejudice being caused by actionable subsidies, for which the adverse effects were to be removed or the subsidies withdrawn by 21 September 2005, a similar procedural agreement has been reached. On 5 October, the Chair of the US Senate Agriculture Committee intimated that the programmes deemed to have caused serious prejudice were unlikely to be altered prior to the next Farm Bill, which would only come into effect in September 2007. The following day, Brazil filed a request for authorisation to apply US$1.037 billion in suspended concessions[33] on goods (including additional import tariffs) and concessions in TRIPs and GATS. With the USA arguing that the countermeasures are not commensurate with the degree and nature of the adverse effects, the matter was remanded to arbitration on 18 October. The two Members have agreed to suspend the arbitration proceeding pending further bilateral talks.

However, stemming from frustrations that no steps at all have been taken to address this group of subsidies, there have been recent indications that Brazil is considering pushing ahead with this latter arbitration proceeding. Whether it will first have to request a compliance panel depends on the actual legal status of the proposed Bill to repeal the Step 2 subsidies. Based on the Step 2 programme being removed from US law, the USA could argue that sufficient steps to mitigate and/or remove the serious prejudice have already been undertaken and that a compliance panel was first required before moving to arbitration.

From the state of play outlined above, it is clear that Brazil is making use of all the legal remedies available to push the USA towards compliance, especially via its requests for cross-retaliation via TRIPs and GATS.[34] However, observers have noted that Brazil is unlikely to actually proceed with the cross-retaliation (should it be authorised)[35] out of concern not to incite a trade war with the USA. Touching on exactly these concerns, former US Trade Representative Robert Zoellick indicated soon after the latest retaliation request that Brazil's GSP benefits (amounting to over US$2.5 billion) could be jeopardised should it decide to proceed down the road of retaliation.

Consequently, while the case would seem to have had some influence on the Hong Kong deal to eliminate cotton export subsides in 2006, meaningful progress on the other programmes that cause serious prejudice seems likely to come from a longer-term negotiating process. This includes direct negotiations between the USA and Brazil, and wider negotiations between the USA and the larger WTO membership on agriculture. Reiterating the point made above, this recognition only reinforces the support for implementing a transitional compensation mechanism in the meantime; this is not, as this chapter will demonstrate, equivalent to the proposal for financial assistance.

## Financial Assistance

The second track under which efforts are ostensibly being undertaken to address distortions in global cotton trade occur outside the purview of the WTO. While having been equated – wrongly in our view – with the compensation proposal contained in the Cotton Initiative, the 'development assistance aspects' of this track have largely been part of a discussion between African cotton producers and the development/donor community. Recent discussions confirm the focus on providing investment resources for the longer-term objectives of promoting greater competitiveness (economy-wide and in the cotton sector), as well as export diversification more broadly. While few observers of the challenges facing cotton-dependent developing countries would dispute the importance of such resources in helping them promote growth and reduce poverty, there is a misconception that this can serve as a substitute for the short-term aim of compensation. Of perhaps greater importance, the prospect of financial assistance in lieu of meaningful reform of the US and EU cotton support programmes carries dangerous implications for the trading system as a whole.

As touched on earlier, the proponents of the Cotton Initiative were initially reluctant to divide it into separate tracks. They acquiesced, however, in the lead-up to the 23–24 March 2005 WTO African Regional Workshop on Cotton, which brought together the 33 African countries engaged in cotton production and trade with the major national and intergovernmental donors. The result was the present situation – with the subsidy-reduction elements of the Initiative subsumed in the much larger and more complex agricultural negotiations, and the compensation-cum-financing elements carved out of the WTO's remit and put into the hands of the donor community.

It is important to highlight the contradiction that although the problems that the Regional Workshop purported to address stemmed from subsidy-induced distortions in the cotton trade, subsidy reduction and recompense, pending its arrival, were explicitly kept off the agenda. As noted by Oxfam (2004b), the programme for the conference had an exclusive focus on 'the Development Aspects, particularly the scope and opportunities for financial and technical assistance', and was aimed at contributing to, *inter alia*, 'a more focussed understanding of some of the policy issues underpinning the [Initiative]...' (WTO 2004b: 22). Surely financial and technical assistance are part of the needed solution. Avoiding discussions on the very source of the problem – the persistence of cotton subsidies, and the adjustment mechanism requested by those most injured appears to be at odds with what should be the core objective of these efforts.

The current state of these efforts, while facilitating a wealth of discussions, conferences and project planning, have produced little in terms of short-term respite from the injury resulting from distorted cotton trade. Emanating from the Cotonou meeting, the International Financial Institutions (IFIs) – the World Bank and IMF – and other multilateral agencies (including FAO, ITC, OECD and UNIDO) have attempted to focus existing instruments on cotton-related challenges. This includes the Bank's PRSPs, the IMF's Poverty Reduction and Growth Facility (PRGF) and numerous technical assistance and capacity building projects aimed at enhancing competitiveness and value-added production in the cotton sector. Especially highlighted have been the Diagnostic Trade Integration Studies undertaken under the auspices of the multi-agency IF.

With respect to bilateral donors, both the pledges and associated actions have been similarly focused. Calls have been made to reflect 'cotton-sector priorities' in country programmes and to provide financial and technical assistance for relevant projects.

There has also been much talk of 'enhanced coordination' and 'follow-up workshops' to ensure that these laudable endeavours proceed as intended.

In this respect, the EU and US programmes are notable both for the paucity of resources allocated (relative to the amount of subsidies provided) and the lack of concomitant commitments to address the core of the problem – the sustained injury resulting from continued subsidising of high-cost cotton producers.

The 'EU-Africa Cotton Partnership',[36] launched at a July 2004 forum in Paris, outlines an action plan focussed on seven areas.[37] While the area on international trade calls for an effective and specific solution amenable to all parties, it maintains that these are best held in the context of the broader agriculture negotiations. Unfortunately, in terms of commitments, there is little more than the April 2004 announcement that 65 per cent of EU support to cotton will be decoupled from production. Leaving a full 35 per cent still tied to production, together with the as yet unknown impact of the announced reforms that will only come into effect in 2006, the extent to which this will alleviate the injury caused by EU subsidies remains to be seen.[38] On technical assistance and capacity building, h40 million is to be allocated to the Initiative proponents' national programmes, with an additional h15 million for ACP-wide cotton-related activities. This h55 million (in the range of US$65–70 million) pales, however, in comparison with the over US$800 million in subsidies provided in 2001/02 alone.

Within the context of their efforts to assist cotton producers, the EU has also highlighted changes in access criteria of the FLEX (Fluctuations in Export Earnings) instrument[39] as a potential financing mechanism to mitigate the effects of export earning shortfalls. It would seem somewhat contradictory, however, that the EU is willing to consider making compensation funds available for earning shortfalls that result, in part, from the EU's own domestic cotton support policies and at the same time opposes the Initiative's request for a similar type of mechanism (see below).

Like the EU, the USA points to various existing aid-related endeavours as examples of efforts being undertaken to support African cotton producers (for example the G8 debt relief announcement and the Millennium Challenge Co-operation). The USA has also recently announced the 'West Africa Cotton Improvement Program',[40] to which it has committed an initial US$5 million in new funding ($7 million in total), aimed at improving the production, transformation and marketing of cotton in the four WCA proponent countries, plus Senegal.[41] However, not only are the resources dwarfed by the billions of dollars paid out in annual US cotton subsidies, but the programme does little to address the injury that continued US subsidies will inflict on these WCA countries, together with the other developing countries, such as Brazil, India and Pakistan, who stand to gain nothing from these endeavours.

In the light of these and other inadequate proposals, it is not surprising that the response from the WCA proponents, together with other African cotton producers, has generally been one of disappointment. While aid activities are welcome, the fact remains that they do little to help cotton producers take advantage of their competitive edge in cotton, or to compensate them for continued loss of market share and export earnings (estimated at US$250 million per annum), while US and EU producers continue to receive extremely generous governmental support. The proponents have thus appealed to subsidising countries to step up their efforts on a scale that is commensurate with the challenges faced. In addition, with so much focus on WCA, and in particular the four proponents of the Cotton Initiative, other African producers have called for a broader continental focus.

This does not imply that there is no role for financial assistance. Indeed, with scarce investment resources contributing to an 'international poverty trap' in much of sub-Saharan Africa (UNCTAD, 2002), additional financial assistance to cotton-dependent developing countries is a necessary, albeit insufficient, condition for their growth and poverty reduction prospects. This includes much-needed resources to facilitate economy-wide productivity-enhancing investments, such as the building of roads, ports and broader institutional infrastructures (for example customs administration), as well as investment focused specifically on the cotton sector, such as relevant local research and development (R&D) to boost labour and land productivity in smallholder farms, and support improved marketing and distribution know-how. In addition, to promote structural transformation and export diversification in the economy, a vast range of skills needs to be developed to facilitate more value-added processing of cotton-based products (including, but not only, the production of textiles and garments).

The fact remains that none of these proposals addresses the continued injury caused by the billions of dollars in subsidies that undermine competitive cotton producers in Africa and elsewhere in the world. Indeed, in this sense, there is a clear and present danger that financial assistance could be targeted expressly at alleviating the pressures on the USA and the EU to do just that – confront their powerful domestic cotton interests and move ahead with reforms of their cotton support programmes. Two concerns arise from the use of financial assistance to undermine pressures for reform in the EU and US cotton sector.

The first is systemic and relates to the legitimacy of the multilateral trading system (MTS) and its capacity to promote the interests of its most vulnerable Members. With such a clear imbalance in the global cotton trade, attempts by the major trading powers to use financial assistance effectively to buy their way out of having to make difficult reforms at home sends a powerful and dangerous signal regarding their commitment to trade liberalisation and more broadly to rules-based economic governance regimes. The loss in legitimacy to the MTS that such signals would engender would be detrimental to all countries involved. It would also be likely to produce, at the very least, a hiatus in the Doha negotiations.

Secondly, there is the risk that financial assistance in the absence of reform in the USA and the EU could worsen the situation brought about by subsidy-induced overproduction in cotton by further depressing global prices and lowering export earnings. As noted above with respect to compensation without subsidy reform, if the assistance was transmitted (even partially) to already competitive producers in such a way as to replicate the market conditions that would have existed without US and EU subsidies, then *ceteris paribus* cotton production and exports from these countries would increase. Without the removal of subsidies in the USA and the EU, and change in their production levels, the global supply of cotton would also increase. Depending on the magnitude of the supply response in the recipient countries, this could further depress global cotton prices and result in lower per unit revenue both on the original and the assistance-induced output. While the net effect would be contingent on the size of the supply response and the impact on global prices, there would be clear potential for further injury.

Additional concerns related to financial assistance include the diversion of international aid resources from other development priorities, the question of whether this would be a judicious use of taxpayer money and the potential, if such assistance were loan-based, to further aggravate the as yet unresolved debt problems facing most developing country cotton producers (Oxfam, 2004a). It would also reinforce the perception that developing countries depend on handouts from rich countries, as opposed to promoting the fact (especially in the cotton context) that they would be capable of generating at least some portion of the additional investment resources required, if there was a more level playing field.

Put simply, financial assistance is not a substitute for compensation: rather, it complements both compensation and the broader subsidy reduction agenda. While it could surely be of benefit (as part of a broader reform agenda) for adequate resources to be made available, current efforts indicate that this is not happening. On its own, however, financial assistance cannot address the structural problem of the persistence of a distorted cotton trade caused by continued subsidies to US and EU cotton producers. Furthermore, financial assistance focused on the WCA countries, or even more broadly on sub-Saharan Africa, offers little to cotton-producing countries such as Brazil, India and Pakistan, which stand to gain far larger benefits (in absolute terms) from global cotton reform.

This discussion highlights the fact that the current agenda for reforming the global cotton trade is both inadequate in its ambition and unlikely to result in meaningful outcomes in the short or even possibly the medium term. For this reason, we turn now to consider areas for improvement, both in the context of the activities discussed above, and beyond.

## What Is Not Being Done?

Having reviewed the initiatives currently on the agenda to promote the reform of the global cotton trade, we discuss potential improvements that might be considered vis-à-vis subsidy reduction, compensation, financial assistance and dispute settlement litigation. We also touch briefly on some systemic commodity issues that require attention if developing country cotton producers are to have the opportunity of maximising the benefits of their competitive advantage.

While it would appear that there will be little subsidy reform in the short term, it is of the utmost importance that when it does occur, adequate proposals will have been put forward to ensure that payments are not simply shifted to the uncapped and loosely-defined green box. In addition, in the light of the slow pace at which deep reforms to the cotton sector are likely to occur – predicated as they are on the overall agricultural negotiations – it is important to put some type of compensation mechanism back on the trade agenda (irrespective of whether it is delivered via a WTO mechanism). If reforms are insufficient, even in the medium term, then it will be up to aggrieved Members to consider the merits of proceeding to dispute settlement.

Outside the WTO, the resources allocated for financial assistance must be greatly enhanced if they are to fill the chronic savings/investment gap in most African cotton-producing countries. In addition, if the global community is serious about helping to create an environment conducive to competitive developing country cotton producers trading their way out of poverty, certain issues endemic to primary commodity dependence must be addressed. These include the long-run secular decline and volatility in cotton prices, as well as the barriers to market access and market entry for cotton and higher value-added cotton products. Other areas include low productivity in the cotton sector and poor access to technology and finance to facilitate increased competitiveness and export diversification.

### Subsidy Reduction

As confirmed by the dynamics that played out in Hong Kong, subsuming the subsidy reduction component of the Cotton Initiative into the broader agriculture negotiations will make reforms in the cotton sector much slower. While this amalgamation is unlikely to be reversed procedurally, it does not necessarily preclude an accelerated track for cotton within the talks on agriculture. Despite some additional language which could further these aims in the Hong Kong text, there is still a need for improvements in both the substance and timing of the current discussions, especially if Members are to live up to the Doha Development Agenda and in particular the July Framework mandate of addressing cotton 'ambitiously, expeditiously, and specifically [...]' (WTO, 2004a).

Recognising the political difficulties in the immediate elimination of all cotton support measures in the USA and the EU, consideration of other avenues to address the distortions resulting from these measures is probably the most appropriate initial approach. Baffes (2004) notes the increased popularity of decoupled support measures (i.e. payments not tied to the level of production). However, for such measures to have the beneficial impacts intended, he highlights three essential conditions: (a) replacing 100 per cent of support mechanisms with decoupled support; (b) ensuring that the decoupled support is explicitly time limited so as to be an effective transitory mechanism towards elimination; and (c) ensuring that eligibility for decoupled support is not predicated on the obligation to keep resources in agriculture (thus facilitating a reduction in supply and an increase in world prices).

The EU's proposed cotton reforms are an example of attempts to move in this direction.[42] Equally, for the USA, with the Panel decision finding that decoupled payments (PFC/DP) notified as a green box measure were ineligible for such classification, domestic legislators have since alluded to the need to 'tighten up' up such programmes to ensure that they are eligible in the future.

Consequently, with the key subsidising Members increasingly looking to the decoupling of their existing support as a mechanism to mitigate distortions, a key area for improvement on substance is the need to develop specific proposals to ensure that support measures moved from the amber box to the green box are minimally trade-distorting. Without such a mechanism, the currently uncapped – and in the view of numerous WTO Members ill-defined – green box offers too much leeway for subsidising Members to avoid real reforms to the sector.[43]

While a detailed discussion of such mechanisms lies beyond the scope of this chapter, it seems clear that such preparation will be essential when the window to negotiate meaningful reform opens. One could, for example, envisage proposals such as cotton-specific reduction commitments based on the amount and classification of support measures as notified in the base period (i.e. committing to reductions *before* support measures can be reclassified under the green box). In addition, in line with Baffes' criteria, the introduction of some concept of time limitation for such measures could be an effective way of garnering greater support amongst developing countries for box-shifting in the initial stages, thereby offering more breathing room for subsidising Members to make the necessary domestic reforms.

In addition, while agreement-wide calls for expenditure caps and more specific criteria for the green box have been strongly rejected by many developed country Members, a more receptive climate may be generated for such disciplines focused specifically on cotton. For example, Members might consider a requirement that no cotton is produced on land which receives support under the green box. While offering some clarification of existing green box guidelines, at least with respect to restricting current land usage for payment eligibility, the Panel ruling provides a floor for such discussions in this area. Furthermore, both the panel ruling and the concerns highlighted above underscore the importance of ensuring that the review of green box criteria, as mandated in the July Framework and reaffirmed in Hong Kong, is as comprehensive as possible, as well as that cotton-specific requirements are embedded in the envisaged amendments to future subsidy notifications and that they are monitored. What seems clear is that the issue of finding appropriate disciplining mechanisms for the green and blue boxes is a priority area for future research.

Another area of substance requiring urgent attention is the base year used for reduction commitments. As it stands, Members are considering either 1995–2000 or 1999–2001 as the base period for agricultural support expenditures. For either of these periods, however, and especially the latter, government expenditures to support cotton were extremely high in both the USA and the EU; using them as a base for reduction commitments would greatly undermine the potential to reduce existing distortions. In this regard, competitive cotton-producing countries may want to propose a more appropriate time-frame for the base year for cotton-specific reductions, either one with a longer time-frame to dampen the effects of higher subsidy expenditures in the last decade, or an earlier time-frame that better reflects historical expenditures prior to the recent increase.

With respect to the timeline of reforms, fixed dates for concrete action are required. On export subsidies, developed countries (i.e. the USA) have already committed to the removal of all forms of export subsidies for cotton in 2006 (in line with the USA's stated intentions pre-Hong Kong to comply with elements of the Brazilian challenge). What remains to be seen is whether the USA intends to reform its export credit guarantee programme beyond the June 2005 amendment to the fee cap, or the potential influence explicit disciplines to be negotiated on such guarantees for all agricultural goods might come into play.

On trade-distorting domestic support, however, agreement on a firm date – or even a blueprint for a timetable – remains elusive. The case made by some Members is that without the foundation of similar dates being made in the overall agricultural negotiations, one cannot be forthcoming for cotton. Acknowledgment of the political origins of such a position does not, however, prevent the search for a middle ground. Predicated on a transitional compensation mechanism, this might include an early harvest, followed by a structure on agreed reductions over time, contingent on the overall starting date (to be determined later). While a similar approach put forward by the WCA proponents before the Hong Kong Ministerial Meeting was not then adopted, it remains an approach that may garner support as the negotiations progress.[44]

Assuming, for example, that the reduction commitments made as part of the Doha Round are to start in year *x* (which in all likelihood will not be before the next US presidential election scheduled for late 2008), one could envisage 'front-loading' in year *x* a 40 per cent reduction of trade-distorting domestic cotton support. By doubling the 20 per cent reduction already agreed to in the July Framework, this would help assuage concerns that these commitments represent only theoretical cuts and ensure that actual cuts are made immediately upon implementation. At the same time, a cut of this degree acknowledges the political difficulty of exacting deeper cuts (especially from the USA) at that point in time. These could be followed by an additional 20 per cent reduction in year x+1 and 15 per cent in year *x*+2. Add to this an early harvest reduction in amber box domestic cotton support of 25 per cent upon agreement (but to be implemented under the 2007 Farm Bill), and over half trade-distorting domestic support measures would be eliminated by 2009 and all such support eliminated by 2011.

While the early harvest reduction, in particular, would pose some difficulties for the US administration, offers for domestic compensation to facilitate acceptance of changes in the next Farm Bill – similar to those proposed in attempts to repeal the Step 2 subsidies – could help facilitate such a move. Indeed, the resistance of the US administration to agree to recent calls to extend the 2002 Farm Bill until the end of the Doha negotiations would seem to indicate some flexibility towards such an approach. For its part, just prior to Hong Kong, the EU proposed to eliminate the most trade-distorting support for cotton immediately upon implementation of the Round; the EU is therefore unlikely to exhibit much resistance to the structure outlined above.

However, as already emphasised, the acceptance of such an elongated timeline should be predicated on the development of a transitional compensation mechanism to offset the injury inflicted on the competitive net exporting LDCs pending such reforms.

### Compensation and Financial Assistance

Recognising the lengthy negotiations ahead before reforms to the US and EU cotton support programmes can be achieved, the issue of transitional compensation (as distinct from financial assistance) deserves renewed consideration by WTO Members. In terms of financial assistance, commitments already made should be translated into practical action plans, and the resources allocated to these should be greatly augmented.

As discussed above, to be most effective, the delivery of compensation should be tied explicitly to the reduction of subsidies. This does not, however, preclude the creation of such a mechanism outside the auspices of the WTO, including on a contractually binding bilateral (as opposed to multilateral) basis. The example of the EU's FLEX mechanism to compensate developing countries for unstable export earnings offers an interesting avenue for further investigation – one which the text of the Hong Kong Declaration could support.

Under the FLEX mechanism, the EU could create a sub-scheme under which the funds allocated were proportionate to the injury caused to LDC net exporting cotton producers, and were tied (voluntarily) to the EU's WTO reduction commitments. Distribution to the beneficiaries could be determined on the basis of net exports and delivered directly to producers in order to replicate the world cotton prices that would have existed if there were no subsidy-induced distortions. Such a mechanism could mimic in many ways the Africa Group's proposed 'emergency support fund' (WTO, 2005a), albeit in a bilateral context. Constructed in this way, it could also temper some of the developed country concerns over setting a precedent for a WTO-sanctioned financial compensation mechanism.

A similar bilateral mechanism could be considered for the USA, perhaps in exchange for the proponents, together with Brazil, accepting a delay in the implementation of reductions to domestic support until mid-2007 (with a time-limited 'Peace Clause'-type agreement not to bring these measures to the DSB in the meantime). Cotton producers not scheduled to receive compensation would receive benefits by way of the agreed subsidy reduction (for which the US reforms would have a relatively larger impact). Indeed, according to Gillson *et al.* (2004), countries such as Australia, Brazil, India and Pakistan would stand to gain much more by such an arrangement.

While possible mechanisms are not limited to those proposed above, it would seem appropriate that the aggregate amount of compensation should be in the range of US$150–300 million per annum for it to effectively redress the injury that continued subsidies cause to net exporting LDCs. To act as an effective additional incentive for reform, the amount would have to be at least 3–4 times that amount. It is unlikely that this could be achieved, so the compensation mechanism is perhaps best directed at addressing continued injury.

Similarly, if financial assistance is to be a truly effective tool for promoting the competitiveness of cotton producers and the pursuit of export diversification, the resources allocated would need to be greatly enhanced. To illustrate the magnitude of the funding required, a 2001 UNECA study estimated an investment rate of 40 per cent of GDP to facilitate diversifying into higher value-added products. For the four proponent WCA countries alone, this would amount to approximately US$1–1.5 billion *each* per annum.

Furthermore, as stressed by Oxfam (2004b), it is essential that such assistance is not made conditional on the reduction of pressure in the WTO for subsidy reform; nor should it exacerbate the beneficiaries' indebtedness. In addition, the development of programme activities should include all stakeholders. A final caution, equally applicable to compensation, is the importance of ensuring that all the funds allocated to these initiatives are in addition to those already earmarked for aid-related activities. Without such assurances, there would be a danger of diverting existing funds to the detriment of other important initiatives.

### Dispute Settlement

With respect to litigation via the WTO's DSB, there are two areas for potential improvement. The first relates to the initial ruling in favour of Brazil against the USA, while the second addresses the potential for additional cotton-related disputes (focused on either or both the USA and the EU). On the former, we touch briefly on some recommendations made in Sumner (2005) that might mitigate the serious prejudice caused by US trade-distorting support measures. On the latter, should the negotiations fail to deliver on meaningful reform in a timely fashion, we discuss some issues that should be considered if the proponents wish to consider a DSB case.

On the Brazil-USA case, Sumner (2005) has made some useful suggestions that could contribute in the near term to mitigating the adverse effects caused by US amber box support measures. Specifically, he focuses on those measures shown to be most distortionary in the 2004–07 period – namely the marketing loan assistance and counter-cyclical payments (Sumner, 2003). On the former, he suggests lowering the loan rate and changing the formula so as to raise the effective loan repayment rate (and thus tighten the degree of subsidy paid to farmers). For counter-cyclical payments, he suggests reducing the target price to lower overall expenditures and removing restrictions on the types of production allowed on land previously used for cotton, so as to more effectively decouple the payments and minimise their distortionary effects.

As noted earlier, however, the lack of specificity about the extent to which these subsidies must be reduced or removed means that there is uncertainty as to what is actually required of the USA for compliance. A compliance panel could contribute to the push for deeper and more expeditious reforms by clarifying this aspect of the ruling.

On dispute settlement options for other cotton producers, such as the WCA proponents of the Initiative, the lack of timely movement in the negotiations could prove a sufficient incentive to proceed with litigation. Two reasons commonly offered as to why this is unlikely to occur are the high costs associated with bringing a case to the WTO's

DSB and the systemic shortcomings of the available remedies. While funding could probably be obtained to support such a case, the latter concern is held by many developing countries, who perceive themselves to be at a systemic disadvantage in making use of the DSU remedies available to them.[45]

Specifically, in the context of this discussion, the remedies are usually limited to the suspension of tariff concessions against the offending Member. Imposing additional duties would raise the costs of imports, which for a small developing country which may be highly dependent on the other Member for consumer and producer imports, would have negative socio-economic impacts. It is partly for this reason that Brazil has requested cross-retaliation in the form of suspending concessions on intellectual property rights and services. Again, however, for small developing countries such as those in WCA, this would confer little benefit; nor would it inflict much damage on the offending country. In this regard, the controversial issue of temporary monetary compensation once again comes to the fore.

A problem that is often cited in relation to the proposal for monetary compensation is the lack of any legal precedent for it in GATT/WTO history. However, the fact that it is not explicitly excluded would appear to be an implicit recognition that compensation is at the very least a potential outcome should it be so deemed in a dispute ruling. Furthermore, such considerations have gained weight once again in the context of the Doha-mandated DSU review. In other words, while it would be a challenging position to argue, legal grounds for monetary compensation appear to exist.

The Brazilian case could also offer guidance that may mean that a new case is less difficult (and expensive) to undertake. For example, as US subsidies have already been deemed to cause serious prejudice according to the Brazil ruling, it would probably be easier to prove that they continue to harm other countries if sufficient US reforms are not forthcoming. Indeed, although the Panel did not base its ruling on the existence of serious prejudice to other Members, it accepted such allegations as 'evidentiary support' (WTO, 2005b). Thus it would seem possible for other Members to pursue a new case based on similar evidence.

As the EU is a net cotton importer and is therefore unable to influence world prices, a serious prejudice claim in terms of price depression would be difficult to pursue. However, with the analysis offered by Gillson *et al.* (2004) on the disproportionate effect of EU subsidies on WCA producers due to their close competition in similar markets, an argument for the cause of serious prejudice resulting from displaced imports could be an alternative avenue. Such an approach, however, would need to be tempered by the EU reforms touched on above, and it would be some time before relevant analysis could be undertaken to determine whether a case would still exist.

## Systemic Commodity Issues

Global cotton subsidy reforms and associated compensation pending their achievement, together with technical and financial assistance, are only a few elements of the broader trade-related primary commodity strategy that is required to address the systemic problems related to dependence on cotton production and more generally on primary commodities. Indeed, such dependence is a key component of what UNCTAD (2002) has termed the 'international poverty trap', whereby the increasing marginalisation of commodity-dependent developing countries (CDDCs) in world trade, together with their continued dependence on a weak and slow growing primary commodity sector exhibiting declining real commodity prices and high price volatility, reinforces generalised poverty and contributes to a vicious low income-savings/investment-productivity trap. As a result, these countries are hard pressed to pursue export diversification, which, via learning-related externalities, can contribute to mitigating risks associated with prices and the upgrading of productive capacities, thus stimulating more dynamic economic growth.

While a comprehensive review of these issues is beyond the scope of this chapter, and has been well documented, for example in a recent UNCTAD (2003b) publication, *Economic Development in Africa: Trade Performance and Commodity Dependence*, we touch briefly on some key areas below so as to highlight the wider context of subsidy reform. In particular, the chapter focuses on the need to address the long-term decline and volatility of cotton prices, and barriers to market access and entry.

On the long-term decline and volatility of cotton prices, we underscore the need to develop international mechanisms to help stabilise prices and thus facilitate more predictable economic management. Price volatility in particular, which is said to be caused largely by supply conditions, can greatly increase the level of economic uncertainty in the economy, and as a result hamper macroeconomic management and frustrate investment decisions. With respect to cotton, while supply concerns have been a factor (for example, the 2002/03 price increase resulted from a poor crop in China), the above analysis shows clearly that subsidies have also played a key role. (Baffes (2004) observes that cotton price volatility increased after 1985 when the USA moved from supply management to price support measures to stabilise farm incomes.)

Declining prices have been attributed to both demand and supply factors. Prebisch and Singer discussed demand side factors in the 1950s. It has been argued that the low income elasticity of demand for primary commodities relative to manufactures (i.e. that increases in income lead to slower demand growth for primary commodities than for manufactures) leads to declining long-term primary commodity prices and thus to deteriorating terms of trade (i.e. a lower purchasing power for imports derived from primary commodity exports). More recently, UNCTAD (2003b) has expounded a supply-side explanation, pointing to structural over-supply resulting from new high-productivity producers[46] (for example Asia in tropical beverages), as well as subsidies to high-cost producers. Cotton is, of course, an example of the latter – although remedies to remove subsidies and provide compensation alone will not rectify the problem (as they predate the recent rise in US and EU subsidies).

With decreasing and uncertain revenues,[47] less foreign exchange[48] to import productivity-enhancing goods and pay off debts,[49] and lower levels of investment,[50] many CDDCs are thus confronted with widening savings, foreign exchange and fiscal gaps, higher debt loads and increasing difficulties in accessing international finance. Taken together with other national and international economic policy-making reforms,[51] these difficulties highlight the far-reaching benefits that mechanisms to stabilise commodity prices could deliver.

In this regard, many in the international community, including in the context of the 'development dimensions' of the cotton issue, have increasingly focused on market-based tools to mitigate price risk, such as forward and future contracts, swaps and put options. While increasing familiarity with such tools in the more vulnerable CDDCs, and the maturing of financial markets, might mean that they became more widely used and help stabilise commodity revenues, they would seem more useful for doing so during a growing season than between seasons (UNCTAD, 2003b). To help address the problem of fluctuations in commodity revenues between seasons, a mechanism would need to influence prices received by producers between seasons. Here the role of price support is important, although admittedly a challenge when the long-term declining trend of cotton prices is considered. While the history and challenges surrounding price stabilisation go beyond this chapter, a bilaterally-funded cotton compensation mechanism could be deployed to help bolster, and facilitate the improvement of, existing national institutions offering price stabilisation, and thus go some way to mitigate the problem of increasing poverty in many competitive cotton producers. To date, however, this suggestion has not met with a warm reception.

Alternatively, there has also been renewed interest in recent years in revisiting the potential benefits of producer–consumer or producer–producer commodity arrangements to manage the demand and/or supply (and by extension, price) of traded commodities. While there are a number of legitimate concerns regarding such mechanisms, not the least of which is the often dismal history of previous international commodity organisations, this does not preclude the potential for new approaches to improve their effectiveness and ensure a better accommodation of current political and economic realities (UNCTAD, 2003a). Indeed, with respect to cotton, there has never been an attempt at supply management, making it perhaps an ideal candidate for a new initiative, with no historical baggage.

Another key area requiring attention if competitive cotton-producing developing countries are to maximise the benefits of their competitive advantage in cotton production relates to market access and entry for cotton and higher value-added cotton products. Market access issues include traditional trade issues, such as the subsidy considerations dealt with in this chapter, as well as tariff peaks and escalations (which can impede value addition in the producing countries) and NTBs, such as market defence measures (anti-dumping and safeguards), product standards, and health and food safety regulations. While MFN import tariffs on raw cotton are generally low for most countries,[52] they tend to increase as additional processing (and value added) occurs. Quantitative restrictions on textiles (under the now-expired ATC or the safeguards that have now replaced it) typify such treatment, which can impede diversification out of cotton production.

Market entry issues, however, are of greater importance in the cotton sector. These include the monopsony and oligopsony power in purchasing and distribution channels that results from the integration of multinational firms which effectively control international trade in specific commodities, as well the need to meet the product quality standards demanded by consumers for entry into specific markets.[53] Although far less concentrated than other commodities such as cocoa and coffee, the role of international cotton traders (who mediate between producers and processors) is often highlighted. According to an ICAC survey, Gillson *et al.* (2004) report that the 19 largest companies accounted for approximately 33 per cent of global production in 2003, with expanded activities in the area of inventory storage and helping to ensure stable supply availabilities. As a result of higher transaction costs stemming from these and other new activities, traders have increasingly attempted to pass them on to captive producers, resulting in lower farm-gate prices and lower domestic earnings (Gibbon, 2003).

In addition, with a greater focus on new quality standards – the 'High Volume Instrument' (HVI) classification (Gibbon, 2003) – traders are increasingly looking to suppliers who can consistently provide uncontaminated high-quality cotton grades, and are willing to pay a premium on the world price in return. These new exacting standards, combined with instances of contamination that have damaged the image of WCA cotton in recent years, have resulted in their cotton being traded at a discount rather than at the premium price it should command due to its otherwise high quality (Estur, 2005).

In light of these constraints on market access and market entry, a wide range of international efforts needs to be considered, including addressing specific measures within WTO rules (such as tariff escalations, market defence measures, and TBT and SPS disciplines), as well as mechanisms to promote better integration into global commodity chains. The development of niche markets and alternative marketing channels (for example fair trade networks) has also been identified in this regard (UNCTAD, 2003a). Domestically, efforts to upgrade production structures and build the the capacity to develop quality assurance and testing facilities could prove highly beneficial.

However, to be able to undertake such activities requires a large pool of investment resources. Indeed, the lack of investment resources underlies two other key systemic issues requiring attention, namely low productivity in the cotton sector (and CDDC economies more generally), and poor access to technology and finance to facilitate these and other improvements in competitiveness and stimulate export diversification. The welcome efforts to provide greater technical and financial assistance to cotton-producing developing countries reviewed earlier are essential. To be effective, however, the resources allocated need to be greatly augmented.

The need for subsidy reform illustrates just some of the systemic challenges facing CDDCs and cotton-producing developing countries in particular. While it forms only one part of the solution to their problems, subsidy reform is essential. If developing countries were allowed to take advantage of their competitive advantage in cotton production, they would be far better equipped to generate at least a portion of the investment resources they need to begin addressing these systemic concerns. In this context, compensation pending these reforms is all the more important.

In conclusion, the chapter considers some potential areas to be pursued post-Hong Kong, as Members approach the 30 April deadline of finalising modalities for agriculture.

## Looking Beyond Hong Kong

The discussion above demonstrates that despite both economic and moral arguments supporting immediate reforms in the cotton sector, political reality dictates that the process of negotiating meaningful agricultural reform in the WTO, including for cotton, will be a long one. There is unlikely to be much in the way of serious implementation before the end of the decade. Indeed, the end date for eliminating trade-distorting domestic support could be even later, if the 2013 date agreed in Hong Kong to eliminate all agricultural export subsidies is any indication. Either way, 2006 will be crucial as agricultural negotiators ambitiously attempt to finalise the modalities. Some cotton-specific elements could be included in the modalities, with the aim of meeting the mandate to find an 'ambitious, expeditious, and specific' resolution to the cotton issue.

If there is failure to achieve explicit numbers and dates in the near term, modalities that ensure the accelerated treatment of cotton (predicated on an agreed baseline to be agreed in the future) could serve as a foundation for further reforms.

### Digging at the Roots – Dealing with Domestic Support

In terms of the reduction and eventual elimination of trade-distorting domestic support, a key sticking point continues to be the timeline for implementation. As proposed above, one avenue for investigation is a structure around which specific dates can be agreed upon in the future. To this end, just before the Hong Kong Ministerial Meeting, the WCA producers proposed a three-step reduction approach of 80 per cent on the day of implementation of the round, an additional 10 per cent after 12 months and the last 10 per cent a year later. However, with the political difficulties surrounding the reform of domestic support measures in the USA discussed above, the degree of 'front-loading' proposed is probably too ambitious. An alternative construction could see a combination of an early harvest, with a lower year 1 reduction and with higher year 2 and 3 reductions (which in the face of a temporary compensation mechanism could be a much easier scenario for the WCA proponents to accept).

In addition, the proponents may wish to pursue cotton-specific mechanisms to prevent the reform commitments that have already been made from becoming an exercise in shifting expenditures to support categories with lower (or no) reduction commitments (such as the blue and green boxes). As mentioned above, cotton-specific commitments based on the categorisation of existing support programme notifications (i.e. before 'box-shifting' can occur) may prove helpful in this regard. Other possible measures include agreement that the envisaged reductions in the total aggregate measure of support (AMS) and/or *de minimis* threshold will be a fixed percentage that is greater for cotton-specific measures (for example, by agreeing that cotton-specific reductions will be *x* percentage greater than the horizontal reductions in this area to be implemented as part of the Round).

Another key issue is that of the base year for reduction commitments. With the high levels of support extended to cotton producers in the USA and the EU in the two baselines currently under consideration (1995–2000 or 1999–2001), the proponents could advocate for an alternative methodology to be established such that the combination of the base year employed for cotton and the reduction commitments accepted ensure real and meaningful cuts in the level of existing support. An earlier (or longer) time-frame to reduce the impact of these particularly generous years of support would seem appropriate.

While perhaps not offering the specificity and depth of reforms that the proponents are seeking, provisions such as these offer concrete and binding commitments that could help implement the mandate to address cotton 'ambitiously, expeditiously and specifically', and at least help move the agenda forward until a more amenable political climate is in place.

### Compensation and Litigation – Where Next?

Little progress has been made on the issue of a mechanism for temporary monetary compensation, although there is increasing justification for it as reform is further delayed. A recent window of opportunity has emerged from the Hong Kong Ministerial Meeting, where Members 'urged' the WTO Director-General to engage, via the donor institutions, in discussion of a possible mechanism to address declining incomes in the cotton sector. Whether or not the 'explorations' of this produce results, and if so how effective they will be, remains to be seen. In light of the view offered above on a realistic timeline for meaningful cotton reforms, it is important to continue to press for the issue of compensation to be reinstated on the WTO agenda.

One option is to create a delivery mechanism outside the WTO, based on a contractual bilateral agreement between subsidisers and LDC net exporting producers, whereby funding would be inversely related to continued cotton support. While there is a danger that such an arrangement could become an institutionalised cost of doing business for the subsidising countries (and a marginal one relative to the subsidies provided), the maintenance of links with the agreed mandate to address the trade-distorting policies that affect the sector would help mitigate this. In addition, the support and involvement of those competitive non-LDC producers who would receive no benefit from such a mechanism would help ensure that momentum towards deeper reforms was not lost.

While the donor community prepares its response to this new opportunity, the proponents would do well to come forward with specific and practicable suggestions on how they envisage such a mechanism being most effective.

On litigation, should the proponents (or other competitive producers) feel that inadequate attention is being given to their needs, and that there is little likelihood of this changing in any acceptable time-frame, they still have the option of reconsidering additional dispute challenges to either the USA and/or the EU. Recent comments by the new US Chief Agricultural Negotiator, Richard Crowder, to the annual convention of the American Farm Bureau Federation (the self-proclaimed 'Voice of Agriculture') confirm that the US administration (if not Congress) clearly recognises the potential threat of continued challenges if reforms fail to move ahead. '[...S]imply put', he stated, 'if the Doha talks stall, if our timetable is overshot, and current US policies continue as they have, the United States faces the prospect of additional challenges to its current programs' (Crowder, 2006). Indeed, the irony is that the outcome upon which such 'stalling and overshooting' would be based would provide the most fertile of environments (with no Peace Clause protection) for a wide range of challenges to the OECD agricultural support programme for cotton and other commodities.

Unfortunate as it may be, deep reforms to the cotton sector are unlikely to take place in the near future. This is not to say that the producers who face the loss of their livelihoods and are on the brink of poverty must sit idly by and wait. In the meantime steps can be taken to help facilitate meaningful reforms when these become possible. Most importantly, some type of temporary compensation mechanism must be developed. While the proponents may have backed off from their position that insufficient movement on cotton at the Hong Kong Ministerial Meeting would translate into a lack of consensus on the overall package, the concerns of all competitive cotton producers – and especially the most vulnerable countries in WCA and sub-Saharan Africa – will need to be taken into account before any modalities on agriculture can be completed. To attempt to do otherwise would call the 'Doha Development Agenda', and the institutional foundation upon which it is based, into farcical disrepute.

## Notes

1 Two key areas of divergence in Cancun were agriculture (including cotton) and the basket of 'Singapore Issues' (which included investment, competition, transparency in government procurement and trade facilitation). See ICTSD (2003) for the collapse in Cancun.
2 On Hong Kong, see the statement from Commonwealth Secretariat Secretary-General (*http://www.thecommonwealth.org/Templates/System/LatestNews.asp?NodeID=147867*), ICTSD (2005) and Oxfam (2005).
3 Cotton producers in WCA for which cotton comprised at least 1 per cent of GDP in 2000 include Benin, Burkina Faso, Cameroon, Central African Republic, Chad, Côte d'Ivoire, Ghana, Guinea, Mali, Senegal and Togo (Fortucci, 2002).
4 Despite difficulties in comparing costs across countries, a 2001 ICAC study ranked WCA amongst the lowest cost cotton producers globally (alongside Uganda and Tanzania).
5 The most widely used cotton price measure is the 'Cotlook A Index', which provides an average (in US$) of the five lowest offering prices traded in North European ports for 16 styles of cotton (all of the Middling 1–3/32 inch fibre length grade). All cotton prices used will be in terms of the Cotlook A Index (hereafter A Index).
6 This decline would have been even more pronounced were it not for a 34 per cent increase in 2002/03, after cotton prices reached historic lows in 2001/02. This upswing was stimulated primarily by a poor 2002/03 crop in China and the resulting increase in global demand. However, the ICAC (2005) projected a 22 per cent decline for 2004/05 after a six-year high the previous season.
7 Real prices were calculated using the US Bureau of Economic Analysis GDP deflator with 2000 as the base year.
8 Government support is disaggregated between 'domestic support measures' and 'export subsidies'; the former have traditionally been viewed as less price distorting than the latter. However, it is commonly believed – and confirmed by the recent WTO ruling, at least in relation to cotton – that domestic support measures can also result in meaningful price distortions and injury to other producers. For present purposes, we shall use the terms interchangeably, unless otherwise specified. We note that the lack of consensus over the definition of what constitutes a subsidy has resulted in the reporting of differing figures across studies.
9 For example, the definition of what constitutes a subsidy (and hence the level of support accounted for), the base year for levels of production and government support, assumptions on market structure, demand and supply elasticities, and the estimation model employed.
10 For those studies that do not themselves consider forgone earnings, FAO (2004) uses a supply response equation for WCA countries to offer a rough calculation of their forgone export earnings.
11 Tables 4.3 and 4.4, sourced from FAO (2004), offer a glimpse of the key conclusions and assumptions relating to the major econometric studies undertaken.
12 See ICTSD (2002) for a review of the TRIPs and public health issue at Doha.
3 Goreux's 2003 study estimated losses for WCA cotton producers, as opposed to the LDC net-exporters referenced in the WTO submission. However, as he outlined later (Goreux 2004a), the degree of overlap between the two groups results only in a 2 per cent difference in cotton production and exports. As such, his calculations remain a reasonable approximation of the compensation required.
14 Adopted in May 2002, the 2002 Farm Bill is officially known as the 'Farm Security and Rural Investment Act of 2002'.
15 Prohibited subsidies are those that require recipients to meet certain export targets, or to use domestic goods instead of imported goods.
16 Subsidies (allowed or otherwise) are deemed 'actionable' in the sense that they are countervailable if they confer a benefit to a specific enterprise or industry (*de jure* or *de facto* specificity), such that they cause (or threaten to cause) material injury to domestic industry.
17 Serious prejudice is said to occur (based on ASCM Article 6(c)) where the effect of a subsidy is to displace imports or exports, significantly depress or suppress prices in the same market or increase the world market share of the subsidising Member (WTO, 1995).
18 Third parties to the case included Argentina, Australia, Benin, Canada, Chad, China, Chinese Taipei, EU, India, New Zealand, Pakistan, Paraguay and Venezuela.
19 Due to the AB report upholding the key finding of the Panel, unless otherwise specified, 'ruling' refers to both the DSB and AB ruling.
20 On the claim of 'threat' of serious prejudice for a basket of subsidies to be granted in the future, the Panel found it unnecessary to rule. They did so in light of the potential for the significant transformation of future support measures resulting from the withdrawal of relevant subsidies (either prohibited and/or causing present serious prejudice) prescribed in their ruling (as seen below).

21 See Table 4.1; this excludes cottonseed payments (number 7), which were not included in his analysis but did form a part of the case.

22 Step 2 payments are provided to domestic users of US cotton and/or exporters to cover the difference in cost between (higher) US cotton prices and (lower) world prices.

23 The US Schedule of commitments on domestic support and export subsidies on agricultural products can be found in Schedule XX of the United States of America, Part IV, Section II entitled 'Export Subsidies: Budgetary Outlays and Quantitative Reduction Commitments' in the GATT Schedule of Commitments.

24 The marketing loan programme (comprising marketing loan gains, loan deficiency payments and commodity certificate exchange gains) is intended to minimise potential loan forfeitures by providing interim financing to eligible producers on their eligible production, and to facilitate the orderly distribution of eligible commodities throughout the year. Rather than selling the crop at harvest when prices tend to be at their lowest, the proceeds of the interim loan enable producers to pay off their expenses when they become due, while storing their pledged harvested crop as collateral and repaying the loan when market conditions are potentially more favourable.

25 Market loss assistance (MLA) payments were annual *ad hoc* emergency measures from 1998–2001, aimed at making up losses sustained to producers' income as a result of recently low commodity prices. These were formalised in the 2002 Farm Bill as the counter-cyclical payments (CPP) programme, which filled a gap in revenues whenever 'effective' domestic cotton prices fell below a target rate of $0.72/pound (effective domestic prices include direct payments and, where applicable, loan gains) (WTO, 2005b).

26 Green box (domestic) subsidies, as defined in Annex 2 of the AoA, must have no, or at most minimal, trade-distorting effects. They often include government services, as well as direct payments made to farmers that do not stimulate production (i.e. they must be 'decoupled' from production). Importantly, they do not currently have expenditure limits, nor are they subject to reduction commitments.

27 Amber box subsidies include all domestic support measures not eligible for the blue (production-limiting) and green (see note 26) boxes, such as measures to support prices, or subsidies directly related to production quantities. They are subject to limitations (a *de minimus* level of support up to 5 per cent of agricultural production for developed countries; 10 per cent for developing countries), as well as reduction commitments (based on an 'aggregate measure of support' or AMS figure).

28 Three such programmes run by the US government's 'Commodity Credit Corporation' were considered by the Panel: GSM 102, which guarantees the repayment of credit made available to finance commercial export sales of agricultural commodities on credit terms that do not exceed three years ; GSM 103, which guarantees the repayment of credit made available by financial institutions in the USA to finance commercial export sales of agricultural commodities on credit terms of between three and ten years; and SCGP, which issues guarantees for the repayment of credit made available for a period of not more than 180 days by a US exporter to a buyer in another country (WTO, 2005b).

29 Other products not included in the Schedule include corn, oilseed, oil products and soybeans.

30 See Steinberg and Josling (2003) for an in-depth legal discussion on the vulnerability of US and EU agricultural subsidies in light of the Peace Clause expiry.

31 The other was Indonesia – Autos; WT/DS54, WT/DS55, WT/DS59, WT/DS64.

32 The GSM-103 programme was also eliminated. However, this programme had not been used for cotton in the past and had only been used marginally for other commodities.

33 Corresponding to the annual average value of US surplus production resulting from subsidisation from 1999–2002 (as estimated by Sumner, 2003) multiplied by international prices for that period.

34 Cross-retaliation has been authorised once before in the WTO, as part of the 1999 banana dispute between Ecuador and the EU. With the two Members having arrived at a negotiated agreement however, Ecuador opted not to exercise its cross-retaliatory rights.

35 See Basso and Beas (2005) for an overview on the potential difficulties in utilising TRIPs as an instrument of retaliation.

36 See the EU 'Proposal for an EU-Africa partnership in support of cotton sector development' at *http://www.cotton-forum.org/docs/partenariat-en.pdf* and the summary of proceedings of the July meeting at *http://www.cta.nl/pubs/coton/Cotton_Forum.pdf*

37 This includes international trade; national and regional cotton strategies; policies and institutions; technological innovation; risk management; chain integration; and coordination.

38 Goreux (2004a) notes that the changes implied by the proposed EU reforms (and the remaining coupled subsidies) would not necessarily alter the level of cotton production in Greece.

39 The FLEX instrument was introduced in 2000 in the framework of EU-ACP cooperation to assist governments facing sudden losses of export revenues. Due however to restrictive eligibility criteria, from 2000–02, only

g35.65 million had been distributed as part of six successful applications (out of 51). Had the new criteria been in place originally, the applications submitted would have resulted in a g255 disbursement.

40 See 10 November 2005, USDA News Release No. 0486.05, *http://www.usda.gov*

41 The programme will focus on: promoting the use of good agricultural practices; strengthening private agricultural organisations; providing training for West African ginners; improving the quality of WCA cotton via better classification; improving linkages with relevant US research organisations; improving the enabling environment for biotechnology; and policy/institutional reform.

42 As noted above, however, with less than full transition to decoupled measures and thus 35 per cent of their support still tied to the amount of area under cotton production, the degree to which these reforms will deliver the professed benefits remains to be seen. Goreux (2004a), for example, speculates that the changes implied will not necessarily alter the level of cotton production in Greece.

43 Indeed, without a cap on green box spending, it is altogether conceivable that support to inefficient cotton producers could increase in the future.

44 The WCA proposal envisaged an 80 per cent cut in trade-distorting domestic support upon implementation, with an additional 10 per cent cut in each of the following two years.

45 For a detailed discussion on such concerns vis-à-vis the DSU, see Shaffer, Mosoti and Qureshi (2003), 'Towards a Development-Supportive Dispute Settlement System in the WTO'.

46 This relates to the 'fallacy of composition', whereby a small commodity producer may be able to increase production without affecting world prices and thus, *ceteris paribus*, increase export earnings; whereas many producers proceeding in this manner will work to depress the world price and lower unit revenues for all. A similar trend is now said to be occurring in low-skilled manufactures.

47 The World Bank (2000) suggests losses (1970–1997) for African non-oil CDDCs (excluding South Africa) exceeding 110 per cent of their combined 1997 GDP and 68 per cent of cumulative net resource flows (cited in UNCTAD, 2003b).

48 Razzaque *et al.* (2004) estimate the average foreign exchange losses for 1995–2000 for the LDCs alone at between US$946 and 2181 billion. For details on the estimation procedures, see Razzaque *et al.* (2004), Chapter 4.

49 See Nissanke and Ferrarini (2001) for a discussion on the commodity-debt relationship.

50 UNCTAD (2003b) notes that the investment ratio would have been on average 6 percentage points per annum had terms-of-trade losses for non-fuel CDDCs not occurred.

51 UNCTAD (2003a) highlights the following possible policy measures: stabilisation of real exchange rates; better management and control of capital flows; debt reduction (including debt write-offs) for HIPCs; financing for diversification, particularly in LDCs and Africa; more effective and wider coverage of compensatory finance; use of risk management instruments; and the consideration in the structural adjustment and stabilisation programmes of the implications of competitive devaluation for international commodity prices, due to the potential of fallacy of composition.

52 For example, the EU has no import tariff on cotton, while that of the USA is fairly low (14 per cent). Additionally, as a result of the Hong Kong Ministerial Meeting, duties in developed countries for LDC exports are scheduled to be eliminated from the start of the implementation of the Doha Round. On the other hand, some exporting countries who have large textile sectors have high tariffs – with China's 90 per cent tariff standing as the only one above 40 per cent (Baffes, 2003; Gillson *et al.*, 2004).

53 This area is addressed most directly in the global commodity chain literature, which examines the range of activities and actors from primary production to final consumption in specific commodity value chains, considering the linkages that bind them and the distribution of value added between them. See Gibbon (2003) and *http://www.globalvaluechains.org/*

## References


Baffes, J. (2004). 'Cotton: Market Setting, Trade Policies, and Issues', World Bank Policy Research Working Paper 3218, Washington, DC: World Bank.

Basso, M. and Beas, E. (2005). 'Cross-retaliation through TRIPs in the Cotton Dispute?'. BRIDGES Monthly Trade News Digest, 9 (5): 19–20. Geneva: International Centre for Trade and Sustainable Development.

Becker, G.S. (2002). 'The 2002 Farm Law at a Glance', CRS Report for Congress RS21233. Washington, DC: Congressional Research Service.

Clay, J. (2004). *World Agriculture and the Environment: A Commodity-by-commodity Guide to Impacts and Practices*. Washington, DC: Island Press for WWF-USA.

Crowder, R.T. (2006). Remarks to American Farm Bureau Federation Annual Convention, 9 January. Nashville, Tennessee. *http://www.ustr.gov/Document_Library/Transcripts/2006/January/Remarks_of_Richard_T_Crowder,_USTR_Chief_Agricultural_Negotiator,_before_the_American_Farm_Bureau_Federation_Annual_Convention.html*

Estur, G.E. (2005). 'Commodity Risk Management Approaches For Cotton in West Africa'. Washington, DC: International Cotton Advisory Committee.

FAO (2002). 'Dependence on Single Agricultural Commodity Exports in Developing Countries: Magnitude and Trends', in FAO Papers on Selected Issues Relating to the WTO Negotiations on Agriculture. Rome: United Nations.

FAO (2004). 'Cotton: Impact of Support Policies on Developing Countries – A Guide to Contemporary Analysis', FAO Trade Policy Technical Note No. 1. Rome: FAO.

Fortucci, P. (2002). 'The Contributions of Cotton to Economy and Food Security in Developing Countries'. Rome: FAO.

Gibbon, P. (2003). 'Commodities, Donours, Value-Chain Analysis and Upgrading', Paper prepared for UNCTAD. Copenhagen: Danish Institute for International Studies.

Gillson, I., Poulton, C., Balcombe, K. and Page, S. (2004). 'Understanding the Impact of Cotton Subsidies on Developing Countries'. London: Overseas Development Institute.

Goreux, L. (2003). 'Prejudice Caused by Industrialised Countries Subsidies to Cotton Sectors in Western and Central Africa', Background document to the submission made by Benin, Burkina Faso, Chad and Mali to the WTO (TN/AG/GEN/4).

Goreux, L. (2004a). 'Cotton After Cancun', mimeo. Paris: Sahel and West African Club (OECD).

Goreux, L. (2004b). 'Prejudice Caused By Industrialised Countries Subsidies to Cotton Sectors in Western and Central Africa', Update of the 2003 background document to the submission by Benin, Burkina Faso, Chad and Mali to the WTO (TN/AG/GEN/4).

Halverson-Cross, K. (2005). 'King Cotton, Developing Countries, and the "Peace Clause": The WTO's US – Subsidies on Upland Cotton Decision', mimeo.

ICAC (2001). 'Survey of the Cost of Production of Raw Cotton'. Washington: International Cotton Advisory Committee.

ICAC (2005). 'The World Cotton Outlook', Paper presented to the 3rd International Cotton Conference, 24–25 May 2005. Uzbekistan: Tashkent.

ICTSD (2002). 'Access to Medicines: WTO Members May Snatch Defeat Out of the Jaws of Victory', *BRIDGES Monthly Trade News Digest* 6(8): 1–3. Geneva: International Centre for Trade and Sustainable Development.

ICTSD (2003). 'Cancun Collapse: Where There's No Will There's No Way', *Bridges Daily Update*. Geneva: International Centre for Trade and Sustainable Development. *http://www.ictsd.org/ministerial/cancun/wto_daily/ben030915.pdf*

ICTSD (2005). 'Low Ambitions Met: Members Adopt Declaration', *Bridges Daily Update*. Geneva: International Centre for Trade and Sustainable Development. *http://www.ictsd.org/ministerial/hongkong/wto_daily/19_December/en051219.pdf*

Josling, T. (2005). 'Unraveling the Cotton Case', *BRIDGES Monthly Trade News Digest* 9(4): 3–5. Geneva: International Centre for Trade and Sustainable Development.

Minot, N. and Daniels, L. (2002). 'Impact of Global Cotton Markets on Rural Poverty in Benin', MMSD Discussion Paper 48. Washington, DC: International Food Policy Research Institute.

Nissanke, M. and Ferrarini, B. (2001). 'Debt Dynamics and Contingency Financing: Theoretical Reappraisal of the HIPC Initiative', UNU-WIDER Discussion Paper 2001/139. Helsinki: UNU-WIDER.

Oxfam (2002). 'Cultivating Poverty: The Impact of US Cotton Subsidies on Africa', Oxfam Briefing Paper 30. Oxford: Oxfam International.

Oxfam (2004a). 'Dumping: the Beginning of the End? Implications of the Ruling in the Brazil/US Cotton Dispute', Oxfam Briefing Paper 64. Oxford: Oxfam International.

Oxfam (2004b). '"White Gold" Turns to Dust Which Way Forward for Cotton in West Africa?', Oxfam Briefing Paper 58. Oxford: Oxfam International.

Oxfam (2005). 'What Happened in Hong Kong?', Oxfam Briefing Paper 85. Oxford: Oxfam International.

Oxfam America. (2003). 'US Export Credits: Denials and Double Standards', Oxfam America Briefing Note. Boston: Oxfam America.

Razzaque, M.A., Osafo-Kwaako, P. and Grynberg, R. (2004). Commodity Prices, Aid and Debt: Implications for LDCs, Small Vulnerable States and HIPCs, Commonwealth Economic Paper 72. London: Commonwealth Secretariat.

Steinberg, R.H. and Josling, T. (2003). 'When the Peace Ends: The Vulnerability of EC and US Agricultural Subsidies to WTO Legal Challenge', *Journal of International Economic Law* 6 (2): 369–417.

Sumner, D.A. (2003). 'A quantitative simulation analysis of the impacts of US cotton subsidies on cotton prices and quantities', mimeo.

Sumner, D.A. (2005). 'Reducing Cotton Subsidies: The DDA Cotton Initiative', in Martin, W. and Anderson, K. (eds), *Agricultural Trade Reform and the Doha Development Agenda*, Chapter 10. Washington, DC: World Bank.

UNCTAD (2002). *The Least Developed Countries Report 2002: Escaping the Poverty Trap.* New York: United Nations and Geneva: UNCTAD.

UNCTAD (2003a). Background notes prepared for meeting of eminent persons on 'Commodity Issues, Including the Volatility inCommodity Prices and the Impact these have on Development Efforts on Commodity-dependent Developing Countries', TD/B/50/CRP.3. Geneva: UNCTAD.

UNCTAD (2003b). *Economic Development in Africa: Trade Performance and Commodity Dependence*. New York: United Nations and Geneva: UNCTAD.

UNCTAD (2005). 'Cotton', in *InfoComm: Market Information in the Commodities Area*, available online at *http://r0.unctad.org/infocomm/anglais/cotton/sitemap.htm*, updated on 23 August 2005; accessed on 3 September 2005.

UNECA (2001). *Economic Report on Africa 2000: Transforming Africa's Economies*. Addis Ababa: UN Economic Commission for Africa.

WTO (1995). *The Legal Texts: The Results of the Uruguay Round of Multilateral Trade Negotiations*. London: Cambridge University Press.

WTO (2002). 'United States – Subsidies on Upland Cotton', Request for Consultations by Brazil', WT/DS267/1. Geneva: WTO.

WTO (2003a). 'Poverty Reduction: Sectoral Initiative in Favour of Cotton, Joint Proposal by Benin, Burkina Faso, Chad and Mali', TN/AG/GEN/4. Geneva: WTO.

WTO (2003b). 'Poverty Reduction: Sectoral Initiative in Favour of Cotton', Joint Proposal by Benin, Burkina Faso, Chad and Mali, Proposal on Implementation Modalities', TN/AG/GEN/6. Geneva: WTO.

WTO (2004a). 'Doha Work Programme Decision Adopted by the General Council on 1 August 2004', W/T/L/579. Geneva: WTO.

WTO (2004b). 'WTO African Regional Workshop on Cotton, Cotonou, Republic of Benin, 23–24 March 2004. Note by the Secretariat', WT/L/587. Geneva: WTO.

WTO (2005a). 'Proposed Elements of Modalities in Connection with the Sectoral Initiative in Favour of Cotton, Communication from the African Group', TN/AG/SCC/GEN/2. Geneva: WTO.

WTO (2005b). 'United States – Subsidies on Upland Cotton', Report of the Panel, WT/DS267/R. Geneva: WTO.

WTO (2005c). 'United States – Subsidies on Upland Cotton', Report of the Appellate Body', WT/DS267/AB/R. Geneva: WTO.

WTO (2005d). 'Doha Work Programme, Preparations for the Sixth Session of the Ministerial Conference, Draft Ministerial Text', JOB(05)/298, 26 November 2005. Geneva: WTO.

WTO (2005e). 'Doha Work Programme, Preparations for the Sixth Session of the Ministerial Conference, Draft Ministerial Text', JOB(05)/298/Rev.1, 1 December 2005. Geneva: WTO.

WTO (2005f). 'Doha Work Programme, Hong Kong Ministerial Declaration', WT/MIN(05)/DEC. Geneva: WTO.

## Data Sources

UNCTAD (2005). *Commodity Price Bulletin.*

US Bureau of Economic Analysis (2004). 'National Income and Product Accounts Tables'.

USDA (various). 'Monthly Summary of Export Credit Guarantee Program Activity', *http://www.fas.usda.gov/excredits/Monthly/ecg.html*, last accessed: 12 November 2005.

World Bank (2004). *World Development Indicators 2004.*

# Index